D0141777

A HOLLOW THREAT

Recent Titles in
Contributions in Military History
SERIES EDITOR: THOMAS E. GRIESS

Reconsiderations on the Revolutionary War: Selected Essays
Don Higginbotham, editor

The Leavenworth Schools and the Old Army: Education, Professionalism, and the Officer Corps of the United States Army, 1881-1918
Timothy K. Nenninger

In Peace and War: Interpretations of American Naval History, 1775-1978
Kenneth J. Hagan, editor

Pacifying the Plains: General Alfred Terry and the Decline of the Sioux, 1866-1890
John W. Bailey

Divided and Conquered: The French High Command and the Defeat of the West, 1940
Jeffery A. Gunsburg

The Army and Civil Disorder: Federal Military Intervention in Labor Disputes 1877-1900
Jerry M. Cooper

History of the Art of War: Within the Framework of Political History, The Germans
Hans Delbrück, translated by *Walter J. Renfroe, Jr.*

The Art of Leadership in War: The Royal Navy From the Age of Nelson to the End of World War II
John Horsfield

A Wilderness of Miseries: War and Warriors in Early America
John E. Ferling

Iron Arm: The Mechanization of Mussolini's Army, 1920-1940
John Joseph Timothy Sweet

American Sea Power in the Old World: The United States Navy in European and Near Eastern Waters, 1865-1917
William N. Still, Jr.

A HOLLOW THREAT

STRATEGIC AIR POWER AND CONTAINMENT BEFORE KOREA

HARRY R. BOROWSKI

CONTRIBUTIONS IN MILITARY HISTORY, NUMBER 25

GP

GREENWOOD PRESS
WESTPORT, CONNECTICUT • LONDON, ENGLAND

Library of Congress Cataloging in Publication Data

Borowski, Harry R.
A hollow threat.

(Contributions in military history, ISSN 0084-9251 ; no. 25)
Bibliography: p.
Includes index.
1. United States. Air Force. Strategic Air Command—History. 2. United States—Military policy. 3. United States—Foreign relations—1945-1953. I. Title.
II. Series: Contributions in military history ; no. 25.
UG633.B684 358.4'2'0973 81-4228
ISBN 0-313-22235-5 (lib. bdg.) AACR2

Library of Congress Catalog Card Number: 81-4228
ISBN: 0-313-22235-5
ISSN: 0084-9251

First Published in 1982

Greenwood Press
A division of Congressional Information Service, Inc.
88 Post Road West
Westport, Connecticut 06881

Printed in the United States of America

10 9 8 7 6 5 4 3 2 1

For
Bobbie, Janet, and Michael
and all my family

CONTENTS

ACKNOWLEDGMENTS

Many individuals have supported my work. My principal debt is to the United States Air Force, for granting me the opportunity to continue my studies, and W. Elliot Brownlee, who always provided direction and encouragement. Thanks must also go to Alfred F. Hurley, Alfred M. Gollin, Carl V. Harris, Lloyd J. Mercer, Robert Ferrell, Elliott Converse, Joe Dixon, Fred Shiner, and the archivists and librarians at the Library of Congress, the National Archives, and the Albert Simpson Historical Research Center at Maxwell Air Force Base, Alabama. I owe a great debt to James Eastman, Jr. who alerted me to newly opened material, and to Joe Trester and Raymond Fredette. For discussions and correspondence I thank John Bohn, Herman Wolk, and Tom Sturm. Generals Curtis E. LeMay and John B. Montgomery generously gave time for personal interviews. The reader must understand that the views and conclusions expressed here are solely those of the author and cannot be construed as representing the opinions of those already cited or of the Department of the Air Force or the Strategic Air Command.

H.R.B.

ABBREVIATIONS

AAC	*Alaskan Air Command*
AAC	*Army Air Corps (became AAF in March 1942)*
AAF	*Army Air Forces (became AF in September 1947)*
ADC	*Air Defense Command*
AEC	*Atomic Energy Commission*
AF	*Air Force (United States)*
AFB	*Air Force Base*
AFCC	*Air Force Combat Command*
AGCT	*Army General Comprehensive Test*
AMC	*Air Materiel Command*
APGC	*Air Proving Ground Command*
ASF	*Army Service Forces*
ASR	*Adjusted Service Rating*
ATC	*Air Training Command*
BW	*Bomb Wing*
CAF	*Continental Air Command*
CIA	*Central Intelligence Agency*
DOD	*Department of Defense*
ERA	*European Recovery Act*
FEAF	*Far East Air Forces*
FEAS	*Far East Air Service*
GAC	*General Advisory Committee (of the AEC)*
GHQ	*General Headquarters (of the AAC)*

ICBM	*Intercontinental Ballistic Missile*
JCS	*Joint Chiefs of Staff*
JIG	*Joint Intelligence Group*
JIS	*Joint Intelligence Staff*
JSPC	*Joint Strategic Planning Committee*
JSSC	*Joint Strategic Survey Committee*
MOS	*Military Operations Specialty*
NACA	*National Advisory Committee for Aeronautics*
NDRC	*National Defense Research Committee*
NSC	*National Security Council*
OAB	*Operations Analysis Branch*
OCAC	*Office of the Chief of the Air Corps*
OJT	*On the Job Training*
PACUSA	*Pacific Air Command United States Army*
PPS	*Policy Planning Staff*
SAC	*Strategic Air Command*
SAG	*Scientific Advisory Group*
TAC	*Tactical Air Command*
TDY	*Temporary Duty*
TN	*Thermonuclear*
TO&E	*Tables of Organization and Equipment*
UMT	*Universal Military Training*
USAFE	*United States Air Force in Europe*
VHB	*Very Heavy Bomber*

A HOLLOW THREAT

INTRODUCTION

Since World War II, orthodox and revisionist historians have debated heatedly the responsibility of the United States and the Soviet Union for the cold war. Orthodox scholars, reflecting official government views, stressed the need to stem the Communist tide in Europe. Revisionists, in turn, have pointed to capitalism's drive for markets and the United States threat to deploy atomic weapons as the primary factors. Since the late 1960s, however, most scholars have argued that both nations share responsibility for the cold war. Each country simply pursued its own self-interest, creating misunderstanding and misconceptions.

Whatever their views, most cold-war historians have neglected an important topic: the military capability of the major powers. Most would agree that military strength largely determines how vigorously or extensively a nation may pursue foreign policy objectives, but few historians have paid serious attention to such capabilities in their studies. This neglect is easily explained. Historians have never enjoyed access to Soviet military documents, and only after 1973 could they examine crucial United States records. As a result, scholars have made uncritical assumptions about military capability, particularly that of the United States.

Most historians have maintained that the United States enjoyed a preponderance of military power during this period, and they have used this assumption in writing their cold-war histories, regardless of their interpretive perspectives. Many of these scholars, and the American public, were overly impressed by the devastating atomic attacks on Japan in 1945; within days of the two detonations, the costly Pacific War ended. Americans did not understand the exact power or limitations of nuclear weaponry, but they realized its enormous potential for destruction. They appear to have forgotten that Japan was a nearly defeated nation in August of 1945; it was easy to assume that American atomic capability could have a similar decisive effect against another enemy, at another time, under different circumstances.

The matter of capability, specifically United States atomic capability between 1946 and 1950, is important to any thorough understanding of that period and should no longer be ignored, particularly by historians who largely blame the United States for the cold war. Although the United States ended World War II as the world's most powerful industrial and military power, the nation reduced its military force and capability to a low level immediately thereafter. The United States monopoly in atomic weapons did not automatically translate into a powerful and effective military tool; the stockpile of atomic bombs was limited in number and the organization responsible for delivering these weapons, Strategic Air Command, was poorly trained and ill-prepared for its mission. When the Soviet Union imposed the Berlin blockade in 1948, the United States entered into its first confrontation of the cold war with little preparation and few options—a condition recognized by the USSR. An Allied airlift into West Berlin unexpectedly defused the crisis. During the blockade, however, American military leaders and governmental officials directed closer attention to the capability of Strategic Air Command to deliver atomic and conventional weapons. Greater dependence upon atomic weapons followed the Berlin crisis, not because atomic bombs offered the best means of supporting the nation's foreign policy, but because they represented the least expensive approach. Truman's economic policies did not permit the Defense Department to build a strong, balanced force, even after the Soviets achieved atomic capability in 1949. Instead, the president elected to proceed with thermonuclear research and tried to reduce his defense budget even further. Meanwhile, the strength of American conventional military forces drastically declined, as demonstrated early in the Korean War. United States military capability during the first five years of the cold war was severely limited, a fact ignored or unknown to orthodox and revisionist historians alike.

The United States, then, did not base its postwar foreign policy on a strong existing capability, but rather on the potential provided by America's huge industrial complex. What Americans frequently overlooked following World War II, and later historians have tended to ignore, is that the element of time had become much more critical. With a highly mechanized army, the Soviets could overrun most of Europe within weeks, while the Strategic Air Command, with its limited capability and supply of atomic weapons, required nearly a week to react and launch an initial attack. Moreover, the Soviets would be able to control much of Europe before the United States industrial machine could begin expanding its production. Some defense leaders understood this and believed that the next general war would differ from World War II in that forces-in-being would play the key role in determining the nation's useful military capability. When faced with mounting commitments and declining budgets, military leaders were forced to move away from the ideal of a balanced force and to place greater emphasis on atomic deterrence. Nonetheless, it was not until late 1949 that the air force and General Curtis E. LeMay's Strategic Air Command began to acquire the governmental support necessary for even a modestly credible deterrent. Realistic atomic diplomacy, then, was virtually impossible before that time. Only the Korean invasion ended the period of restricted capability.

The other side of the coin, however, is also important in understanding the early cold-war period. The Soviet military capability remains more of a mystery; Russian authorities tightly control access to their military documents, leaving scholars no hard data to work with. While American intelligence organizations matured rapidly during World War II, they were decentralized after hostilities ended and remained so until the Korean War, despite the creation of the Central Intelligence Agency in 1947. Military intelligence gathering, often limited, formed the basis for United States understanding of Soviet capability. Lacking a solid intelligence base, military and civilian planners naturally placed more emphasis on what they judged to be the intent of Soviet foreign policy. By combining their knowledge of Soviet intent and military capability, they tried to determine, however imprecisely, the degree of threat posed to American interests by the USSR. Perceptions, then, played a very important role in the minds of United States planners. Year after year, Americans perceived a growing intent toward expansion and aggression on the part of the Soviet Union. In the absence of good intelligence, planners believed Soviet capability matched intent and urged corresponding policies on the part of the United States. Conversely, American society, far more open to intelligence gathering, posed a lesser problem to Soviet intelligence collection and analysis. The Soviets probably understood more about United States capability than did the American public and were not so intimidated by atomic weapons as some have suggested. Though scholars need more knowledge about United States and Soviet capability, little is conclusively known about the latter. We do, however, understand certain perceptions that American leaders held, perceptions that affected the formulation of military and foreign policy. Again, we know little about Soviet perceptions.

The following chapters will examine the military capability of the United States, specifically that of Strategic Air Command between its inception in early 1946 and the Korean War. Capability cannot be determined solely by the type and amount of hardware; geography, morale, leadership, and human skills must play a prominent role in the analysis. Many questions remain unanswered and new ones will arise, but with more knowledge of military capability, historians can better understand the origins of the cold war.

1 LOOKING AHEAD

During World War II, army aviators gained their first opportunity to employ air power on a grand scale, but they had limited experience to guide them. The air battles of World War I offered little assistance; aircraft and equipment had changed radically since 1918. For airpower tactics and strategy, the flying generals adopted the unproven ideas of generals Billy Mitchell and Giulio Douhet, but the Army Air Corps (AAC) had been unable to test these theories in peacetime.[1] Military aviators could subject their tactics and strategy to combat-trial after 1941; and after four years of experience, they had formed definite ideas about air power in war.

Collectively these experiences convinced aviators of three central points, which air leaders carried into the postwar era. First, they believed the air arm had to preserve the autonomous status temporarily achieved within the War Department. (The more optimistic among them advocated an independent service, equal to the departments of Navy and War.) Autonomy would guarantee the Army Air Forces (AAF) continued development of their own military strategy, tactics, and doctrine. Moreover, independence would enable the air arm to procure and distribute its own supplies, men, and weapons.

Second, the generals understood well the heavy reliance they had placed upon scientific knowledge and personnel. The nation that devoted its resources most vigorously to research and development, they reasoned, would enjoy victory in future wars.

Last, their faith in air power, specifically strategic bombing, had strengthened greatly. Although they acknowledged air power as only one part of the military arm, most airmen believed that properly applied strategic bombardment could effectively destroy or halt a nation's war machine. Many placed greater value on aerial bombardment after the AAF dropped two atomic bombs on Japan; some even suggested that air power alone could win a war. The *Summary Reports of the United States Strategic Bombing Survey*, which appeared in 1945 and 1946, confirmed this belief. The postwar air force developed around these three convictions; the most important plans and programs proposed or instigated by the AAF aimed for autonomy, better scientific technology, and an improved strategic bombing force.

America's flying force failed to achieve autonomy after World War I and remained under the War Department until 1947. The army chiefs considered their air units auxiliary elements, support forces to assist the ground attack. The air corps, so called, assumed the organization used by the ground forces, with little regard to differences. Until 1935 geographical corps commanders controlled all tactical units, including air elements. The army divided air combat forces into nine separate commands, each led by a ground officer. Airmen, therefore, had little influence at command levels, and they considered their superiors inflexible and unresponsive to their needs. The air corps would undergo occasional internal reorganization but remained under War Department control.

The secretary of war in 1934 established the Baker Board, under the chairmanship of Newton D. Baker, to study the capability of the Army Air Corps to perform its mission. The board recommended that the air corps add another organization. The existing Office of the Chief of the Air Corps (OCAC) was to continue its control of supply, training, and servicing; a new General Headquarters (GHQ) Air Force would direct combat elements.[2] Since the air arm had acquired a mission independent of the ground force, in 1931, that of coastal defense, the army adopted the Baker Board recommendations in 1935.[3]

The reorganization placed all air combat units into a GHQ AF, operated under the chief of staff and the War Department. The GHQ AF formed four air districts and established a structure of wings and groups. The commanding general of GHQ AF controlled the tactical units while the corps commanders retained responsibility for bases, common supply, and discipline.[4] Despite the division of control, airmen took optimism from their new mission of coastal defense, which encouraged the AAC to expand its development of both pursuit and bomber aircraft. Any new activity kept the hopes of independence alive.

The AAC took another step toward autonomy in June 1941. Secretary of War Henry L. Stimson favored an independent air arm, and under his direction the army issued Regulation 95-5 creating the Army Air Forces. The War Department established this new command level to improve coordination among GHQ AF, OCAC, and other army units. The regulation replaced GHQ AF with an Air Force Combat Command (AFCC) and gave direct responsibility for aviation to the chief of the AAF, General H. H. Arnold. Stimson added to the War Department the office of "assistant secretary of war for air," reflecting the increased importance of the air arm.[5] Aviators, nonetheless, wanted more influence within the War Department.

To this end, General Arnold proposed a plan in late 1941 that placed ground, air, and service forces on equal footing, with the chief of staff to coordinate the branches. Under Arnold's plan, overseas theater commanders would exercise control over units within their territory and would report only to the army's chief of staff. The army delayed action on Arnold's proposal following the attack on Pearl Harbor but later accepted part of his suggestion. In March 1942 the War Department issued Army Circular No. 59, dividing the army into three equal components: the Army Air Forces, the Army Ground Forces, and the Army Services of Supply. The circular also abolished the Army GHQ, an intermediate level of control and made the chief of staff the unquestioned military commander of the United States Army. Now the chief of staff commanded through four officers: his assistant chief of staff and the commanders of the air forces, ground forces, and service supply.[6] The air arm at last enjoyed an equal position within the army.

The new status permitted more internal freedom. The AAF dissolved the OCAC and AFCC and placed air elements under a single commander and staff. Arnold gained authority "to procure and maintain equipment peculiar to the Army Air Forces." With its own supply organization, the AAF could continue to seek self-sufficiency and independence.[7]

Although the AAF had achieved greater autonomy, it suffered deficiencies. The air arm needed a body of doctrine and found its few qualified officers spread thinly throughout the organization. Air leaders operated under a loose organization while rapidly expanding for war. As planners struggled with these problems, the first combat reports from North Africa arrived, providing some experience as a basis for planning. Early battle results stressed flexibility. British Lt. Gen. Sir Bernard L. Montgomery recommended central control of air units by an air officer closely associated with ground commanders. Breaking up air resources among ground units had proven inefficient; centralization would allow greater flexibility. The American aviators strongly agreed.[8]

The War Department officially endorsed this view by issuing Field Manual 100-20, *Command and Employment of Air Power*, in July 1943. Thereafter, the army centralized control of air power and exercised command through an air force commander. The manual, described as the "Declaration of Independence" for the AAF, asserted that land and air power were coequal and acknowledged air superiority as the first requirement for successful land operations. The publication recognized the existence of different air missions requiring a strategic air force, a tactical air force, an air defense command, and an air service arm. The Army Service Forces (ASF) supported both aerial and ground units. On this matter of service, the AAF expanded its quest for autonomy.[9]

Although the ASF attempted to perform a uniform service for all units, the AAF wanted the option of refusing service from its coequal branch, to expand its own specialized servicing contingent. The three force commanders, Generals Arnold, Ben Lear, and Brehon Somervell, agreed that one authority should control all service functions. But they disagreed about giving the operational commander responsibility for supply. The AAF held that a commander, given a task, must control supply and the tactical means to complete his objective. The opposing position contended that a commander who administered both supply and operations did neither well; the two functions should remain divided, though coordinated.[10] The argument had appeared before, among ground units, and it held greater validity within the air arm. In combat, air units depend heavily on supplies and service; unlike ground operations, air warfare depends on bases and runways.

Arnold continued to urge his view upon the army. In a memorandum to the chief of staff in 1944, he argued that the air mission involved more than fighting for air superiority. "The administration, supply and service functions related to maintenance of air superiority are and must be so completely integrated with combat and training operations of the Air Forces that their performance by a distinct command produces fatal divided responsibilities."[11] Under the existing arrangement, airmen with supply problems had one recourse—go to the chief of staff. The procedure required time and often failed to correct the deficiencies. Although Arnold recognized that a central service agency could provide common supply and service activities more economically, he strongly advocated that the AAF accomplish its own specialized functions. As much as possible he wanted supply controlled by the AAF, not a coequal army branch. Lear and Somervell correctly considered his objective a further attempt to achieve independence. They believed the superior approach lay in separating functions; the branches, they argued, could define and resolve problems and differences. The army rejected Arnold's proposal.[12]

After the war, AAF leaders were determined to retain their hard-earned although limited autonomy, but they realized the three services needed integration. A unified defense department could satisfy both objectives. The AAF would welcome either an independent air department or a unified organization with an autonomous air arm. The War Department, having given virtual autonomy to the AAF, supported unification. The navy strongly opposed the idea; it feared losing its customary control in a three-service department. In 1945, the admirals recalled, the Joint Chiefs of Staff had established the Twentieth Air Force on Guam and directed the command from Washington. The navy considered this a serious infringement of its authority in the Pacific. To the admirals, unification promised more command erosion. Moreover, they feared losing their aviation arm to a coequal air force.[13] Their apprehension prompted one admiral to suggest a merger of the AAF strategic bombardment units with the naval air forces. The resultant air units combined with the marine corps, he told Arnold, would give the navy a total military force. The admiral's suggestion reflected the navy's concern over unification, the plan that had greater hope for congressional approval. After fighting for independence from the War Department, Arnold had no desire for navy control.[14]

Two military reorganization plans emerged in late 1945; neither succeeded. First, Secretary of the Navy James V. Forrestal established a committee, headed by Ferdinand Eberstadt, to study military unification. Its report supported the navy view and recommended three departments, war, navy, and air, with the navy and army maintaining air contingents.[15]

The proposal had little effect within the executive branch. President Harry S. Truman in December 1945 proposed another reorganization program to Congress. Based on suggestions by the army, navy, and the Joint Chiefs of Staff, the plan called for a Department of National Defense with three branches. The navy would retain its marine corps, aircraft carriers, and water-based aviation.[16] During 1946 each service put forth its position before congressional committee hearings. The navy strongly attacked the plan, and the Congress took its opposition seriously. The unification bill failed.

Before any reorganization could occur, the army and navy would have to resolve their differences. In late 1946, Maj. Gen. Lauris Norstad, director of Plans and Operations of the War Department General Staff, and Vice Admiral Forrest P. Sherman, deputy chief of Naval Operations, began developing an acceptable plan. After two months they resolved their basic differences and incorporated their recommendations into a National Security Act draft. In February 1947 the president submitted the proposal to Congress; in July an amended bill passed and Truman signed it.[17]

The National Security Act of 1947 contained several flaws. The new National Military Establishment included three separate and coequal branches and each service secretary enjoyed freedom in administering his branch; each had direct access to the director of the budget and the president. Navy leaders urged such authority to protect their independence within the military establishment. The arrangement permitted the services to bypass the secretary of defense on contested issues, undercutting one reason for unification. The National Security Act had not clearly defined the functions of each branch because the services could not agree on their missions. To facilitate passage of the bill, the planners overlooked the matter. After Forrestal became the first secretary of defense he attempted to establish service missions through executive order, but disagreement among the branches continued.[18]

Gaining autonomy required nearly two years of postwar effort by the AAF and its supporters. During that time, the air arm reorganized into a peacetime force and sought to improve its capability, but its leaders never forgot the key issue of autonomy. In their view the best and most efficient air arm could develop only from an independent status within the military establishment. For the AAF, the National Security Act of 1947 finally fulfilled that goal.[19]

The scientific developments that emerged during World War II had greatly impressed AAF leaders. Advances in weapons technology and other fields had come rapidly and made victory possible. General Arnold and his aviators, however, believed American research and development trailed that of other nations in certain fields, specifically in rocketry. Future military success, they reasoned, would go to the nation that pursued a continuous, well-funded, and carefully planned research and development program for its defense arm. The organization of this effort would prove important. Germany had improperly used scientists and technical knowledge during the war while Great Britain effectively coordinated scientific and military efforts.[20] The American record proved commendable, given the military's prewar arrangement of limited contact with scientists.[21] After the war the AAF placed great interest in the quality and control of military research and development.

Before World War II, scientific efforts relating to military use in the United States centered on two organizations. The National Advisory Committee for Aeronautics (NACA) acted as a consulting and research agency for the Joint Army and Navy Aeronautical Board and predated the war by twenty-five years. Following the outbreak of fighting in Europe, one member of that board, Dr. Vannevar Bush, saw the need to organize science for war. He proposed a national defense research committee to coordinate, supervise, and conduct research on problems unrelated to aeronautics. In 1940, President Franklin D. Roosevelt accepted his plan and named Bush to head the new committee of scientists and representatives from the War Department and Navy Department.

During the war, the National Defense Research Committee (NDRC) sought to correlate government and civilian research in military fields and, with executive support, enlisted aid from scientists, institutions, and organizations throughout the United States. The army and navy welcomed the new committee; General Arnold anxiously gave his more troublesome nonflying problems to NDRC.[22] He later described cooperation between the AAF and the scientists as excellent.[23]

But Arnold did not wish to relinquish all his research and development to nonmilitary groups, for he recalled an earlier experience. When Dr. Theodore von Karman, a pioneer in aerodynamics, in 1939 urged the AAC to construct a wind tunnel that would hold a full-scale plane and could generate winds of up to 400 miles per hour, the NACA objected and questioned the procedure for conducting research. Nevertheless, the AAC let contracts for the huge tunnel, built it, and used the facility extensively and with great rewards. Contrary to the advice of one official group, the AAC had embarked on its own experimental program. Arnold realized that before the AAF could reach and maintain top aviation status, a variety of experimental programs must follow. Nonmilitary groups might reject projects; therefore, the AAF needed to retain its own program.[24]

Arnold feared complete civilian control and excessive dependence on nonmilitary agencies, for they could overlook defense needs and operational requirements. The AAF would need scientific assistance in peacetime; yet, without the pressures of war, the necessary assistance might not develop. Arnold also worried about the direction of military aviation, as aviators would face danger if wedded to old ideas. The AAF first needed a plan based upon future requirements. To determine needs, he concluded, the AAF must bring together knowledgeable men from all fields. On the basis of collective opinion, they could best suggest the technological direction the air force should take for the next twenty to thirty years. If future requirements were addressed first, better organization and control of research and development would follow.

Arnold consulted Dr. Robert Millikan at the California Institute of Technology and quickly received his support. Millikan recommended a colleague, Theodore von Karman, to head the planning committee.[25] Arnold arranged a meeting with von Karman in September 1944 and expressed his concerns and objectives. Von Karman agreed to chair the committee upon receiving assurances of independence and of responsibility to Arnold alone. After reaching agreement, von Karman invited scientists from educational institutions, government agencies, and private business, along with military advisers, to join his committee. By December, he had completed the committee membership, and shortly afterward General Arnold addressed his new Scientific Advisory Group (SAG) to outline his thoughts and directives. Arnold wanted creative thinking; he warned against old ideas simply rehashed. He reminded the committee that the "new" air arm would form around mechanically minded aviators who would look to science to build an invincible force.[26] In an earlier memorandum, Arnold had enumerated facts and problems regarding the AAF and asked for recommendations. He wondered what assistance the AAF should give to or ask from educational and commercial scientific organizations during peacetime. More pointedly, he asked the committee what proportion of available money the AAF should allocate to research and development.[27]

After Arnold's instructions, the committee began work, but it quickly encountered opposition. Bush of the NDRC objected to the committee's premise. In his view, military research and development should restrict its efforts to improving weapons. Civilian agencies should plan and create new products. Bush considered military men incapable of comprehensive planning, for they could not master all the sciences. Circumstances made civilian scientists indispensable. The time had passed, Bush asserted, when military men could call in advisers at will, then reject all or part of the advice given them. The new status of scientists would not permit any bending of the knee to the military hierarchy. He suggested a partnership between the two groups, with neither subordinate. If the military attempted to provide experts, second-rate results would follow. Minor military men would chafe at this form of organization, but "men of stature" would realize its necessity.[28]

Von Karman, by contrast, fully supported the military to conduct research and development; his position had not altered since 1939. SAG reflected his view in *Toward New Horizons*, its final report, issued in late 1945. It considered the air force the major defensive arm of the nation and reaffirmed its need for scientific and technological progress. But the committee disagreed with Bush on the matter of control. Von Karman and the SAG considered civilian control potentially injurious to research in military aviation. The AAF, they advised, should determine its course and seek assistance from any group.[29]

The AAF adopted the Arnold-von Karman position and retained control over research and development, although advisory boards would aid future efforts. Merit existed in Bush's argument, but the decision on application of scientific gains remained with the military. The generals would have to accept the success or failure of any operation as theirs alone.

Bush had correctly raised the issue of coequal status. Although aviators appreciated the scientists, their attitude did not encourage cooperation. Many officers tended to treat scientists as mere employees. Even the air force's regulations assigned the scientists to an inferior position. The AAF paid employed civilians less than comparable officers for identical travel expenses—a sore issue. After the war, the military had difficulty retaining scientists. This worried commanders. They wished to keep technical people, both military or civilian.[30]

Perhaps influenced by interest in rocketry, von Karman's group stressed the future of intercontinental missiles and supersonic flight. Von Karman had supported rocket research before World War II, and captured German documents confirmed its potential.[31] Defensive rockets and intercontinental ballistic missiles (ICBM), he reasoned, would permit the United States to maintain air superiority. Again Bush disagreed. At the time von Karman's committee made its first recommendation, Bush disparaged missiles before the Senate Committee on Atomic Energy. He scoffed at the idea of a 3,000-mile rocket shot from one continent to another, precisely enough to hit a target. At the moment no one knew how to do this, and he doubted that it could be accomplished for a long time.[32] The AAF favored von Karman's advice.

The committee advised a broad research and development program; early in 1946, the AAF Air Material Command (AMC) adopted most of its recommendations, which included letting a contract for the study and investigation of missiles and rockets.[33] The AAF decided to conduct its own research and development whenever the private sector proved unwilling.[34] Although atomic energy would certainly play a future role, the AAF had little hope of influencing nuclear research and development. After August 1945, the War Department had attempted to divest itself of responsibility over atomic energy, and opinion held that control would soon pass from the military. While Congress and the executive debated arrangements, the Joint Chiefs of Staff remained isolated from the issue. Therefore the AAF believed its purposes would be better served by concentrating on nonatomic research.[35]

General Arnold's most difficult task lay ahead: securing the necessary appropriations. Von Karman estimated that the AAF should allot between 25 and 33 percent of its budget to research and development.[36] The postwar years proved disappointing, for the air arm found 5 percent the highest share it could provide, given its mission to maintain a first line of defense. Congress in 1946 had approved $174 million for AAF research and development, but during the year the Bureau of the Budget reduced that amount by $75 million and transferred this portion to army pay.[37] Next year, the figure again fell below $150 million as Truman and Congress grew more mindful of economy. These sums would not support all the programs envisaged by Arnold and his planners, and the budget cuts threatened many new programs underway. If compensatory increases failed to appear within several years—and this seemed likely—certain projects would terminate with limited results to show for the initial investment.

Given a lower level of funding than had been requested for AAF research and development, the generals faced difficult decisions. They needed an aerial reconnaissance capability and bombers with extended range. The promising jet engine demanded much more work before it could become operational, while missile research needed to include shorter-range weapons for air defense and use by conventional bombers. (The burden for further ICBM research rested with private enterprise.)[38] The most pressing demands fell on current forces, which depended upon existing weapons and aircraft. With newer weapon systems now further removed in time, the air arm diverted more research and development funds into short-term improvements of old aircraft. Arnold had warned against this approach, which would permit obsolescence to enter the postwar air force; but the AAF had no alternative.

To insure the best use of limited resources, Arnold established a new staff position and encouraged a permanent civilian research organization. In late 1945, he added a deputy chief of staff position for Research and Development. This move separated procurement from research, elevated research and development to a higher organizational position, and made Air Materiel Command the field agency for this new post.[39] To provide a balance between realistic operational needs and research, he placed a field commander at its head, Maj. Gen. Curtis E. LeMay.[40] With a limited background in engineering, LeMay felt uneasy about the command; but he recruited highly qualified scientists and concentrated on managerial problems.[41] To the general's credit, von Karman described LeMay as a military man who "had his feet in both camps."[42]

LeMay's new position figured in Arnold's second effort to encourage air force research and development. In late 1945, Arnold talked with the aircraft manufacturer Donald Douglas and proposed to divert ten million dollars from the AAF budget for a long-term project. Douglas agreed to the proposition and entered into a three-year contract with the AAF. From this beginning, the Research and Development Corporation (later known independently as the RAND Corporation) emerged.[43] The air force remained its largest customer, and RAND research teams supplied extensive planning information. The new deputy chief of staff for Research and Development coordinated the early efforts between RAND and the AAF.

When Arnold retired in early 1946, he left a framework for AAF research and development: one controlled by the air arm but connected with civilian scientists, institutions, and commercial corporations. His successors struggled with limited funds and dropped certain long-term projects, such as the ICBM, in an effort to improve current air strength. Their decision supported the last postwar goal of the AAF generals, a strong air arm or "forces in being."

The air arm that developed in the postwar period was shaped by a strong faith in strategic bombing. Although the conviction varied in strength among them, practically all aviators believed that strategic bombing had critically damaged the German and Japanese war effort, while certain military leaders and civilian observers remained more skeptical. During the war the Allies constantly evaluated the success of strategic bombing. The Royal Air Force (RAF) had attempted daylight bombing and suffered devastating losses from German defenses. British fliers then turned to night attacks, which required new tactics. Instead of bombing specific targets, they blanketed cities with explosives to destroy material and morale. Although RAF losses fell, Britain enjoyed only modest success with these attacks.[44] By contrast, Americans continued daylight bombing and sought specific targets rather than cities. In early 1944, long-range P-47 and P-51 escort fighters provided fighter cover deep into Germany. As American fighter planes increased in number and the Luftwaffe weakened, the Allies gained control of the air and more bombers reached their targets. Americans and their adversaries considered daylight precision bombing more damaging and effective than the British approach.[45] Aviators believed World War II had proven the preeminence of air power in war.

Long before the conflict in Europe concluded, however, critics had raised questions about the value of strategic bombing. In 1944 a group of air officers headed by Maj. Gen. Muir S. Fairchild proposed that a civilian-controlled committee conduct a bombing survey in hopes of obtaining an assessment of bombing effectiveness.[46] President Franklin D. Roosevelt directed a survey of the European effort, and President Truman expanded the study to include Japan. The findings in Europe, given to the president in September 1945, supported the belief of the air generals and concluded, "Allied air power was decisive in the war in Western Europe."[47] Concerning the effort against Japan, the Summary Report (Pacific War) stated, "It further supports the findings in Germany that no nation can long survive the free exploitation of air weapons over its homeland."[48] Critics charged that both enemies were nearly beaten by 1944 and that much of the bombing effort had proven ineffective.

The AAF generals argued that true strategic bombing did not appear until late in the war: in Europe only the last ten months brought a massive effort against Germany. Less than 17 percent of the bombs dropped in that theater during the war fell before 1 January 1944, and only 28 percent before 1 July 1944.[49] Aviators believed that General Dwight D. Eisenhower too frequently directed American bombers to tactical targets, such as submarine pens or V-1 and V-2 rocket sites, rather than to strategic targets as he prepared for the forthcoming Normandy invasion. When air strikes focused on strategic targets, such as the synthetic oil industry instead of submarine pens, they had a devastating effect. Years later, Germany's Armaments Minister Albert Speer supported this view when he described an attack made on 12 May 1944:

> On that day the technological war was decided. Until then we had managed to produce approximately as many weapons as the armed forces needed, in spite of their considerable losses. But with the attack of nine hundred and thirty-five daylight bombers of the American Eighth Air Force upon several fuel plants in central and eastern Germany, a new era in the air war began. It meant the end of German armaments production.[50]

Speer puzzled over the inconsistency of Americans in selecting their targets, but his view supported that of the AAF.

In the Pacific, the efforts against Japan did not reach massive proportions until General LeMay began his operations from the Marianas in early 1945. Incendiary bombs proved most damaging against cities, and one attack destroyed more than either of the atomic bombs of August 1945. By June of that year, LeMay estimated that continued strikes would destroy the Japanese industry by October. Although atomic weapons ended the war in early September, LeMay never altered his assessment.[51] The generals conceded that Germany and Japan were battered in the last year of fighting, but their condition did not diminish the damage inflicted by the bomber fleets. All aviators believed air power had made a major if not decisive effect on the war, and the critics of strategic bombing could not shake their belief.

Within a year of Japan's surrender, General Carl Spaatz, now head of the AAF, described his impression of strategic air power in *Foreign Affairs:* it could not have won the war without surface vessels, but air power had offered the spark of success. Strategic bombing, he argued, must be an independent air campaign, intended to be decisive and directed against the essential warmaking capability of the enemy. In his mind and in those of allied leaders, the turning point in Europe had come with Big Week in February 1944, when Luftwaffe strength fell dramatically. Air power had proved decisive.[52]

Spaatz's concluding sentences revealed his purpose; he worried about the current AAF. World War II had found the United States ill-prepared; luckily, time permitted the buildup of a powerful air arm. Not until 1944, he reminded his readers, had Americans been able to drop large numbers of bombs. "It is even conceivable," he continued, "that the fact of an American Air Force in being with full potential in 1939, might have prevented the outbreak of war."[53]

Other military men shared Spaatz's view. LeMay believed in strategic bombing; he argued that his efforts against Japan had reduced its ability to wage war and that surrender would have come late in 1945 without the atomic weapons. The conversion of General Joseph W. Stilwell, theater commander in China-Burma-India, impressed LeMay. In 1944, Stilwell doubted that LeMay's plans for bombing Japan would prove useful in defeating Japan. After the surrender ceremonies in Tokyo Bay, Stilwell traveled to Guam and told LeMay, "I recognize now the terrible military virtues of strategic bombardment."[54] Arnold best expressed the view of many air leaders: the effect of strategic bombardment, he stated, was not always apparent; rather, it lay concealed like a "cancer" that kills from within.[55] Arnold believed that the same bombing principles would apply in future wars, although aircraft and bombs would change and carry more destructive power. The effect would come more quickly and decisively, he predicted, but "fundamentally, it will be the same."[56]

Critics such as Bush disagreed. He believed future wars would find bomber fleets obsolete. Bush held that an enemy using proper defensive equipment and jet pursuit aircraft could cause a bomber fleet unacceptable damage and end the day of great bomber attacks. He conceded that atomic bombs in quantity might alter his conclusions, but he considered the short-range guided missile (not the ICBM) a better weapon to develop. Other means, like submarines, existed for delivering atomic weapons, and excessive reliance should not be placed upon strategic bombing.[57]

Bush's view found little support within the AAF, although aviators agreed with some of his ideas; they too wished for further developments in guided missiles. But the third goal of the AAF involved the maintenance of a strong fighting force, and air leaders had to base their strength on the existing aircraft inventory, heavily laden with B-29 bombers. Moreover, they had a strong faith in strategic bombing. When later confronted with limited procurement funds, they recalled their wartime successes and elected to improve their bomber force.

World War II provided clear impressions to AAF leaders. The independence gained during the war reinforced their conviction that only through autonomy could the strongest possible air arm emerge. They realized the great contributions science had made to victory, and General Arnold made great efforts to insure that a strong research and development program existed for the postwar air arm. When appropriations fell well below the expected level in 1947 and 1948, the flying generals sacrificed their research and development funds in order to secure their third goal, the maintenance of the strategic bombing force that was crucial to their concept of strength in the air.

Between September 1945 and the Korean War in mid-1950, the AAF worked toward these three ends. Although autonomy came in September 1947, air leaders found the remaining goals more elusive. Research and development appropriations remained disappointingly low during the postwar period and encouraged the United States Air Force to place even greater stress on a strategic bombing force.

NOTES

1. The army's aviation section operated under the Signal Corps until World War I when it was designated the Army Air Corps in 1926, and became the Army Air Forces in 1941. See Chase C. Mooney and Edward C. Williamson, *Organization of the Army Air Arm, 1935-1945* USAF Historical Studies no. 10 (Montgomery: Air University, 1956), pp. 1, 7.

2. Mooney and Williamson, p. 1.

3. Alfred Goldberg, ed., *A History of the United States Air Force, 1907-1957* (New York: D. Van Nostrand Inc., 1957), p. 39.

4. Otto L. Nelson, *National Security and the General Staff* (Washington, D.C.: Infantry Journal Press, 1946), p. 323.

5. Mooney and Williamson, pp. 5-7.

6. Nelson, p. 389.

7. Goldberg, p. 96.

8. Robert F. Futrell, *Ideas, Concepts, Doctrine: A History of Basic Thinking in the United States Air Force, 1907-1964* (Montgomery: Aerospace Studies Institute, 1971), p. 121.

9. Futrell, pp. 122-23. The objectives of strategic and tactical forces often overlap. Generally, strategic air forces bombarded industrial plants, military targets, and transportation systems within the enemy's interior. These forces also maintained defensive fighters to accompany the bomber attacks. Tactical air forces controlled all other air operations, primarily those of close air support for ground attack and offensive air-to-air combat. The air defense organization protected the continental United States and provided training, while the air service procured and distributed aviation supplies and performed some specialized maintenance.

10. Nelson, p. 445.

11. See "Memorandum for the Chief of Staff" (circa 1944), reprinted in Nelson, pp. 446-49.

12. Nelson, pp. 446-48.

13. Futrell, p. 170.

14. H. H. Arnold, *Global Mission* (New York: Harper and Brothers, 1949), pp. 537-38.

15. R. Earl McClendon, *Unification of the Armed Forces* (Montgomery: Air University, 1952), p. 5.

16. McClendon, p. 8.

17. Futrell, pp. 173-74.

18. McClendon, p. 49. Forrestal initially opposed a strong secretary of defense; however, after he had served in that capacity for one year, he advocated more centralized authority for that office. See National Military Establishment, *First Report of the Secretary of Defense* (Washington, D.C.: Government Printing Office, 1948), pp. 3-4.

19. For a discussion of AAF efforts toward autonomy late in the war, see Perry McCoy Smith, *The Air Force Plans for Peace 1943-1945* (Baltimore: Johns Hopkins University Press, 1970), pp. 15-26.

20. Gordon Wright, *The Ordeal of Total War* (New York: Harper & Row, 1968), pp. 79-82.

21. For an excellent history of American scientific effort during World War II, see James P. Baxter, *Scientists Against Time* (Boston: Little, Brown & Co., 1950).

22. Baxter, pp. 14-16.

23. Arnold, *Global Mission,* p. 165.

24. Theodore von Karman, *The Wind and Beyond* (Boston: Little, Brown & Co., 1967), pp. 225-27.

25. Arnold, *Global Mission,* p. 272. Millikan had had contact with the air arm since World War II, and Arnold placed confidence in his judgment.

26. Von Karman, pp. 267-71.

27. Memorandum General Arnold to Dr. von Karman, subj: AAF Long Range Development Program, 7 November 1944, 203.1, Vol. 14, Albert F.

Simpson Historical Research Center, Maxwell Air Force Base, Alabama (hereafter cited as AFSHRC).

28. Vannevar Bush, *Modern Arms and Free Men* (New York: Simon and Schuster, 1949), pp. 252-53. See also Bush's July 1945 report, *Science, the Endless Frontier: Report to the President on a Program for Postwar Scientific Research* (Washington, D.C.: Government Printing Office, 1945), pp. 33-34.

29. Von Karman, pp. 272, 291-94.

30. See General Curtis E. LeMay file, 168.64-3, AFSHRC.

31. Von Karman, p. 227.

32. Futrell, p. 199.

33. U.S. Congress, House, Committee on Appropriations, *Military Establishment Appropriations Bill of 1948: Hearings before a subcommittee of the Committee on Appropriations,* 80th Cong., 1st sess., 1947, pp. 649-50 (hereafter cited as *Hearings,* 1947).

34. U.S. Congress, House, Committee on Appropriations, *Military Establishment Appropriations Bill of 1947: Hearings before a subcommittee of the Committee on Appropriations,* 79th Cong., 2d sess. 1946, p. 475 (hereafter cited as *Hearings,* 1946).

35. Richard G. Hewlett and Oscar E. Anderson, Jr., *A History of the United States Atomic Energy Commission,* vol. 1, *The New World, 1939-1946* (University Park: Pennsylvania State University Press, 1962), pp. 429-30. See also George F. Lemmer, "The Air Force and the Concept of Deterrence 1945-1950" (USAF Historical Division Liaison Office, Washington, D.C., 1963), p. 11.

36. Von Karman to General Arnold, 15 December 1945, 203.1, Vol. 14, AFSHRC.

37. See *Hearings,* 1946, p. 487, and *Hearings,* 1947, p. 613.

38. Futrell, pp. 200-201.

39. Previously, Arnold's staff had consisted of five assistant chiefs of air staff (AC/AS): Personnel, Intelligence, Operations, Materiel, and Plans.

40. Futrell, pp. 188-89. See also H. H. Arnold, "Science and Air Power," *Air Affairs* 1 (December 1946): pp. 184-95.

41. Curtis E. LeMay, *Mission with LeMay* (Garden City, N.Y.: Doubleday and Company, Inc., 1965), pp. 394-95.

42. Von Karman, p. 302.

43. Futrell, p. 188.

44. Bernard Brodie, *Strategy in the Missile Age* (Princeton: Princeton University Press, 1959), pp. 120-24.

45. Wesley Craven and James Cate, eds., *The Army Air Forces in World War II,* vol. 2, *Europe—Torch to Pointblank* (Chicago: University of Chicago Press, 1949), pp. 227-29. See also Sir Charles Webster and Noble Franklin, *The Strategic Air Offensive Against Germany 1939-1945,* vol. 2, *Endeavor* (London: Her Majesty's Stationary Office, 1961), pp. 5-7, 268-69.

46. David MacIsaac, "What the Bombing Survey Really Says," *Air Force Magazine,* June 1973, pp. 61-62.

47. *The United States Strategic Bombing Survey Over-all Report, European War* (Washington, D.C.: Government Printing Office, 1945), p. 107 (hereafter cited as USSBS [European War]).

48. *The United States Strategic Bombing Survey Summary Report, Pacific War* (Washington, D.C.: Government Printing Office, 1946), p. 28. The Strategic Bombing Survey and its findings have long been a subject of controversy. One serious charge came in 1950 when Marshall Andrews alledged the air force illicitly slipped Report 71a into the survey, seeking to alter certain unpleasant truths about the success of strategic bombing. Several scholars later accepted and expanded this view; but the whole charge of air force misconduct, specifically with 71a, has been effectively countered by David MacIsaac in his *Strategic Bombing in World War Two* (New York: Garland Publishing, Inc., 1976), pp. 119-35. See also his Introduction to David MacIsaac, ed., *The United States Strategic Bombing Survey*, vol. 1 (New York: Garland Publishing, Inc., 1976), pp. xxi-xxvi.

49. USSBS (European War), p. 71.

50. Albert Speer, *Inside the Third Reich* (New York: The Macmillan Company, 1970), pp. 412-13.

51. Arnold, *Global Mission*, p. 564.

52. Carl Spaatz, "Strategic Air Power," *Foreign Affairs* 24 (1946): 388-92, 395-96.

53. Spaatz, pp. 394-95.

54. LeMay, pp. 388-90.

55. H. H. Arnold, *Third Report of the Commanding General of the Army Air Forces to the Secretary of War* (Baltimore: Schneiderith & Sons, 1945), p. 62.

56. Arnold, *Global Mission*, p. 580.

57. Bush, *Modern Arms*, pp. 53-56.

2 BEGINNING ANEW

Between V-J Day and 1947, the Army Air Forces directed two critical activities. The air arm drastically decreased its size through demobilization and attempted to build an independent, modern air force, the most advanced possible under existing technology. The effort was directed toward a strategic bombing force and extensive research and development. The purposes often conflicted. The AAF succeeded in demobilizing but emerged with little strategic power. During the initial months, aviators made only small steps toward a modern air arm.

The AAF reduced its size quickly and haphazardly because war-weary Americans wanted their citizen army disbanded and begrudged further defense spending. Fighting had ended; no apparent need existed for a large military. Congress reflected the public mood and urged rapid demobilization. In the first months, military leaders expected a large reduction, but they underestimated the contraction during 1946. This miscalculation hindered their rebuilding efforts.

Reduced budgets threatened AAF goals. A small air force might weaken the case for independence; with funds limited, research and development would suffer the most cuts. War was not imminent, and little pressure existed for extended scientific work. The extensive demobilization in late 1945 and early 1946 permitted the most experienced airmen to leave the service, and with them the AAF lost the foundation for a strong force.

The AAF had begun preparations in 1943 for a peacetime force. Air leaders worked without a plan because no one knew what military obligations the United States would incur after the war. In the following year, AAF planners proposed a force of 105 groups.[1] General George C. Marshall strongly disapproved, stressing the traditional opposition of Americans to a large peacetime establishment. By August 1945, after repeated revision, the AAF settled on seventy groups, with fifty-four separate squadrons.[2] The War Department found the proposal reasonable, and the air arm predicated its planning on a peacetime force of seventy groups.

After demobilization the AAF encountered great difficulty maintaining seventy groups and never gained this strength until the Korean War. Limited funds and a thriving postwar economy prevented the AAF from retaining an adequate number of men, the more highly trained specialists in particular. When demobilization concluded in mid-1946, air commanders found themselves struggling to build a modern force with low budgets and high turnovers, and they discovered many men were incapable of learning or performing highly technical tasks. Consequently, the AAF suffered in quantity and quality.

During the sixteen months following the war, aviators made small gains, but they failed to achieve their major objectives. The AAF established a command to build and direct its strategic force and provided a new organization for research and development. Other commands received and refined their postwar missions and could boast of minor accomplishments. But by late 1946 the AAF had been reduced to a fraction of its wartime strength, and modernization had proceeded slowly. Congress failed to grant independence as long as the navy strongly opposed any new status for army aviators. Nevertheless, despite the turmoil and uncertainty of this period, the AAF made a beginning.

When the War Department began planning for demobilization, two years before World War II ended, the army assigned the task to its Special Planning Division, which included a single AAF member, Col. F. Trubee Davison, chief of the AAF's Special Projects Office. The division's planners, believing that the European conflict might end by 1 September 1944, first made preparations for redeploying certain ground and air forces from Europe, through the United States, and into the Pacific Theater.[3] The army planned to redeploy only part of its European forces; many men would revert to civilian status after arriving in the United States. The War Department wanted to replace as many returning men as possible with new recruits; then the required units would depart for the Far East. The army compiled an Adjusted Service Rating score (ASR) for each man, which reflected his overseas service, combat time, and family status. A certain score would permit a man to leave if there were no particular need for his skill.[4]

For the air arm, the army assigned the task of formulating plans for redeployment and demobilization to Continental Air Forces (CAF), a command established partly for that purpose on 15 December 1944.[5] As groups and squadrons returned from Europe and lost their experienced personnel to high ASR scores, CAF was either to deactivate the units or to upgrade them with new recruits. CAF would determine the necessary personnel requirements for deployments, schedule all training and unit moves to meet the commitments of Headquarters AAF, and properly distribute men and aircraft. On 1 April 1945, the AAF activated CAF with Maj. Gen. St. Clair Streett as Commander.[6]

The following month the deployment from Europe, labeled White Plan, began. With much confusion and some delay, airmen and aircraft entered the United States through two centers: Bradley Field, Connecticut, and Hunter Field, Georgia. By 31 August 1945, the operation had ended with 73,643 airmen and 5,462 aircraft returned to the United States.[7]

With White Plan concluded, CAF concentrated on demobilization. By early September 1945, the AAF had accepted CAF's reduction program, and within the month the command assumed responsibility for demobilization. CAF established thirty-two separation bases and discharged a growing number of airmen each day. When the volume declined in late December, CAF began closing its centers. On 20 February 1946 demobilization concluded, with 734,715 officers and enlisted men released.[8] Air leaders could now begin their building task; but they also faced the immediate prospect of reorganization.

The AAF required an organization that would support autonomy and permit optimum use of air power. In determining a proper postwar arrangement, planners encountered two problems. First, the United States had not established firm peacetime missions and commitments for the AAF; therefore, aviators lacked political guidance and were left to their own assumptions. The AAF planners chose to use the seventy-group program as a basis for reorganization.[9] Second, the organization of flying commands required a decision: combat air forces could be divided into commands based upon the mission or function, or units could fall under a central command much like CAF. Leaders of CAF faced their versions of these problems; they realized the need to prepare a peacetime organization, yet their missions remained unchanged from those embodied in the initial (1944) instructions. Moreover, CAF then held responsibility for all the combat units located in and returning to the United States, and any division of forces according to function would alter CAF's status as a centralized organization.[10]

On 14 November 1945, CAF prepared an early reorganization proposal that offered centralized control of all combat units, with forces organized by function. Planners suggested four subordinate commands: western, eastern, central, and tactical. Western and eastern would operate and maintain strategic forces and tactical units as necessary, while central command would administer advanced training for individuals and units. Tactical command, which contained tactical, light bomber, and troop carrier aircraft, would cooperate with the army and navy in joint operations.[11]

The CAF plan offered an arrangement consistent with autonomy, because it supported related AAF goals. Only one command would work directly with the other services. Tactical would control all units assigned to assist other services in such operations as air support of ground troops. Central and the two coastal commands would control all strategic and air defense aircraft and would work independently of the other services. The proposal also gave CAF control over combat commands, permitting flexibility and coordination. Air forces would organize according to function or mission, making command easier.

The AAF rejected the CAF proposal and established its own ad hoc committee to devise a reorganization plan. Lt. Gen. Hoyt S. Vandenberg, assistant chief of Air Staff, Operations, directed CAF to reevaluate its every activity for possible elimination, reduction, or merger and to submit its findings by 31 December.[12] Meanwhile, between early December and late January, the ad hoc committee met frequently and suggested postwar organization plans based upon different circumstances: a separate air force, a single defense department, and an autonomous status within the War Department. The committee's last proposal, which closely resembled CAF's November plan, divided the combat forces in the United States into a strategic force, two air defense organizations, and a tactical force to coordinate activities with the army.[13]

While the ad hoc committee was deliberating, CAF received new directions. On 22 January 1946, General H. H. Arnold advised CAF that the primary mission had changed from demobilization to rebuilding the AAF, because problems had arisen from the drastic reductions.[14] Too many trained personnel had departed the AAF, yet manpower requirements remained for overseas positions and primary instructor duties in the United States. On-the-job training would help resolve the problem, but rebuilding depended on recruits. During the preceding four months over half a million airmen had left, a circumstance that was forcing AAF leaders to undertake intensive recruitment. Arnold expected CAF to continue its base utilization study and cautioned its planners to recognize financial and political constraints. Their plans would require continual reexamination to insure the best organization.

Arnold expanded the missions of CAF. The command gained

responsibility for reconnaissance, photographic, and mapping units; and Arnold directed CAF to develop an aircraft search and rescue service in conjunction with the United States Coast Guard. He concluded by urging his commanders to anticipate an integrated, mobile AAF, capable of attack and maintaining "the first line of defense of the United States and its possessions."[15] Although Arnold considered aviation's new mission the most important of all responsibilities, the AAF had to rebuild and reorganize its forces.

The ad hoc committee and the AAF modified their earlier plans several times. In late January, planners proposed to eliminate CAF and to reorganize operational commands by function. With a mobile air force, they correctly reasoned, the AAF did not require regional divisions. Each command headquarters could direct its activities and the AAF would provide coordination, eliminating the requirement for CAF as constituted. The committee wanted this plan working in mid-February and redesignated CAF as Air Defense Command (ADC), as two of the four air forces in CAF were concerned with air defense.[16] Two other commands, Strategic Air Command (SAC) and Tactical Air Command (TAC), would develop their own command structures. The decision to organize combat forces into commands based on function became the basis for AAF organization.

In February 1946, the AAF suddenly and without explanation directed CAF to transfer its entire headquarters organization to SAC; ADC and TAC would now build their commands with other air forces. The War Department established the three combat commands, effective 21 March 1946, and redesignated CAF headquarters at Bolling Field, Washington, as Strategic Air Command. The Army directive gave SAC a single combat force, the Fifteenth, to be activated at Colorado Springs, Colorado, by 31 March 1946.

In a letter dated 12 March 1946, General Carl Spaatz, now commanding general, AAF, outlined SAC's new mission.

> The Strategic Air Command will be prepared to conduct long range offensive operations in any part of the world either inde-

> pendently or in cooperation with land and naval forces; to conduct maximum range reconnaissance over land or sea, either independently or in cooperation with naval forces; to provide combat units capable of intense and sustained combat operations employing the latest and most advanced weapons; to train units and personnel for the maintenance of the Strategic Forces in all parts of the world; to perform such special missions as the Commanding General, Army Air Forces may direct.[17]

The mission directed essential activities: offensive air attack, training of strategic forces, and special missions as required. Yet at its inception SAC lacked an offensive force and could not train its personnel adequately. The command's most competent men were participating in a mission with the navy, Operation Crossroads.[18] To fulfill the missions given them by Spaatz, the commander and deputy of the new command faced a difficult task, one that would require resourcefulness. The AAF selected General George Churchill Kenney to command the new organization, with General Streett, then CAF deputy commander, as deputy.[19]

Kenney was a logical choice to command SAC. His rank and combat record in the Pacific made him a natural selection for a large operational command. At the end of World War II, the AAF had four full generals: Arnold, Spaatz, Kenney, and Joseph T. McNarney. Spaatz and Kenney had directed combat operations during World War II, while McNarney had served in administrative positions. After V-J Day, McNarney became acting supreme allied commander in the Mediterranean, and Arnold selected Spaatz as the next commanding general, AAF. Kenney remained commander of the Pacific Air Forces until his reappointment in early 1946.[20]

General Kenney's prewar career had resembled that of many other AAF leaders. In 1917 he left the Massachusetts Institute of Technology and enlisted as a flying cadet in the aviation section of the Signal Corps Reserves. He established a strong combat record during World War I and earned the Distinguished Service Cross and Silver Star. After the war he remained with the AAC and attended the Army Engineer School at Dayton. His interwar assignments included flying, professional schools, staff work at the Office of the Chief of the Air Corps, and service as chief of production at Wright Field, Ohio.

World War II gave Kenney his opportunity. He assumed command of the Fourth Air Force at Riverside, California, in March 1942; three months later, he received his most important assignment. General Douglas MacArthur, commander in chief of the army forces in the Pacific, had become dissatisfied with his air arm and its commander, Lt. Gen. George H. Brett. When MacArthur requested a replacement, Arnold recommended Kenney. MacArthur agreed, and Kenney took command of the Allied Air Forces in the Southwest Pacific in July 1942.[21]

General Kenney, a short and dynamic man, soon demonstrated aggressive leadership. He stressed upgrading the combat forces and improved their capability by introducing new tactical techniques, such as skip-bombing. Impressed, MacArthur gave his new commander authority to reshape the command, and Kenney quickly replaced several older officers with younger and more energetic men.[22] Kenney's first test came in March 1943, when his units encountered a heavily defended Japanese convoy in the Battle of the Bismarck Sea and brilliantly defeated the enemy's larger force. Admiration grew between the two generals. During the war Kenney described himself as a MacArthur man. He later wrote, "I consider him [MacArthur] one of our greatest statesmen and the best general this country has ever produced."[23] MacArthur wrote similarly: "Of all the brilliant air commanders of the war, none surpassed him [Kenney] in . . . essentials of combat leadership."[24] MacArthur had reason for his praise; within months of Kenney's arrival he had an effective air force in his theater. Kenney continued his success through New Guinea and the Philippines battles, ending the war with a strong reputation.[25]

In October 1945 he returned to the United States and contributed his support to the movement for AAF autonomy. Although the AAF still considered independence its goal, wartime operations in the Pacific had demonstrated a need for coordination between services. Autonomy without reorganization could make coordination difficult. Kenney favored a department of national defense with equal branches, an arrangement similar to that which brought coordination among the three services late in the Pacific War.[26] He considered it unwise for each to operate without coordination in peacetime; such a system would fail during war. Kenney believed a department of defense would facilitate coordination.

Virtually all airmen supported a defense department; they believed a separate air department too difficult to achieve. They considered autonomy within the War Department the least desirable status. Air leaders knew that the navy would oppose unification for fear of losing its own air arm. Both services, particularly the AAF, strongly advocated air power and strategic bombing, but the navy wished to retain its air force. The admirals did not consider strategic bombers as a decisive force and stressed tactical aviation from fast carriers. The navy believed the AAF wanted to control both land- and sea-based aviation and would slight the latter. The navy resisted unification, the AAF's hope for independence.[27]

To gain autonomy, the AAF presented the strongest possible case for airpower. Aviators publicized World War II accomplishments, stressed aviation in future conflicts, and emphasized land-based flight. A single commander, they argued, must control this force. The AAF denied any desire to control sea-based aviation; many airmen believed aircraft carriers would soon reach obsolescence (a point still debated thirty-seven years later).[28]

Despite the years of planning and publicizing airpower, the decision on autonomy rested with the Congress. On 2 November 1945, Kenney testified before the Senate Military Affairs Committee, urging a merger of the services. He began his testimony forthrightly: "I state categorically that I am in favor of a single department of armed forces with co-equal arms of land, sea, and air."[29] Citing examples from his Pacific command, he argued that air power would have yielded poor results if it had not been entrusted to one commander. He acknowledged the navy's tactical mission, but he believed "primary responsibility for air warfare must rest with the co-equal coordinate air force, whatever the character of the earth surface underneath."[30] The senators hardly challenged his remarks; they expressed more interest in his wartime experiences, and Kenney eagerly obliged with appropriately prepared visual aids and charts. The United States Strategic Bombing Survey Report on the Pacific War had not yet appeared, and Kenney's impressions of airpower accomplishments carried great weight. The navy, unorganized in its opposition to unification, paid attention to Kenney's comments and later contested his views before the committee.[31] Kenney nevertheless had given a strong performance before friendly senators.

Kenney returned to the Pacific to undertake a reorganization of his command. He wanted to merge the largely tactical Far Eastern Air Force (FEAF) and the strategic units located in the Marianas, a move that General MacArthur supported.[32] Within two weeks, Kenney returned to Washington for temporary duty and, on 30 November, revealed that his proposed merger had begun. Kenney strongly hinted he would play an important role in the future Pacific reorganization; and shortly afterwards the Dayton, Ohio, press announced that Kenney would command the now-merging FEAF.[33] On 27 December, MacArthur declared in Tokyo that all five Pacific air forces had consolidated into one Pacific Air Command United States Army (PACUSA), commanded by General Kenney.[34]

Important assignments followed. Kenney appointed his top wartime generals to key positions; Lt. Gen. Ennis C. Whitehead became his deputy commander, Maj. Gen. Clements McMullen assumed the chief of staff post, and Maj. Gen. K. B. Wolfe took command of Fifth Air Force and PACUSA's headquarters.[35] Then, suddenly, the War Department named Kenney special advisor on military affairs for the United States delegation to the United Nations.[36] Kenney quickly departed for Europe on 3 January 1946, leaving his Pacific command and embarking upon a new career.

As General Kenney began work in London, AAF leaders were considering how to build an atomic striking force. On 2 January 1946, Lt. Gen. Vandenberg sent a memorandum to Lt. Gen. Ira C. Eaker, chief of staff, that outlined plans for establishing a strategic force using atomic weapons.[37] His proposal considered only the men and equipment currently available, and neither required nor precluded creation of a special command. Vandenberg simply wanted an adequate force to exploit the potential of atomic weapons. The United States had a limited supply of bombs, perhaps a dozen, and the AAF needed only one group to deliver this small number.[38] That unit, however, demanded the most competent personnel and modern equipment available. Vandenberg wanted the atomic force located near the Manhattan District Project assembly and storage facility at Albuquerque, New Mexico, with scientific and technical personnel from both the striking force and the district mutually accessible for full coordination. He believed the force and its special equipment should be centrally controlled while in the United States.

Vandenberg recommended that the 509th Composite Group form the nucleus of an atomic striking force. The 509th had delivered the two atomic weapons against Japan and recently returned from the Pacific. A self-contained attack group, it included all the support sections: troop carrier, air service, material, engineering, ordnance, and military police. Vandenberg suggested these units locate at Sandia Base and Kirtland Field near Albuquerque. Later the atomic force could expand by adding two additional groups, the 444th and the 40th, all placed under the 58th Bomb Wing (BW). During World War II, the very heavy bomb (VHB) groups used such organization; with three or more units, a wing had sufficient strength to deliver a heavy attack and the flexibility to deploy groups independently. But, unlike other wings, the 58th BW would direct a far wider mission than any wartime group.

The 58th BW would conduct specialized training, provide its own technical support, supply atomic bombs whenever a group deployed overseas, and insure the capability to deliver atomic weapons to enemy targets. The atomic bomb groups would operate in the United States and deploy to forward bases when needed, while the wing's specially trained transport squadron would ferry the necessary weapons to the same location. Air Transport Command could handle most supply requirements for the deployed groups, but Vandenberg reserved responsibility for bomb transport to the 58th BW. Despite the wing's new operational functions, Vandenberg's suggestions essentially followed the organization used in World War II. With atomic bombs, the president made the decision on using the weapons.

Vandenberg avoided comment on potential enemies and possible targets, but the Soviet Union and the range of United States bombers weighed upon his mind. As early as 1943, planners had considered the Soviet Union a long-term threat.[39] During early 1945, relations between the two countries deteriorated; and, after the war, government leaders considered the Soviet Union a threat to American interests.[40] Scientists believed that the USSR could develop atomic weapons within two to five years, and military leaders accepted this estimate.[41] When the Soviet Union attained atomic capability, Vandenberg reasoned, the possibility of war between the two nations would increase and limited bomber range would make strategic attack against the USSR difficult. From the United States, the AAF could not reach Soviet targets with B-29s carrying bombs; aviators needed forward bases. The polar routes to northern Europe and Asia offered the shortest distances from the United States, but the arctic climate presented a formidable obstacle. Vandenberg's memo did imply use of the polar routes; improved range might allow groups to strike directly from the United States. But Vandenberg's first concern was with the immediate problem of building a capable atomic force that could reach Soviet targets from forward bases.

To form this striking unit, Vandenberg recommended the 509th Composite Group for top priority in obtaining the latest equipment and the best men available. In the immediate future the AAF would receive B-50s (enlarged B-29s with greater speed, ceiling, and carrying capability) and, later, the huge B-36s. At the moment the AAF had twenty-seven B-29s modified to carry atomic weapons, but these bombers lacked an adequate radar bombing system. With atomic weapons scarce, the group's mission demanded precision bombing. Vandenberg hoped a newly developed radar system, the AN/APQ-23, would meet the need. Furthermore, the 509th was to practice combat missions to achieve a high state of readiness. Vandenberg left no doubt that accuracy in bombing "*can* and *must* be attained" and that, in the end, only skilled manpower could build and maintain a capable organization.[42]

Vandenberg wanted this plan adopted as the first phase of a program to equip and train all medium and heavy bombardment units for atomic weapons. His proposal retained the system and tactics used during World War II. He stressed the need for close cooperation with the Manhattan Project, as the AAF knew little about atomic weapons and recognized the contributions science and technology could make toward extending range and improving equipment, especially airborne radar. Vandenberg's proposal for developing an atomic striking force found support with the formation of Strategic Air Command nearly three months later.

The direct responsibility for building a strategic force, capable of both atomic and conventional attack, fell to SAC's commanding generals, Kenney and Streett, and the old CAF staff. In March 1946, Kenney returned from London but continued his United Nations work in New York until October. His dual assignments forced him to pass more responsibility to his deputy and burdened his early effort to form his own staff.

General Kenney wanted men from his former Pacific command. He contacted the new PACUSA Commander, General Whitehead, to ask if MacArthur would release Whitehead from his Japanese assignment for duty with SAC. Whitehead politely replied that he had not discussed the matter with MacArthur and would not inquire; therefore, he had no idea. Instead, Whitehead proposed several other generals for Kenney's future staff, giving his strongest recommendations to General McMullen.[43] Whitehead held McMullen in highest esteem and credited his own success in the Pacific to McMullen's outstanding supply and logistical support work. Whitehead hated to lose his top deputy, but he believed McMullen the most readily available and the best possible man for Kenney. He considered SAC the most important military command and wanted Kenney to have the most capable men on his staff. Kenney held McMullen in high regard, too, and later wrote of him,

"He was tops in the supply and maintenance field."[44] Kenney proceeded slowly with selecting a staff and devoted much time to his United Nations duties. Meanwhile Streett and his old CAF staff continued directing SAC's day-to-day operations.

Between March and June 1946, several generals concluded that the United Nations demanded too much attention from Kenney. From Japan, Whitehead sent a word of caution to his former superior.[45] To him, the more important task was organizing the new Strategic Air Command. Whitehead placed little faith in the U.N. activity, terming it a "dead pigeon," and urged Kenney to free himself from that responsibility. Whitehead's associates in Japan shared his opinion. Kenney, however, publicly expressed strong support for the United Nations. On 6 April 1946, he optimistically addressed the Military Order of the World Wars, claiming the Big Five military planners were learning to compromise. He urged his audience to read the U.N. Charter, warning that another generation would wage war unless the charter was followed.[46] Whitehead nevertheless felt that Kenney had more important work to perform, for SAC.

Whitehead believed SAC should prepare for guided missiles. The AAF did not control the missile program. In early 1946 the War Department had embarked upon a research and development project for ballistic missiles, but differences of opinion existed within the army over responsibility for the project.[47] For technical reasons, the program belonged to the Ordnance Branch; before the AAF could claim control, the missile would have to depend upon an airfoil to sustain its flight. Aviators challenged this interpretation and fought to direct missile research and development. The technical argument could not stand up for long, Whitehead argued, and the AAF had to actively seek responsibility for the program. If the air arm failed in this quest, the conservative leadership at Army Ordnance would stifle the project and perhaps allow civilian scientists to gain control. Either arrangement would yield tragic results. In Whitehead's opinion, the guided missile program belonged to the AAF, and SAC should develop a missile force.

General Whitehead closed his letter by cautioning Kenney

once more about SAC's importance and his U.N. duties. He believed Kenney to be the only air general who had the stature to secure the guided missile program, and then only if he devoted full attention to SAC. Whitehead warned that the navy might team up with the civilian scientists to undercut the army, thereby denying the AAF any appreciable share of the guided missile program.

General Whitehead's concern persisted into the summer. On 4 July 1946, he sent another letter, hand-carried to Kenney by General McMullen, from Japan.[48] Whitehead, McMullen, and Wolfe had discussed the SAC staff problem and concluded that two of them should return to the United States for duty with the new command. Still concerned over Kenney's U.N. duties, Whitehead warned, "If anything should happen and units of the Strategic Air Command be called upon for combat operations, the only thing which people would remember would be that George Kenney was the commander."[49] Whitehead believed that a navy campaign against the AAF was imminent and that the admirals would declare the AAF combat units unprepared. If this happened, aviators would "lose their shirts" because the AAF had its authorized strength and still could not carry out its mission; the drive for independence would suffer a damaging blow.[50] The AAF had entrusted its most critical mission to SAC, Whitehead reasoned. If aggressive enough, Kenney could prove its readiness and thus withstand any navy attempt to reduce its strategic role. He urged a decision on General McMullen and offered his full support to Kenney and SAC.

From his distant Pacific post, Whitehead had touched the critical issues for the AAF in 1946. The air arm had been seriously weakened since V-J Day; demobilization had decimated the strategic forces and the navy was strongly opposed to AAF autonomy. The AAF had given SAC its principal offensive force, but neither command had control of the most promising weapon, the guided missile. Assigned dual responsibilities, General Kenney had to depend heavily upon a deputy and staff (not selected by him) to direct SAC's early activities. Kenney could not give SAC his full attention until November;

he did not obtain General McMullen as his deputy commander until late December 1946. Meanwhile, General Streett and his assistants first had to struggle with Project Wonderful, an unrealistic commitment of occupation forces to Europe SAC could not fulfill. In attempting to meet this obligation, SAC would conclude 1946 with only two groups capable of complete offensive operation. Whitehead's fears had validity.

Project Wonderful, SAC's initial concern, originally evolved in August 1945 as part of the occupation program. It directed the overseas deployment of four wings, sixteen bombardment groups, and fifteen air service groups. After the Japanese surrender, the War Department retained Project Wonderful, although CAF immediately discontinued its intensive training program in order to concentrate on demobilization. Consequently, the command failed to meet this large commitment, forcing the War Department to reduce the project goal to six VHB groups. Five would join the occupation forces in Europe; the 449th would deploy to Alaska.[51] The turmoil of demobilization completely ended effective training, and groups could not obtain sufficient or qualified manpower. During the last months of 1945, the army repeatedly postponed the deployment dates; yet by January CAF had still failed to send a single group. In March 1946, SAC assumed the commitment and found Project Wonderful groups only 18 percent manned, with virtually no training underway.[52] Military leaders refused to cancel the plan; to do so would reflect poorly on the air arm. The AAF continued its efforts to organize a total of seventy groups; but, given the effects of demobilization, that goal too, became unrealistic.

The seventy-group plan assigned thirteen VHB groups to SAC, but the command's assistant chief of staff for plans, Col. Arno Luehman, correctly considered this goal too optimistic for 1946. Luehman knew the War Department had approved 400,000 men for the interim and postwar air arm. He estimated that approximately a fourth would serve overseas. Combining manpower figures with economic constraints and political considerations, Luehman believed SAC should try for just nine groups.[53] Other SAC leaders supported the thirteen-group goal, a policy that would have permitted more skeleton groups but less efficiency.[54] The AAF still expected SAC to properly man six VHB groups by 1 September and to deploy the 449th to Alaska. As weeks passed, little success followed. In June the commitment fell to three groups; in July the European deployment program collapsed. SAC deactivated unmanned units or retained them on paper only. By December, Luehman's forecast had proven accurate. The command contained just nine groups; six were completely or partially manned, and only five were maintaining training programs.[55] SAC had fallen far short of its goal.

During 1946 the AAF suffered most from a shortage of trained manpower, a deficiency that prevented SAC from building a global striking force capable of delivering weapons to an enemy target. SAC even lacked the qualified instructors to prepare its new men. To compound the difficulty, the command inherited many inept airmen recruited during the war, who could contribute little to a highly technical force. SAC simply lacked the quality and quantity of manpower needed to build a capable air arm.

In May 1946, the AAF authorized a SAC strength of 43,729 military men from the 400,000 provided by the seventy-group plan.[56] At that time SAC had 37,426. Throughout the year, the command's authorization declined, but the number of men decreased drastically. By 31 December, the figure had fallen by 14 percent, and, during the same period, civilian strength had plummeted from 12,144 to 4,902.[57] SAC's shrinking manpower pool, reduced by 12,478, made planning and building a strategic force difficult. But an imbalance and shortage of skills posed a more serious problem. SAC attempted to man its groups with sufficient specialists during 1946, but shortages immediately appeared in critical fields such as radar, power plant, and aircraft maintenance. At the same time the command had many men trained for technical specialties not needed by SAC; until they were retrained, these men could only perform unskilled tasks. By 31 December 1946, the AAF had fallen short of its total authorized strength by 7,000 men and needed 6,000 specialists.

The shortages stemmed from several causes. After the war, the more highly trained airmen found more alluring employment opportunities in the market economy. Those with technical skills in aircraft maintenance and repair departed from military service in great numbers, leaving in the ranks a large proportion of unskilled airmen. The AAF also lost many veterans who had qualified for retirement during the war but had been retained for duty by the War Department. During demobilization, these experienced supervisors left first. Within months, the AAF had lost the experience and the training potential needed to build forces; commands had to place men far less qualified in important supervisory positions.[58]

To obtain specialists, SAC took action. Despite the inexperience of many supervisors, the command initiated more on-the-job training (OJT) and returned its own men to Air Training Command (ATC) for formal instruction in technical skills.[59] In the latter arrangement SAC lost all use of these men until they returned to their units.

While selecting men for technical retraining, SAC found a surprising number unsuited for learning technical skills, a problem with its roots in World War II recruiting. To meet vast wartime needs, the War Department had emphasized quantity in its recruiting. The army gave each recruit an intelligence examination, the Army General Comprehensive Test (AGCT), to determine an individual's capabilities for assignments. Many had IQ scores below 85. Most of the men going to the AAF undertook some specialized training, and each carried a Military Operations Specialty (MOS) number that reflected his skills. Airmen earning low AGCT scores usually performed unskilled tasks. When the war ended, they remained with the AAF while the more highly skilled left the service.[60]

SAC wanted to give technical training only to those airmen with AGCT scores of 100 or more. After surveying its force, the command found an insufficient number with the required score, so it reduced the level to 85.[61] Commanders generally considered airmen with scores lower than this to be unable to learn technical skills. But the screening revealed that many had scored below 85, and a few under 60. Such men enlisted for three-year tours, and commands could not discharge them without long administrative procedures. Commanders usually avoided this unpleasant task by transferring them to other units. This reshuffling posed a danger. If wartime conditions returned, groups would quickly expand and SAC would need a highly skilled force for training new recruits; few unskilled airmen could be utilized in this training corps.[62]

The problem permeated all the commands. General Spaatz supported efforts to separate the inept from all commands; this "deadwood," he stated, only impeded development.[63] After the war, the AAF had raised the minimum acceptable AGCT score from 60 to 70—a figure still considered low.[64] The AAF streamlined its elimination process in November 1946 and reduced the waiting time required for separating inept personnel. Air Training Command, however, failed to discharge substandard recruits. In one instance, out of thirty-three men sent to a SAC station all but one had AGCT scores between forty-two and sixty-nine.[65] When SAC finally separated these recruits, the commander waited long for their replacements: the AAF could not recruit enough qualified men.

Four months after demobilization had ended, the AAF appealed publicly for enlistees. The War Department prepared press releases for local newspapers, stressing opportunities in the new peacetime air force.[66] Although recruiting campaigns started in May, SAC never received its authorized number of airmen during 1946. First-time enlistments increased during the summer and numbered 6,527 by 31 December. Assigned strength on that day came to 27,871; therefore, nearly 25 percent of the SAC force had six months of military experience or less.[67] With so many inexperienced airmen, and still suffering from a shortage of 7,000 men, mostly specialists, SAC could do little rebuilding.

To alleviate the manpower shortage, SAC stressed retention. In late 1946, SAC polled its short-term enlistees and found 60 percent undecided or unwilling to reenlist. Their tours would terminate in 1947, and if this percentage actually departed, SAC's serious personnel shortage would continue. The command ordered personal interviews to determine the reasons for discontent and to attempt to correct the problems.[68] As a result of these meetings, SAC decided that commanders had given insufficient attention to personal welfare, a charge which covered many areas. In reality, commanders had little power over changing assignments and duties and the general instability that was discouraging the men. Moreover, airmen had incentives to leave. The AAF had used promises of technical training to attract recruits and, indeed, had prepared many for a variety of specialized tasks. When an airman completed his service commitment, he could join private industry at much higher pay and could enjoy greater stability in living and working conditions. The AAF trained technicians for both military and civilian needs but could not compete strongly enough to retain its first-term specialists.[69]

The AAF and its commands aggravated their manpower difficulties by tolerating inadequate record-keeping and poor administrative control at group and squadron levels. Frequently, SAC was unable to determine the number of airmen it controlled. The directives and procedures for maintenance of personnel records had been adequate, but during demobilization airmen with various skills were temporarily used as administrative clerks and personnel assistants. They worked without knowing procedures and separated men as directed, quickly. Some airmen remained in these administrative posts, never learning personnel record-keeping. At some bases they instituted their own methods. In June 1946, AAF planners conducted an inventory of the air arm's personnel. To their dismay, they found that the AAF controlled—on paper, at least—more men than served in the entire army.[70]

With inaccurate records, SAC could not readily determine its specific shortages or surpluses on a given base; thus, it could not effect changes to correct imbalances. Squadron and group commanders traditionally viewed personnel record-keeping as a low-priority item, but the responsibility belonged to them nonetheless. As operational fliers, they usually concentrated on their unit's training and combat capability. In a personal letter to Brig. Gen. Charles F. Born, Fifteenth Air Force Commander, General Streett placed the blame on field commanders and noted that inadequate record-keeping predated SAC.[71] In view of the critical shortages, however, that approach could not continue. Streett established two boards from his headquarters to visit each station and to evaluate its administrative and personnel procedures.[72] The examiners would point out deficiencies to base commanders and, whenever necessary, help establish properly organized personnel sections. By late 1946, SAC had finally taken an active interest in personnel matters at the squadron and wing levels. The delay reflected poorly on command leadership, for, without doubt, manpower shortages had given SAC its most serious developmental problem in 1946.

After sixteen months of peace and reorganization, the AAF had failed to gain either autonomy or strong financial support for research and development. AAF leaders had laid the foundation for a strong air arm by reorganizing combat forces according to function and had established definite peacetime missions for each. Improved aircraft and new equipment held promise for a global capability. Yet by 1947 the strategic bombing force numbered six bomb groups, four incomplete. The AAF had fallen far short of expectations.

Demobilization and personnel management presented the most critical problems; the first left the air arm woefully short of qualified personnel. Properly, the War Department had approached reduction on the basis of prior length of service, but this approach allowed the more needed and experienced airmen to depart first. Thereafter, the AAF even lacked instructors to train men. As commands deactivated units and attempted to use their available manpower better, instability in personnel records assignments followed, causing dissatisfaction and a poor rate of retention. Many groups and squadrons maintained inadequate personnel records and did not always know the number of men or specialists they controlled. When commanders discovered airmen ill-qualified for service or training, they preferred to tolerate or to transfer the inept to other units. With severe shortages in terms of specialists and total manpower, the AAF could maintain only a fraction of its wartime strength.

Military and civilian leaders had recognized the effects of demobilization early but did not appreciate their severity. On 8 October 1945, General Streett sent General Arnold a warning: the air force had almost reached the point of being a mere "symbolic instrument of National Defense."[73] The departments of State, War, and Navy recognized this danger during an October 1945 meeting. Representatives from each agreed that, when the army and navy reached their postwar authorized strength, the services would have an insufficient number of men to operate.[74] All military leaders realized that they could not stem demobilization, but AAF planners continued to retain an ambitious postwar goal of seventy air groups. In attempting to achieve this objective, the AAF and SAC spread their limited manpower and resources among too many groups; they concluded 1946 with a weak combat capability. General Spaatz candidly described that capability in a later report to the secretary of the air force. By 31 December 1946, he recalled, fifty-five groups were listed on paper; only two were effective.[75]

NOTES

1. The AAF reached a peak size of 243 groups and 2,411,294 men in 1944. See Wesley Craven and James Cate, eds., *The Army Air Forces in World War II,* vol. 7, *Services Around the World* (Chicago: University of Chicago Press, 1958), pp. 566-69, 581.

2. Perry McCoy Smith, *The Air Force Plans for Peace 1943-1945* (Baltimore: Johns Hopkins University Press, 1970), pp. 73-74. For a breakdown of the seventy groups by description, see AAF letter 20-91 to CG and CO Major Commands, subj: Interim and Peacetime Air Force Plans, 14 February 1946, 168.116020-91, Albert F. Simpson Historical Research Center, Maxwell Air Force Base, Alabama (hereafter cited as AFSHRC).

3. John C. Sparrow, *History of Personnel Demobilization in the United States Army* (Washington, D.C.: Office of the Chief of Military History, 1951), p. 42.

4. Sparrow, pp. 98-99.

5. AAF letter 20-29, subj: Activation of Headquarters Continental Air Forces, 16 December 1944, 415.01B, AFSHRC. Other CAF responsibilities included: the command of the four continental air forces, the I Troop Carrier Command, continental air defenses, joint air-ground training, organization and reorganization of training programs for redeploying units, and the formation and command of a continental strategic reserve.

6. Continental Air Forces, "Summary of CAF Activities" (Printed report of CAF, 1946), p. 4 (hereafter cited as "CAF Summary"), AFSHRC.

7. "CAF Summary," p. 19. Air Transport Command had responsibility for ferrying troops back to the United States; CAF carried passengers on a space-available basis when flying back aircraft. White Plan was also known as White Project.

8. Craven and Cate, pp. 568-69.

9. Robert F. Futrell, "Preplanning the USAF," *Air University Review* 21 (1971): 66-67.

10. On V-J Day, commands in the United States included CAF, Air Training Command, Air Transport Command, AAF Center, and Air Technical Service Command (a combination of Air Service and Material Command).

11. "History of Strategic Air Command 1946" (Typescript history prepared by Hdq. Strategic Air Command, Offutt AFB, Nebr., 1950), p. 5 (hereafter cited as "SAC-1946"), AFSHRC.

12. General Vandenberg to CG CAF, subj: Survey of Personnel and Organization, 19 November 1945, 416.01-46, AFSHRC.

13. "SAC-1946," pp. 9-12.

14. CG AAF to CG CAF, subj: Mission of the Continental Air Force, 22 January 1946, 168.64-16, AFSHRC.

15. Ibid.

16. "SAC-1946," pp. 10-11.

17. CG AAF to CG SAC, subj: Interim Mission, 12 March 1946, 416.01-46, AFSHRC.

18. In Operation Crossroads the military detonated two atomic bombs on Bikini Atoll during the summer of 1946. The navy had positioned captured Japanese and other ships nearby, to learn the effect of atomic weapons.

19. War Department to CG AAF and CG CAF, subj: Establishment of Air Defense, Strategic Air and Tactical Air Command, 21 March 1946, 416.01-46, AFSHRC.

20. Flint O. DuPre, ed., *U.S. Air Force Biographical Dictionary* (New York: Franklin Watts Inc., 1965), pp. 123, 155-57.

21. Office of Public Relations, Hdq. AAF, "General George Churchill Kenney." Public relations release, n.d., K141.2421, AFSHRC.

22. George C. Kenney, *The MacArthur I Know* (New York: Duell, Sloan and Pearce, 1951), pp. 50-51.

23. Kenney, *MacArthur,* p. 9.

24. Douglas MacArthur, *Reminiscences* (New York: McGraw-Hill, 1964), p. 157.

25. For Kenney's own evaluation of his activities during the war, see George C. Kenney, *General Kenney Reports* (New York: Duell, Sloan and Pearce, 1949).

26. *New York Times,* 13 October 1945, p. 4.

27. Vincent Davis, *Postwar Defense Policy and the U.S. Navy, 1943-1946* (Chapel Hill: University of North Carolina Press, 1962), pp. 226-28.

28. U.S. Congress, Senate, Committee on Military Affairs, *Department of Armed Forces Department of Military Security: Hearings before Committee on Military Affairs,* 79th Cong., 1st sess., S.84 and S.1482, p. 308. See testimony of Lt. Gen. James Doolittle, 9 November 1945 (hereafter cited as *Hearings,* 1945).

29. *Hearings,* 1945, p. 219.

30. *Hearings,* 1945, p. 232.

31. *New York Times,* 1 December 1945, p. 23.

32. *New York Times,* 15 November 1945, p. 4. See also Radio CAX 54428, General MacArthur to General Marshall, 7 November 1945, 168.6008-3, AFSHRC.

33. *New York Times,* 10 December 1945, p. 2.

34. *New York Times,* 27 December 1945, p. 3.

35. Ibid.

36. *New York Times,* 30 December 1945, p. 5.

37. Memorandum, Lt. Gen. Hoyt Vandenberg to Lt. Gen. Ira C. Eaker, subj: The Establishment of a Strategic Striking Force, 2 January 1946, 416.01-46, AFSHRC.

38. "The Balance of Military Power," *The Atlantic Monthly,* June 1951, p. 23.

39. Smith, p. 51.

40. Walter Millis, ed., *The Forrestal Diaries* (New York: Viking Press, 1951), p. 106.

41. Bernard Brodie, *The Atomic Bomb and American Security* (New Haven: Yale Institute of International Studies, 1945), p. 23.

42. Memorandum, Lt. Gen. Hoyt Vandenberg to Lt. Gen. Ira C. Eaker, subj: The Establishment of a Strategic Striking Force, 2 January 1946, 416.01-46, AFSHRC.

43. General Whitehead to General Kenney, 16 March 1946, 168.6008-3-Kenney, AFSHRC.

44. Kenney, *Reports,* p. 435.

45. General Whitehead to General Kenney, 5 June 1946, 168.6008-3-Kenney, AFSHRC.

46. *New York Times,* 7 April 1946, p. 27.

47. John L. Chapman, *Atlas: The Story of a Missile* (New York: Harper and Brothers, 1960), pp. 27-29. In early October 1946, the AAF did gain control over the missile research and development program. See Memorandum for CG; AAF, AFG, and Chiefs, Technical Services, Subj: Guided Missiles, 7 October 1946, Spaatz Collection, Library of Congress, Washington, D.C.

48. General Whitehead to General Kenney, 4 July 1946, 168.6008-3-Kenney, AFSHRC.

49. General Whitehead to General Kenney, 26 July 1946, 168.6008-3-Kenney, AFSHRC.

50. Ibid. Actually SAC had reached 90 percent of authorization in July. See "Strategic Air Command Statistical Summary I, 1946." A summary prepared by Hdq. Strategic Air Command, Andrews AFB, Md., 1947, Sec. II, p. 1 (hereafter cited as "Statistical Summary 1946"), 416.01-46, AFSHRC.

51. "SAC-1946," pp. 66-69.

52. "SAC-1946," p. 73.

53. Untitled memorandum, Col. Arno Luehman, A-5 to Chief of Staff, SAC, 9 April 1946, 416.01-46, AFSHRC.

54. "SAC-1946," p. 73.

55. "SAC-1946," pp. 82-85.

56. AAF Ltr., 20-91, to CG and CO Major Commands, subj: Interim and Peacetime Air Force Plans, 14 February 1946, 168.116020-91, AFSHRC.

57. "Statistical Summary 1946," pp. 1-5.

58. "SAC-1946," pp. 157-59.

59. The AAF considered technical skills as those which required a specialized knowledge in a scientific or mechanical field such as electronics, instrument repair, or engine maintenance. These skills required an organized training program, usually conducted in classrooms and workshops. Although duty in supply or security police also required organized training, these were not considered technical fields at the time.

60. Wesley Craven and James Cate, eds., *The Army Air Forces in World War II*, vol. 6: *Men and Planes* (Chicago: University of Chicago Press, 1955), pp. 539-42.

61. Hdq. SAC to CG 15th AF, subj: Critical SSN Shortages, 11 July 1946, 416.01-46, AFSHRC.

62. Hdq. AAF to CG SAC, subj: Elimination of Inept Personnel, 13 September 1946, 416.01-46, AFSHRC.

63. Hdq. 15th AF to CG SAC, subj: Survey of Training Command Transferees, 23 December 1946, 416.01-46, AFSHRC. Among commanders, the term inept came to describe any airman not suited for military duty, from low intelligence, poor attitude, or general inability to fulfill military duties.

64. General Streett to Col. William Hudnell, 20 November 1946, 416.01-46, AFSHRC. Streett wanted the scores raised to 100-110 and noted he had a few airmen who could not read.

65. Hdq. 15th AF to CG SAC, subj: Survey of Training Command Transferees, 23 December 1946, 416.01-46, AFSHRC.

66. CG AAF to CG SAC, subj: Local Recruiting Features, 28 May 1946, 416.01-46, AFSHRC.

67. See "Strategic Air Command Statistical Summary I," Personnel. A summary prepared by Hdq. Strategic Air Command, Andrews AFB, Md., for September 1946, p. 20. See also "Statistical Summary 1946," 416.01-46, AFSHRC.

68. Hdq. SAC to CG 15th AF, subj: Short Term Enlistees, 13 December 1946, 416.01-46, AFSHRC.

69. With officers, SAC struggled with a surplus. During 1946, the AAF established procedures for discharging excess officers according to their past records and future potential. See "SAC-1946," pp. 172-76.

70. Hdq. AAF to CG Major Air Commands, subj: Personnel Inventory of the Army, 24 October 1946, 416.01-46, AFSHRC.

71. General Streett to General Born, 30 September 1946, 416.01-46, AFSHRC.

72. Hdq. SAC to CG 15th AF, subj: Survey of Personnel Accounting Procedures in 15th AF, 8 October 1946, 416.01-46, AFSHRC.

73. Sparrow, p. 362.

74. Millis, p. 102.

75. Carl Spaatz, *Report of the Chief of Staff USAF to the Secretary of the Air Force* (Washington, D.C.: Government Printing Office, June 1948), p. 13.

3 A WRONG TURN

Maj. Gen. Clements McMullen became deputy commander of Strategic Air Command in January 1947 and assumed extensive responsibility both for the command's daily operations and for its long-range development. Like Kenney, McMullen believed SAC would face two related problems in the forthcoming year. There was little hope for additional personnel during 1947, and SAC would have to restructure its forces and command to achieve greater efficiency. SAC needed to improve its ability to move combat and support units to forward bases quickly, although hampered by the manpower shortage. With Kenney's approval McMullen focused on these objectives and neglected realistic training of combat crews. He became closely identified with the command's reorganization and thus strongly influenced SAC's development during the following two years.

SAC needed to improve its mobility to support unification and develop a strong capability. The army and navy issued a joint letter in January 1947 agreeing upon a basis for unification. The following month President Truman sent both Houses of Congress his proposed legislation, giving each service autonomy and equal status under a secretary of national defense. The War Department and Navy Department held reservations about the compromise bill, but aviators closed ranks, supported the executive's plan, and hoped for passage.[1] Each air command had to demonstrate the capability to carry out its assigned mission. SAC held responsibility for the Army Air Force's most critical mission, long-range strategic bombing with atomic and conventional weapons. If the command failed to develop that capability, the drive for independence would suffer. More importantly, SAC's potential as a military force would be limited unless it could deploy men and equipment quickly to forward bases. Existing bombers could not operate adequately from the United States.

During 1947, the AAF enjoyed mixed success in achieving autonomy, expanding research and development and improving its strategic bombing force. In late July, Congress approved Truman's National Security Act, which guaranteed autonomy for the AAF and gave the navy control over its own aviation and over the marine corps. The act further provided for a Research and Development Board to coordinate activities of interest to all the services. Headed by a civilian, the board contained two representatives from each military branch. Research and development, however, encountered severe fiscal restraints. The president was aiming for a balanced budget in 1947, and the War Department reduced funding for AAF research and development from the previous level of $185 million to $145 million. The insufficiency of funds forced the military to terminate work on guided missiles and other long-range projects, but technical work on existing equipment continued with useful results.[2] Manpower shortages continued as the AAF directed the command to activate additional groups. The AAF could outfit only fifty-five groups; many were skeleton units. Nonetheless, SAC acquired more trained specialists, increased its group force, and expanded operational flying.[3] Kenney's and McMullen's first full year with SAC brought considerable improvement to the struggling command. The AAF became an independent U.S. Air Force in September and, despite setbacks, ended the year with optimism.

Kenney had selected McMullen as his deputy on the basis of personal knowledge (and, perhaps, of Whitehead's recommendations). The two generals had enjoyed a long acquaintance; both had entered the Signal Corps as aviation cadets in 1917 and had flown together on border patrol in the southwest. Before joining the army, McMullen had worked as a civil engineer; in 1923 he became an engineering officer for the corps. With only occasional interruptions, he continued a support career and commanded various service squadrons and organizations. McMullen became chief of the Maintenance Division at Patterson Field, Ohio, in December 1942, and two years later he assumed command of the Far Eastern Air Service (FEAS), supporting Kenney's Pacific operation in an impressive manner. Early in 1946, General Whitehead named McMullen chief of staff, PACUSA; but in November, McMullen departed to command SAC's Eighth Air Force at Fort Worth, Texas. Later that year, when the AAF reassigned General Streett, Kenney appointed McMullen as his deputy.[4]

McMullen's selection seemed appropriate for one principal reason. SAC would need an improved operation before it could achieve optimum mobility, and McMullen's contemporaries considered him an expert on organization and efficiency. Although he had not commanded a combat group during World War II, McMullen brought to SAC a strong interest and background in support activities and unit organization. Superiors and subordinates alike considered McMullen a driving, tireless worker, who held strong opinions and would not easily alter his convictions or command decisions. Many believed him obstinate, but Kenney felt that McMullen had the ability to reorganize SAC efficiently under the restraints of a peacetime budget. He described McMullen as "a little tough with iron in his soul."[5] During McMullen's tenure SAC adopted new personnel policies, restructured its combat units, and drastically altered the command headquarters—actions that promised to improve the command's efficiency and permit greater mobility.

McMullen first visited SAC Headquarters in early December 1946 and reviewed future command plans with Kenney. They discussed capability, and Kenney advised McMullen that he wanted to demonstrate SAC's mobility as soon as they became better organized.[6] The commander had specific reasons. Future warfare would demand quick movement of the small strategic force; only with practice could units execute an efficient deployment on short notice. The mobility of the United States strategic forces would also reassure our European allies. In light of World War II experience, the flying generals believed that air and sea power now shared responsibility for America's first line of defense. In articles, speeches, and books, aviators and their supporters constantly stressed this point, a point also used to justify independence for the air arm.[7] Yet the argument would carry little weight unless the AAF could demonstrate mobility and the capability to react. When Kenney and McMullen met in December, prospects for either unification or autonomy appeared dim. For these reasons, the command had to reorganize its manpower and streamline its structure to achieve mobility.

During 1947, General Kenney divided his time between SAC and other AAF activities, including that of public spokesman for air power. Air leaders had urged Kenney to accept as many speaking invitations as possible in order to further AAF objectives, and Kenney needed little prodding. He spoke well, and his wartime reputation made him a welcomed guest at hearings, conventions, assemblies, and public ceremonies. His topics usually included the past accomplishments of air power, its existing capabilities, and the air arm's future role in an atomic age. AAF leaders wanted the air-power story constantly repeated; Americans needed to understand their first line of defense. General Spaatz urged each commander to give public relations serious attention; if strong public support were developed, he argued, an expanded, improved, and independent air arm could follow.[8] Kenney considered his role as spokesman very important to the AAF, and most other fliers agreed. It took him away from SAC headquarters frequently, and, in his absence, greater responsibility for day-to-day command operations passed to McMullen. But Kenney had the utmost confidence in his deputy, considering him loyal and highly capable.

Over the years, McMullen had developed ideas on organization, and, with Kenney's support, he established policies and pursued actions which greatly affected SAC's personnel structure—and, ultimately, its capability. He believed the flying force had failed to reduce itself properly after the war and felt that every wing had a manpower surplus. In his view, units could perform their work with fewer but more capable people. McMullen especially wanted to trim the number of officers and to ensure that each made a genuine contribution to the SAC mission. He had grave reservations about the percentage of rated officers (fliers, including nonpilots) versus nonrated officers in the AAF. His doubts had their roots in the Army Air Corps of the 1930s.[9]

Before 1941, the AAC had strictly limited the number of nonflying officers taken into its command. The corps preferred to have qualified pilots performing all tasks, both in the air (navigation, for instance) and on the ground (including maintenance, administration, and command). The AAC's small size encouraged this practice, which was based primarily on the consideration that those who could fly would best understand the support activities related to aviation. The smoothest and most effective operation, therefore, required qualified pilots at every unit position. In peacetime, the air arm might reach this goal; but in war, everyone considered it impossible to train a sufficient number of pilots to handle every assignment.[10] During World War II, nonflying officers had increased in number and had worked in many support positions previously held by pilots. Aircrew members began their training in just one specialty; they became pilots, navigators, bombardiers, and flight engineers. The wartime experience proved that nonrated officers could expertly accomplish many duties, and it was felt a return to the old practice would waste talent.

General McMullen, however, believed in the prewar system; he was obsessed with the idea that only pilots had value in operational units.[11] Even as FEASC commander, he had asked Kenney for as many competent, combat-experienced fliers as possible for his support organization.[12] McMullen worried that the AAF had accumulated "a large percentage of non-flying officers who will take away the dash and glamour of the Air Forces." The result, he feared, would be a "precedent ridden lifeless activity similar to our prewar Quartermaster Corps."[13] As deputy commander he directed studies of various

SAC units to demonstrate that the most successful squadrons contained the largest proportion of aviators. McMullen believed SAC would improve its operations by taking a higher percentage of pilots into the command and by expanding their training to include nonflying duties.[14] Therefore, he accepted only a minimum number of nonrated officers.

Unfortunately, McMullen found many fliers unwilling to broaden their responsibilities beyond the cockpit; he abhorred this attitude. Young pilots, he reasoned, could never gain the necessary experiences to command units if they limited themselves to flying.[15] Moreover, strict specialization wasted the limited manpower supply. A pilot devoted only part of his working schedule to flying; in the time remaining, McMullen believed, these aviators could fill administrative positions currently held by nonfliers. Aviators could perform the tasks better and would reduce the manpower requirements and expense.[16] The AAF required 70 percent of its officer force to be rated, but McMullen wanted at least 80 percent, with each rated officer performing nonflying duties.[17]

McMullen considered his approach superior for another reason. As the year proceeded, SAC would have to increase its number of VHB groups with approximately the same number of officers.[18] His plan for requiring all aviators to hold assorted positions offered the best hope for success in that undertaking. Therefore, McMullen continually urged his field commanders to cut their officer force and to utilize aviators in several roles.

Most of McMullen's subordinates agreed with the concept of training aircrew members for nonflying duties, but the deputy commander encountered opposition when he expanded the concept to include cross-training of crew members for other aircrew positions. McMullen believed every pilot should become proficient in every aircrew duty (another prewar practice), and he wanted all other crew members trained for each nonpilot task. This would further reduce manpower requirements and make officers far more valuable. Versatile crew members, he reasoned, would ameliorate future shortages in any specialty, as a group would be able to rectify any imbalance by juggling personnel without interrupting operations. Moreover, as fliers learned the tasks of other crewmen, improved flight coordination would follow. Commanders, however, feared the additional training requirements: they would hinder a flier in developing and maintaining his primary specialty and would therefore cause decreased proficiency.

McMullen gave a hint of his intentions in a letter to Brig. Gen. Roger Ramey, commander of SAC's Eighth Air Force, in March 1947. The deputy commander had just reviewed the composition of a VHB squadron, attempting to reduce its officer requirements. McMullen suggested that SAC allow noncommissioned officers to serve as flight engineers and recommended that all navigators receive training as bombardiers and radar observers. These measures would permit a crew to operate with three officers instead of five, and squadrons could reduce their officer force by one-third.[19] The logic behind his proposal failed to impress SAC commanders, however. They believed that cross-training would run counter to SAC's immediate purpose of building a capable combat force, because it imposed a heavy burden on the command's personnel force. In effect, McMullen wanted SAC to develop an additional capability (basic aircrew training), which duplicated an Air Training Command (ATC) mission.

General McMullen remained firm and continued to develop his cross-training program. He unsuccessfully requested ATC to supply SAC with several mobile training units to support his efforts, while SAC planners modeled their new training courses on existing ATC programs.[20] Cross-training would require many months for each flier to complete: for pilots, between one and two years. Therefore, McMullen directed units to prepare detailed records for each trainee, although he imposed no completion deadlines. Experienced crew members would begin cross-training first, while still fulfilling their primary flying duties.

The deputy commander hoped to implement part of his program in August, but he continued to meet resistance.[21] The cross-training program simply found little support within SAC. McMullen's own Operations Analysis Branch (OAB) criticized the plan. The command could not provide the additional manpower needed for training duty, and therefore most crew members would have to assume instructional duties in addition to their usual ones. Training planners had not prepared their programs carefully, and the results were second-rate. Crew members, the OAB warned, would soon discover weaknesses in the approach and would fail to put forth the proper effort. Even if the programs were successful, months would pass before any benefits appeared; in the meantime, the cross-training activity would gravely threaten SAC's combat capability. Resigned to McMullen's insistence on adopting the plan, the analysis branch advised taking more time to prepare for implementing it and recommended a stand-down period at each station in order to concentrate on completing the program as quickly as possible.[22]

Ignoring these basic recommendations, McMullen pushed the program. As most crew members and commanders disliked the plan, he used threatening action to stem any discord. Poor attitudes toward cross-training, he advised his commanders, should reflect adversely on an officer's effectiveness report.[23] SAC began implementing the plan in late 1947, but full-scale cross-training was not possible until 1948. During 1948, the negative results predicted by the OAB and many of McMullen's subordinates became evident. It is ironic that McMullen, a general noted for his efficiency and organizational knowledge, instigated and implemented this disastrous personnel policy.

SAC's new deputy commander also held strong opinions about staffs and about lines of communication between commanders and subordinates. McMullen considered most staffs overmanned, inefficient, and frequently prohibitive to smooth operations and direct communications. He preferred to keep his staff small and, whenever possible, to direct the command's operations personally. Expecting his subordinate commanders to adopt a similar position toward their lower-level staffs, he quickly set an example.

When McMullen arrived at Andrews Field, Maryland (SAC's new headquarters), the command was using a typical staff organization. The general staff consisted of six agencies:

Personnel, Intelligence, Operations, Supply and Maintenance, Plans, and Communications. Eighteen staff agencies (Adjutant General, Chaplain, Finance, and so on) assisted the general staff. In all, twenty-four administrative agencies had direct access to General Kenney and four deputies: McMullen, an executive officer, a chief of staff, and his deputy.[24] McMullen immediately eliminated and consolidated agencies and streamlined the staff; in doing so, he assumed more direct responsibility for operations.

McMullen first reorganized the reporting procedures by requiring special staff groups to work through the general staff, thus reducing the number of groups reporting directly to the commander.[25] He then combined Communications with Operations, abolished the executive officer's position, and assumed chief-of-staff responsibilities himself. Later the AAF reassigned the deputy chief of staff, and McMullen left the position unfilled. By December 1947, the SAC command structure consisted of five general staff agencies that screened most of the special staff activity and reported to McMullen.[26] Within a year, the deputy commander had consolidated the staffs and had assumed a strong command position. Whenever Kenney became involved with public activities or problems at AAF level, SAC's operations were completely directed by McMullen.

Unlike McMullen, many unit commanders lacked the necessary authority to accomplish their missions, a problem that stemmed from army organizational practice. Throughout World War II and for two years thereafter, station commanders, regardless of background, had controlled every unit assigned to their bases. Although the combat group held responsibility for the primary mission, its commander did not control the supporting units. General Spaatz had termed this arrangement intolerable because tactical commanders were often forced to negotiate for proper support; he urged his commands to eliminate the problem.[27] The AAF gave its commands freedom to implement new organizational plans for their bases that would give combat commanders the necessary authority to fulfill their missions.

Commands were given a choice of developing their own

arrangements or adopting the recently designed Hobson Plan, which attempted to solve the command problem by vesting full authority in a wing commander who, in turn, held responsibility for the combat mission. The proposal evolved from a survey conducted immediately after World War II by the AAF Air Inspector, Maj. Gen. Junius W. Jones. His department surveyed thirty-two different installations, interviewed commanders, and compiled suggestions for improving base organizations. The final report, appearing in November 1945, stressed the lack of organizational uniformity within the AAF and the confusion in command channels at station levels. The report recommended that the AAF establish a self-sustaining, standard tactical unit containing the necessary combat, logistical, and administrative elements. Col. Kenneth B. Hobson, chief of the Organizational Division, then developed a reorganization plan that incorporated the report's recommendations.[28] Hobson's final proposal provided a wing organization for each station, comprised of four component groups: combat, maintenance and supply, airdrome, and hospital. This plan formed the basis for AAF Regulation 20-15, which directed all AAF commands to implement a standard organization, effective July 1947.

In June, before the AAF directive appeared, SAC had permitted its two air forces, the Eighth and the Fifteenth, to formulate their own station reorganizations, provided that each left support-group control to the tactical group commander. The Fifteenth AF alone had designed five different plans, each containing a provisional wing structure over all the groups assigned to a base. (Later SAC proposals reflected the command's need for mobility and were better adapted to its atomic weapons capability.) The first two arrangements proved unsatisfactory. Plan ABLE simply superimposed a wing headquarters over three equal groups: combat, service, and airdrome.[29] The wing, with a staff of six branches plus special agencies, played a supervisory role only. A second proposal, BAKER, recognized SAC's mobility requirement and merged the service and combat groups under a wing headquarters. Both groups could then deploy to forward bases with sufficient self-service and maintenance capability. Whenever necessary, the airdrome group would follow the combat units, leaving behind a skeleton section to administer the station. BAKER failed in part because it emphasized group rather than squadron deployment, another organizational legacy from World War II.

When McMullen joined SAC in January 1947, Fifteenth AF presented a third proposal, Plan CHARLIE, to a SAC conference, where commanders enthusiastically approved the new approach. CHARLIE gave greater attention to delivering atomic weapons, using the arctic region, and operating with squadrons instead of groups. To increase mobility, CHARLIE organized combat and maintenance squadrons to deploy anywhere on short notice. The airdrome group would prepack, seal, and store the necessary equipment for a thirty-day operation at any location.[30] Then, when called upon, the airdrome group would form and man a mobile support unit to accompany the combat and maintenance squadrons with the prepared supplies and equipment. Each wing was to be provided with an air transport unit of twelve C-54s to assist in deployment.

Plan CHARLIE clearly suited SAC's needs, but it presented problems. First, the combat group commander, charged with the primary mission, still did not control all support functions; now he depended upon the wing commander. Second, the plan divided the wing into many squadrons, each capable of independent operation, and forced manning to exceed 2,000 men per combat group. SAC could not provide (nor would General McMullen tolerate) such a level. To resolve these problems, SAC was forced to revise Plan CHARLIE.

CHARLIE-REVISED and three additional plans, DICK, DOG, and EASY, made further improvements. Each of them reduced the manning figures—but insufficiently, as SAC's manpower authorizations decreased several times during May and June. On 1 May, SAC established Plan DOG on all bases, which largely solved the control problem. This plan, instead of integrating separately controlled service and tactical units, gave the officer responsible for any mission direct command of all units and personnel authorized to support his operation. Plan DOG, however, became useless when manpower ceilings fell. Plan EASY, adopted on 1 June, resembled the previous proposals but actually made the combat group commander the wing commander, thus firmly establishing the primacy of combat-commander control. With maximum efficiency in mind, SAC gave the wing commander complete freedom in assigning his allotted manpower. The service group commander supported the combat groups and operated the base.[31] This promising plan never received a fair test, as it was superseded by Regulation 20-15, which directed every command to begin adopting the Hobson or Wing Base Plan at all stations on 1 July.

The Hobson Plan appeared compatible with manpower economy, efficiency, and SAC's mobility needs. As in Plan EASY, joint jurisdiction and responsibility rested with a single commander who now held strong central control. With command channels clear, decentralized operations could follow. The proposal reduced the size of basic functional units but actually created more command positions for company-grade officers. The plan contained features that General McMullen could support.

Unfortunately, the AAF implemented the Wing Base Plan with insufficient preparation, and the transition was difficult, confusing, and protracted. The directive to adopt the Hobson Plan came unexpectedly for SAC and the other commands; no warning or realistic testing preceded the announcement. As late as 11 June, McMullen had discussed a new organizational arrangement with his Fifteenth AF commander, unaware of the forthcoming change.[32] Tactical Air Command had even scheduled an organizational conference with the chief of staff for early July, having received no notice before the directive appeared. On 1 July 1947, AAF leaders met hurriedly with command representatives to announce the order.

The new regulation lacked instruction and allowed deviation. ATC and Air Material Command sought and received permission to delay implementation, while TAC was granted one week to draw up recommended manpower authorizations for stations containing tactical groups.[33] SAC proceeded with selected units and directed the 56th Fighter and two VHB Wings to begin operations under the new plan on 15 August. Three additional units would adopt the Hobson Plan in November. Regulation 20-15 offered no new manning documents; instead, it advised commands to use old or modified Tables of

Organization and Equipment (TO&E) in reorganizing their combat groups.[34] Support units relied upon existing distribution tables to determine personnel requirements, although they could request supplemental additions. In effect, the AAF implemented the plan on a small, experimental basis and expected field evaluations and recommendations for changes within three months. Based upon these experiences and information, the AAF would then establish new manning tables.

The Wing Base Plan supported SAC's needs for clear command authority, efficiency, and mobility. McMullen, however, believed the plan permitted too many men in each group. In August he imposed his own manpower ceilings on SAC units. With passive support from the AAF, the command established lower officer ceilings for every station, wing, group, and squadron within the command. The new level, known as the "General McMullen Ceiling," reduced the officers assigned each wing under the old TO&E by 10 to 20 percent.[35] SAC permitted a VHB wing with three combat groups, a maximum of 227 officers, contrasted with 287 under the Wing Base Plan.[36] McMullen's reasoning had remained unchanged. By forcing officers to fill flying and administrative positions and by ambitiously pursuing cross-training, the command could reduce its manpower requirements. These policies would broaden career experiences and produce superior officers and commanders. McMullen's modifications, however, placed a heavy strain on each unit.

After three months, two SAC units filed their evaluations of the Wing Base Plan with Fifteenth AF. The 307th VHB Wing and the 56th Fighter Wing approved the new organization, in general, with minor recommendations for change. Both wings, however, complained of personnel shortages in officer and enlisted ranks.[37]

Two major difficulties had emerged from McMullen's restrictions. The deputy commander had assumed that virtually all assigned officers would be on station to perform their many duties. In reality, an average of 20 percent were attending technical or professional schools, on maneuvers, on leave, or ill. As SAC wanted the maximum number attending technical training with ATC, the command could do little about absences. With 20 percent of the officer force unavailable for duty, unit efficiency fell by at least that figure. Low and poorly planned ceilings had become counterproductive.

The second problem centered on inadequate wing staffs. Because McMullen disapproved of large staffs and deputies, he had limited wing headquarters to thirteen officers, half the usual number. This action precluded a normal general staff of A-1, A-2, and so on, and forced the wing commander to use group personnel in double roles. Now the combat group commander also acted as A-3; the support group commander served as A-4. Both were assisted by their own group staffs. In effect, the group commanders directed the general staff that normally supervised and evaluated group performance; they became their own reviewers. McMullen supported this arrangement, believing that group commanders should have direct responsibility to the wing commander. An intermediate staff of separate officers contributed little and did not justify the cost.[38]

To alleviate both problems, Fifteenth AF requested a 20 percent increase in officer strength. McMullen stood firm and refused the appeal. He suggested that if each unit fully pursued cross-training the manpower shortage would disappear. Moreover, McMullen felt a strong personal obligation to use the taxpayer's dollar wisely, and he forced into practice his often-repeated motto, "Give them half of what they asked for, work them twice as hard, and they will get twice as much done."[39] Kenney supported economy measures; he believed that "the peacetime economy requirements for the manning of units of the United States Air Force is relatively more important than the requirement for maintaining the tactical integrity of our units."[40] More important, Kenney and McMullen could not honor the Fifteenth's request because their command lacked the necessary resources.

Meanwhile, SAC had to continue expanding its number of combat groups. In March 1947, realizing that Congress would not approve funds for a seventy-group air force, the AAF established an intermediate goal of fifty-five. Four months later, all fifty-five groups were ordered to be organized, at least partially manned, and operating at some level of efficiency by 1 January 1948.[41] SAC began placing more combat groups at each station, thus reducing the number of support personnel required, but the command could not provide additional men for established groups and still expand to meet the AAF goal. General Kenney had little choice but to demand manpower economy, and General McMullen considered his policies workable and proper.

SAC's dilemma stemmed from confusion over the proper approach to building and maintaining a peacetime air arm and the effect of its organization on autonomy and appropriations. The AAF could form a small number of highly trained and mobile forces that would operate very effectively at the outbreak of hostilities. That same force would have great difficulty expanding for full mobilization. If the air arm chose to form more units, even at reduced levels of efficiency, emergency expansion could follow more quickly and easily. Many air leaders doubted that the United States would ever fully mobilize again during the atomic age and personally favored the first approach. Other considerations existed. During the first half of 1947, AAF leaders operated under suspense and pressures; they believed the unification bill before Congress had no better than an even chance of passage, and they knew that a small air force, however efficient, would not aid the AAF cause. The three services would divide future defense appropriations; as the first line of defense, the AAF would require more than an equal portion. By maintaining only a few highly capable groups, aviators would place their service at a future disadvantage, politically and economically. Consequently, the AAF undertook a more ambitious program to develop more groups; but that approach placed a burden on every command without doing anything to improve capability.

Strategic Air Command had begun 1947 searching for efficiency in operation and greater mobility. As in 1946, manpower presented the principal obstacle. Improved organization offered the best hope for success; and, when General McMullen became deputy commander in January, he properly sought these goals through reorganization. SAC modified its command structure and organized its combat forces into more mobile units. But, as manpower authorizations declined during the year, instability instead of efficiency followed. When McMullen added his own restrictions to the Wing Base Plan and began a cross-training program, units encountered operating problems. To compound the difficulties, SAC needed to establish additional groups by 1948. At year's end, the command technically manned seventeen combat groups (including five fighter groups), but the capability of each for worldwide operation remained open to question. Insufficient manpower had impeded efforts to build a highly mobile and capable strategic air arm, and SAC's commanders felt compelled to emphasize reorganization and efficiency rather than realistic combat training.

To his credit, General McMullen's efforts yielded some results. Officer strength grew by only 200 during 1947, and enlisted ranks by 5,500, yet SAC formed eight additional groups and tripled the number of B-29s on hand and maintained.[42] The nation's strategic force, however, encountered no threat or test in 1947, and the question of actual capability took second place to autonomy and the struggle for appropriations. Not until early 1948 did the United States fear the Soviet Union's activities in Europe and then examine SAC's capability. The imbalance of the approach taken during 1947 then became apparent.

NOTES

1. R. Earl McClendon, *Unification of the Armed Forces* (Montgomery: Air University, 1952), pp. 32-35.

2. U.S. Congress, House, Committee on Appropriations, *Military Establishment Appropriations Bill of 1948: Hearings before a subcommittee of the Committee on Appropriations*, 80th Cong., 1st sess. 1947, pp. 613-16. See also Alfred Goldberg, ed., *A History of the United States Air Force, 1907-1957* (New York: D. Van Nostrand Inc., 1957), p. 201.

3. *Report of the Chief of Staff United States Air Force to the Secretary of the Air Force* (Washington, D.C.: Government Printing Office, 1948), p. 57 (hereafter cited as *C/S Report-1948*).

4. "History of Strategic Air Command 1947." Typescript history prepared by Hdq. Strategic Air Command, Offutt, AFB, Nebr., 1949,

unpaged Biography Section (hereafter cited as "SAC-1947"), Albert F. Simpson Historical Research Center, Maxwell Air Force Base, Alabama (hereafter cited as AFSHRC).

5. General Kenney to General Whitehead, 14 May 1947, 168.6008-3-Kenney, AFSHRC.

6. General McMullen to General Whitehead, 13 December 1946, 168.6008-3-McMullen, AFSHRC.

7. General H. Arnold made this point in his *Third Report of the Commanding General of the Army Air Forces to the Secretary of War* (Washington, D.C.: U.S. AAF, 1945), p. 72. See also the testimonies of Generals Arnold, James Doolittle, and Kenney, U.S. Congress, Senate, Committee on Military Affairs, *Department of Armed Forces Department of Military Security, Hearings S. 84 and S. 1482*, 79th Cong., 1st sess. 17 October to 17 December 1945. A representative article is found in General Kenney's "Strategic Air Command," *Military Review*, August 1947, pp. 3-7.

8. General Spaatz to General Kenney, 1 May 1946, Spaatz Collection, Library of Congress, Washington, D.C.

9. The term "rated" referred to officers given aeronautical training and official ratings as pilots, navigators, bombardiers, or flight engineers.

10. Monte D. Wright, *Most Probable Position* (Lawrence: University Press of Kansas, 1972), pp. 183-85.

11. Maj. Gen. John B. Montgomery, a private interview held at Los Angeles, California, 14 July 1975. See also Oral History Interview with Lt. Gen. C. S. Irvine by Robert M. Kipp, March AFB, Calif., 17 December 1970, pp. 15-16, Interview no. 734, AFSHRC.

12. Wesley Craven and James Cate, eds., *The Army Air Forces in World War II*, vol. 5: *The Pacific: Matterhorn to Nagasaki* (Chicago: University of Chicago Press, 1953), p. 339.

13. General McMullen to General Whitehead, 17 April 1947, 168.6008-3-McMullen, AFSHRC.

14. General McMullen to Brig. Gen. Roger Ramey, CG 8th AF, 23 July 1947, 416.01-47, AFSHRC. See also General McMullen to General Whitehead, 6 January 1948, 168.6008-3-McMullen, AFSHRC.

15. General McMullen to General Ramey, 11 March 1947, 416.01-47, AFSHRC.

16. In January 1947, General Spaatz established this concept as AAF policy and called upon commands for support. See General Spaatz to General Kenney, 1 January 1947, 416.01-47, AFSHRC.

17. CG/SAC to CG/AAF, subj: Reduced Manning Level, 19 April 1947, 416.01-47, AFSHRC.

18. See *C/S Report-1948*, p. 56.

19. General McMullen to General Ramey, 14 March 1947, 416.01-47, AFSHRC.

20. CG/ATC to CG/SAC, subj: Requirements for Additional Formalized Training, 29 October 1947, 416.01-47, AFSHRC.

21. SAC Ltr., 353, CG/SAC to C/G Eighth and Fifteenth Air Force and C/G MacDill Field, subj: Cross Training, 3 July 1947, pp. 1-3, 416.01-47, AFSHRC.

22. Mr. Carroll L. Zimmerman, Chief, Operations Analysis, to AC/S, A-3 SAC, subj: Proposed Cross Training Program, 22 August 1947, 416.01-47, AFSHRC.

23. See SAC Ltr. 353, AFSHRC.

24. "Strategic Air Command Statistical Summary I, 1946." A summary prepared by Hdq., Strategic Air Command, Andrews AFB, Md., January 1947, p. 3, AFSHRC.

25. Staff Memorandum No. 20-13, Hdq., SAC, subj: Organization Grouping of Staff Agencies, 13 March 1947, 416.01-47, AFSHRC.

26. "Strategic Air Command Statistical Summary 1947." A summary prepared by Hdq., Strategic Air Command, Andrews AFB, Md., January 1948, p. 3, AFSHRC.

27. "History of the Fifteenth Air Force 1947." Typescript history prepared by Hdq. Fifteenth Air Force, Colorado Springs, Colo., 1948, p. 32 (hereafter cited as "15th AF-1947"), AFSHRC.

28. Clarence McCauley, "Evaluation of Wing Organization," research paper, Air University, 1949), pp. 5-6, M-32984 NC, AFSHRC.

29. The following information on Fifteenth AF Plans is taken from "Extracts from Special Staff Study," prepared by Plans Branch, A-1 Division, Fifteenth AF, Colorado Springs, Colo., n.d., 416.01-47, AFSHRC.

30. Mary R. Self, "History of the AMC Supply Support of the Strategic Air Command 1946-1952." Typescript history prepared by AMC Historical Division, Wright-Patterson AFB, Ohio, 1954, p. 36, AFSHRC.

31. "15th AF-1947," pp. 28-29, AFSHRC.

32. General McMullen to Brig. Gen. Leon Johnson, 11 June 1947, 416.01-47, AFSHRC.

33. Ward W. Martindale, "Analysis of the New Wing Base Organization," research paper, Air University, 1948, p. 10, M-32984-R, AFSHRC.

34. "15th AF-1947," pp. 37-42, AFSHRC.

35. Interview notes with Col. Richard King, director of Personnel, SAC, 20 January 1949, 416.01-47, AFSHRC.

36. "15th AF-1947," pp. 42-43, AFSHRC.

37. Brig. Gen. D. R. Hutchinson, C/G 307th VHB Wing to C/G SAC, subj: Comments and Recommendations on Wing Base Organization, 13 November 1947, 416.01-47, AFSHRC. See also ltr., Col. W. Hudnell, CO 56th Fighter Wing, to C/G SAC, subj: Comments and Recommendations on the Hobson Plan, 20 November 1947, 416.01-47, AFSHRC.

38. Headquarters Fifteenth AF, "Study of Reorganization of Units—AAF Regulation 20-15," 17 November 1947, 416.01-47, AFSHRC. See also SAC 320.1, General McMullen to CG/15th AF, subj: Secondary Duties for Group Commanders, 9 October 1947, 416.01-47, AFSHRC.

39. Fifteen Air Force had requested the 20 percent increase before

the Hobson evaluations were submitted. See CG/15th AF to CG/SAC, subj: Officer Manning of Units under AAF Reg. 20-15, 13 September 1947, AFSHRC. See interview notes with Col. Richard King, director of Personnel, SAC, 20 January 1949, 416.01-47, AFSHRC.

40. General Kenney to C/S USAF, subj: Proposed Change in Manning and Housing of SAC Units (circa November 1947), 416.01-47, AFSHRC.

41. *C/S Report-1948*, p. 57.

42. Untitled memorandum, CG/SAC to CG/USAF, 15 January 1948, 416.01-47, AFSHRC.

4 A GLOBAL REACH?

Strategic Air Command's capacity to deliver conventional and atomic weapons to enemy targets during 1947 depended on forward bases in Western Europe, the Far Pacific, and the Arctic region. The command's bombers had limited range, which forced SAC to plan combat operations from overseas stations within reach of the Soviet Union and Eastern Europe. SAC groups needed mobility to move attack and supporting elements quickly to forward bases. Unit reorganization accomplished during the year focused on this requirement. To insure that VHB groups could deploy quickly and operate smoothly from overseas installations, SAC maintained a unit rotation policy. During the year groups or squadrons deployed overseas and conducted training for periods of up to thirty days. Once crew members became familiar with operating in a forward area, the probability of successful operations in the event of war increased.

Not all available bases were equipped or suited for SAC operations. During World War II, B-29s had flown only in the Pacific; European facilities and runways were frequently inadequate. After the war the AAF failed in its attempt to deploy B-29 groups to Europe (Project Wonderful), and the AAF did not maintain any VHB groups in Western Europe. The Pacific offered more encouragement; the United States had greater authority in that region, and wartime B-29 operations had been conducted from the Marianas. Forward bases in the western Pacific, however, were far removed from many important targets. In the Arctic the AAF had one principal base capable of supporting SAC operations: Ladd Field, near Fairbanks, Alaska. But the severe climate, the AAF's lack of experience in cold weather operations, and Ladd Field's inadequate facilities precluded any immediate possibility of dependable operations over the polar routes. The most secure forward area for the United States thus offered the most forbidding environment.

During the year SAC deployed units to all three regions, flew training missions, and conducted daily operations; but of the three, greatest emphasis fell upon the Arctic. Ownership of Alaska and the Aleutians, excellent relations with Canada, and access to Greenland made the northern approaches attractive. Equally important, this area offered the shortest route to enemy targets.

SAC's efforts in 1947 yielded mixed results. Deployments proceeded well in the Pacific, while training in Western Europe proved more difficult. Arctic operations encountered disappointing setbacks, largely because northern bases lacked facilities and equipment to support extensive operations in severe weather. Facing many other demands and a shortage of funds, the new United States Air Force could not provide the resources. Emphasis shifted from the Arctic after 1947 and focused on extending aircraft range and on developing bases in Western Europe and the Middle East.

SAC leaders began to plan operations from forward bases in July 1946. Maj. Gen. St. Clair Streett, then deputy commander, proposed a program of unit rotation and operation from the United States to three forward areas: the North Atlantic (Greenland, Iceland, Newfoundland, and Labrador), the North Pacific (Alaska, and the Aleutians), and the Far East (the Philippines and the Marshall and Ryukyu Islands).[1] Streett based his plan upon the B-29, which had a basic range of 3,000 nautical miles, although he anticipated the B-36 with its 10,000-mile range. Streett believed the strategic forces would remain small and flexible and suggested every SAC unit should deploy temporarily to each theater for training and familiarization.

Streett excluded Western Europe from his early plans, as did General McMullen when he joined SAC in January 1947. Kenney and his deputy placed less emphasis on Europe than on the other theaters, probably for three reasons. Both had fought in the Pacific and considered that region more critical to American interests. The Soviet Army in East Germany would be able to overrun military installations in the American Zone in a matter of days and threaten United States positions to the west. Moreover, the Labor government in England and the leaders of Iceland did not wish to become involved in military arrangements with the United States. Last, both generals believed that General Whitehead would provide excellent training for SAC units deploying to the Far East. McMullen felt the United States Air Forces, Europe (USAFE), were "doing nothing" about training in early 1947, and he did "not want our people to get contaminated with the do-nothing policy."[2] The decision to undertake European rotation, then, did not originate with SAC but with AAF.

The AAF in May 1947 directed SAC to prepare units for thirty-day rotations to Germany, beginning 1 September.[3] The next month, General Spaatz advanced the European deployment date to 1 July and shortened the tour to ten days. The State Department approved a program to send five VHB units to Europe during the remaining months of 1947. Every bomb group except the 509th (which alone had atomic capability) would conduct a rotation. The AAF advised SAC that the primary object of these deployments was to acquaint crew members with European operations and directed the movements to be executed without publicity.[4] The short visits permitted only limited familiarization.

In July the first B-29 squadron arrived at Giebelstadt Air Base in West Germany. Immediately it found operations difficult. Facilities and support proved inadequate, and flights complicated to arrange. Demonstration and training missions over European nations required diplomatic clearance from each country, but Denmark and France objected to B-29s crossing parts of their territory. The AAF had ordered SAC units not to overfly Holland and Belgium.[5] The Soviet Union protested bomber flights through the air corridor into and over Berlin. Obtaining permission for flights caused such difficulty that USAFE limited squadron training exercises to the British Isles, North Africa, and the Mediterranean.[6] Aircrews lacked access to bombing and gunnery ranges and could conduct only long-range and formation flying.[7] With no permanent VHB groups stationed in Europe, units found a shortage of spare parts difficult to overcome.[8] In general, SAC commanders did not feel early deployment to Germany offered meaningful training for units and crews, and SAC planners in September attempted to cancel these short-term deployments in order to concentrate on manning the groups assigned them under the fifty-five group plan.[9]

The air force insisted that rotation continue, and the situation improved by late 1947, as visiting crews began to accomplish more training, including long-range flights to Dhahran Air Base, Saudi Arabia. This facility, leased from the Saudi government, gave the air arm its closest base to Soviet targets.[10] Later in the year deployed groups began using Fürstenfeldbruck in Germany. Lt. Gen. Curtis LeMay assumed command of USAFE in October 1947, and he worked to expand and expedite construction at the base to accommodate three squadrons of B-29s.[11] USAFE obtained permission from the Royal Air Force in December to use more frequently the British-controlled bombing and gunnery ranges at Heligoland and Lubeck, Germany.[12] By year's end, all but two of the designated squadrons had completed a rotation tour to Europe, and several had had two trips.[13]

The European deployments served two purposes. They gave groups the practical experience of deploying overseas and operating from forward bases. They also were a means by which the United States demonstrated interest in Western Europe, consistent with the Marshall Plan and American concern over political events in Greece and Turkey.

SAC commanders continued to display greater enthusiasm for rotating units to the Far East; and when McMullen became

SAC's deputy commander, he and General Kenney began to plan a program of rotating B-29 units to the Pacific. At first, McMullen wanted to deploy six bombers (Kenney preferred an entire group) to Japan by March 1947.[14] Unable to meet this goal, McMullen later submitted a formal plan for rotating single squadrons, the first to arrive by 1 May 1947.[15] Whitehead had already indicated his strong support for the rotation policy; he had even suggested that his own 19th and 22nd VHB groups transfer to the United States and SAC, provided that the command would continually maintain two groups rotating in the Pacific. This arrangement would provide excellent deployment training for every unit and permit better utilization of each group. But Whitehead believed SAC should expand later movements to include far more men and equipment. A group should deploy each month, he suggested, with thirty aircraft and 1,350 men. Whitehead even offered to help transport SAC's personnel and equipment from Hawaii to Guam in the Far East Air Forces' C-54s.[16] A large deployment, he argued, would demonstrate SAC's mobility and self-sufficiency to the army and navy.

During early 1947, AAF leaders worried about the military unification bill before Congress and about the navy, which they considered the biggest obstacle to the bill's passage. Relations between the army and navy in the Pacific had suffered since 1943 because of disputes over theater command and authority. These circumstances led Whitehead to believe the AAF had to "take the play" away from the navy and demonstrate its own potential. "Can you imagine the consternation at Navy Headquarters," he wrote Kenney, "when you make the announcement of a mass move of a VHB Group, complete with its personnel from the Z.I. to Guam or Okinawa?" By using only the navy's facility at Barbers Point, Hawaii, for refueling, SAC could complete the entire deployment without naval assistance. The movement would display mobility and the capability to act alone and thus could aid the cause of air-arm independence. For greatest effect, Whitehead suggested the large group deployments begin on AAF Day, 1 August.[17]

Given manpower shortages, reorganization efforts, and other

commitments, however, SAC chose to continue its plan of deploying only single squadrons to the Pacific. In May 1947 the first unit arrived in Japan, and five more followed during the year. As fall approached, the United States experienced an aviation fuel shortage that limited flying operations. Although rotations to Europe continued, the AF directed SAC to cancel its November and December movements to the Pacific.[18]

In contrast to their experience in Europe, SAC units operated smoothly and efficiently in the Far East. The United States controlled Japan, the Marianas, and the Ryukyus; diplomatic clearances for overflights were not needed. Whitehead maintained active B-29 groups in his command; facilities and supplies presented no problems. After arriving, the deployed squadrons quickly began their familiarization with the theater and undertook a variety of training flights. Units conducted camera-bombing and live bomb drop exercises, as well as reconnaissance and sea search missions. Whitehead, a very capable combat commander, took great efforts to ensure that the visiting crews spent their time wisely; he considered SAC's capability most critical for the United States.[19] The rotation arrangement between the FEAF and SAC worked to the satisfaction of both commands. Although the small Pacific deployments failed to have the dramatic impact that Whitehead had desired, they demonstrated the best use of a forward area.

The shortest routes between North America and most of northern Europe and Asia traverse the polar region, and because the United States owned Alaska and enjoyed access to other portions of the area, SAC hoped to improve its limited bomber range by using forward bases in the Arctic. Unlike Europe and the Far Pacific, the Arctic presented difficult operational problems; the severe climate and the need for special equipment put use of the region out of the question for the immediate period. Soon after World War II, AAF leaders entertained great expectations for the polar routes. They believed a combination of experience and technology would allow the AAF to use the far north.

To operate in the Arctic the AAF needed more knowledge of several subjects. Aviators did not know how equipment would function under extremely low temperatures, nor did they understand how to conduct operations in the polar environment. Of less immediate concern to planners were the men: how would they function during a sustained period of severe weather? Unfortunately, the AAF's cold-weather experience was limited.

Before World War II the War Department had established Ladd Field in Alaska, primarily for cold-weather testing.[20] Previously, the army had directed cold-weather experiments in Minnesota, Michigan, and Maine; but complete testing required extended periods of extreme cold, a condition seldom found in the United States.[21] During the winters of 1940-41 and 1941-42 airmen conducting experiments at Ladd Field became convinced that, given time and preparation, the AAF could operate in extreme low temperatures—but not with equipment currently available. The following winter Japanese activity in the Aleutians interrupted cold-weather testing, although the United States was able to begin delivering aircraft to the Soviet Union via Fairbanks. September and October weather permitted normal operations; but, in November, extreme temperatures suddenly halted the movement. Oil coolers broke, hoses cracked, oil tanks froze, and wheel struts collapsed. The Cold Weather Testing Detachment worked with Materiel Command to complete the immediate task, and eventually thousands of aircraft deployed to the Soviet Union.[22] Most of the operating problems, however, remained unsolved. Interest in cold-weather operations heightened when air leaders learned that sub-zero temperatures had severely limited even the efficient Luftwaffe during Germany's invasion of the USSR. After World War II, the AAF realized that the knowledge necessary for cold-weather operations could be gained only by sending men, equipment, and units to the Arctic.

Although Ladd Field would serve as the primary test site, the AAF hoped to accomplish preliminary work in the United States. Air Proving Ground Command, which directed the Cold Weather Detachment, constructed at Eglin Field, Florida, a climatic hangar capable of duplicating many of the difficulties which combat units would encounter in cold-weather operations. The facility could maintain a low temperature of -70° F., and it enabled airmen to conduct cold-weather experiments throughout the year. In August 1946, APGC first tested a P-38 at -50° F. and found it unable to operate. Fluids leaked and froze when the aircraft's frame and cables contracted unevenly. Electrical wires became brittle, and switches and controls often froze.[23]

Aided by the new climatic hangar, APGC and SAC planned extensive Arctic tests for the 1946-47 winter; the experience would heavily influence SAC's plans for utilizing the Arctic. If the results proved negative, the command would direct greater effort toward extending flying range and would depend more on other forward bases. During that winter, nine different aircraft operated at Ladd Field, and three flying units conducted regular operational flights: SAC's 46th Reconnaissance and 62nd Fighter Squadrons and the 28th VHB Group.[24] Nature provided the AAF with one of the harshest winters on record, putting all operating units and equipment to the severest test possible. The results revealed SAC's inability to operate freely in the arctic environment.

The 28th Bombardment Wing encountered many problems when the unit deployed to Alaska. Commanders had prepared the wing poorly, and crew members received inadequate indoctrination; these deficiencies stemmed from limited cold-weather experience.[25] Air Training Command had hurriedly assembled two mobile training units to conduct orientation briefings for the northbound crews, but many instructors had never served in the Arctic and consequently offered poor instruction.[26] The ill-prepared wing arrived in Alaska in late December 1946, and still its men failed to receive appropriate instruction. Like SAC and ATC, Alaskan Air Command (AAC) had suffered severely from demobilization and its men possessed low experience levels. Airmen began their arctic training unfamiliar with cold-weather problems and their effects upon the body and equipment. During extreme temperatures they had to guard continually against frostbite and to avoid prolonged, rapid, or deep breathing to protect their lungs. Most men knew the danger of grasping cold metal with their bare hands; but few realized other dangers such as spilling gasoline on their hands, which could cause skin burns. Fliers frequently discarded their bulky arctic clothing; and, when temperatures dropped suddenly or aircraft heating systems failed, they quickly lost their effectiveness. Despite the obvious need, commands constantly had to direct airmen to wear proper clothing. Personal equipment required attention; oxygen masks would crumble if roughly handled at low temperatures.[27] Experience, a painful teacher, gave many such lessons before airmen learned to work in the cold climate.

To compound the difficulties, AAC lacked equipment and facilities to receive and support a large tactical unit undertaking full operations. Without adequate hangars, technicians had to perform aircraft maintenance with little protection from wind and snow. During the coldest months, airmen ran their vehicles continuously, because AAC lacked garages. Supplies from the United States came slowly and irregularly; once the wing had fourteen aircraft grounded for lack of parts.[28] Commanders found communication poor between Alaska and the United States, intolerable for any military operation and particularly so for the nation's principal offensive force.

Crew members of the 28th BW also developed personal problems. Adverse conditions alone did not lower morale; but when cold weather and equipment failures stopped their flying operations, the men became discouraged. Flight time decreased by 90 percent from summertime levels; and when aviators missed flying in any given month they lost flight pay, a substantial part of their salary.[29] No other fliers worked as hard to accomplish their mission, often with little success. During off-duty time the men found recreation limited and expensive; a sense of isolation developed among them. They came to feel authorities at higher headquarters had little interest in their work or problems. One observer rated the unit's morale no better than "fair," a term that also described the degree of its operational success.[30]

During January and February 1947 the 28th BW found great difficulty in conducting continuous operations because of inadequate equipment and extreme temperatures. Maintenance personnel found that without proper hangar space the B-29 could not function consistently below $^{-}40°$ F.[31] The squadrons scheduled most take-offs for mid-morning, and preparations began seven hours earlier. During severe cold, airmen slowly applied heat to the engines for at least three hours before starting, and this process was made more difficult by a lack of portable hangars to enclose the engines.[32] If the weather remained favorable after the preflight period, crews moved the aircraft to the runway. Because AAC lacked enough snow- and ice-removal equipment to keep taxiways clear and allow the bombers to taxi under their own power, the aircraft often had to be towed. Moreover, most of the towing vehicles had limited power and traction. At one point the 28th relied upon a twenty-six-ton armored personnel carrier for towing.[33] Aircraft tires often froze to the surface and would not round out easily when rolling.[34] Flight controls would stick, and smaller pilots frequently had trouble working the elevator trim.[35] The crews spent hours attempting to launch their aircraft, but their efforts often ended in cancellation or abort. Even if the B-29s launched, their crews faced other unfamiliar problems.

Inflight weather conditions in the Arctic largely determined the success of each mission. Under extreme temperatures the B-29 carburetors would malfunction because of inefficient heating capacity.[36] Propeller feathering systems could fail and create inflight fire hazards. If equipment functioned properly and the crew completed the mission, local weather could suddenly make the landing hazardous. Temperatures changed rapidly in the Arctic and, at low altitudes, icing conditions and ice fog could quickly develop around an airfield. When flying in poor weather, crews relied upon instruments and proper de-icing equipment, items that frequently failed in winter operations. On one occasion a pilot had to break his ice-covered window with a crash ax to land.[37]

A series of difficult flights placed a cumulative strain on crew members, a stress similar to that found in combat. The flight surgeon for the 28th BW noted such mental strains after observing the group operate for three months.[38] In his opinion the men could handle the cold well enough; but the vast, uncharted region, with its harsh terrain and icy conditions, provided a greater stress than the weather. The Arctic presented navigation problems, and if downed, crew members had little confidence in their survival equipment or in the AAF search and rescue units. The cumulative effect of these pressures forced two of the unit's crewmen to refuse flying duty after arriving in Alaska. These fliers had had no such fears previously. Yet all the aviators shared this anxiety to some degree, and with good reason.

The Arctic presented greater flying hazards than did other regions. If an aircraft developed trouble over a populated area elsewhere, the pilot could make an emergency landing at a nearby airstrip; if over water, the crew had a reasonable chance to ditch the airplane and launch life rafts. Again, if circumstances forced them to parachute in some temperate region, fliers had an excellent chance to survive until they could find help or be rescued by search teams. The Arctic, by contrast, offered none of these comforting possibilities, for two reasons: its size and its climate.

If one were to remove that portion of the globe north of the Arctic Circle and position it over the geographical center of the United States, it would cover the entire nation, Mexico, most of Cuba, large portions of the Pacific and Atlantic Oceans, and nearly all of the Canadian provinces. Only on the periphery of this vast expanse could a crew find an isolated airstrip. Aviators in trouble could only hope for a natural landing site; if the flier bailed out, he would not survive long. Crewmen downed on the polar ice cap or in the area of continual winter darkness had no chance.

Despite these overwhelming obstacles the AAF attempted to provide the best possible chance for survival. Search and rescue units operated in the north, using C-47s and C-54s with added tanks for extended range. If search crews located downed crew members, they faced a difficult pick-up. To remove men stranded on the polar ice cap, the AAF experimented with gliders; two, capable of carrying a B-29 crew, would be put down at the rescue site. When crewmen boarded the gliders and signaled, the plans would be snatched by tow lines from the rescue aircraft and returned to an airfield.[39] These units and procedures, by no means fully reliable, gave some hope to fliers.

Even though rescue was not impossible, downed airmen had to be able to survive while waiting to be located, and aviators lacked confidence in their personal survival equipment. The quality of emergency gear demanded improvement; existing equipment was not adequate for the Arctic. Items useful in tropical and temperate climates often held little value in the far north. Experienced crew members soon began to fashion their own gear, and carried it when flying far from their base. As the AAF recognized the problem, AMC began to design more appropriate survival kits. In the meantime crew members knew little about protecting themselves or about using their limited equipment if downed in the Arctic. Commanders had not prepared their fliers for cold-weather survival.[40]

With good reason the 28th BW flight surgeon listed polar navigation as the primary reason for aircrew stress. Every crew member pondered the possibility of being lost in that vast area, as any extended polar flight depended upon proper navigation, and conditions in the Arctic required procedures not used in the United States.

In the polar region, air navigation involved two critical problems. First, the magnetic compass became highly unreliable in northern latitudes because drastic variations in magnetic force occurred over short distances. Moreover, the vertical component of the magnetic field became stronger near the magnetic pole, making the horizontal force, which determined the compass reading, less accurate. Magnetic storms aggravated the problem by shifting the known magnetic lines of force. Second, inflight charts using the conventional geographic coordinate system proved troublesome in the polar region. Meridians converged at the pole, but each still represented a degree of longitude. To fly a constant course on such a chart, fliers had to continually alter headings, making precise navigation impossible.[41] Therefore, the navigator needed a different compass system and chart in this region.

Technically, aviators could solve both problems easily. They could eliminate compass difficulties by using a gyro system that had no reliance upon magnetic force. A freely spinning gyro will maintain its spin axis in a constant direction, allowing the navigator to determine a heading (based upon a celestial observation) and to set the figure into the compass.[42] The pilot can alter the aircraft's bearing in terms of degrees away, left or right, from the last heading. Magnetic or true-north headings are not used. Because small errors of precession exist in any gyro or compass, periodic corrections, based upon celestial observations, must be made continually and the compass corrected accordingly. By using special grid charts and a gyro compass, polar navigation could be accomplished easily and accurately.

Navigators accepted these drastic changes of technique with reluctance. When using a grid chart, an aircraft flying toward the North Pole might use a heading of 270 or 180 degrees. With a lifetime of true-north reference in mind, a navigator required genuine conviction in his computations before establishing such a heading. Moreover, when flying grid on a Lambert conformal chart, the navigator continually applied large convergence factors to most computations.[43] Compass precession could be excessive, forcing him to correct for both past and predicted drift. Only by using these new techniques could the navigator gain proficiency and confidence in the procedures, but this practice was not common in the United States.

The navigator contended with other problems unique to the Arctic. He could not depend upon the usual ground aids, because only a few stations transmitted directional signals in this vast area. Moreover, airborne radar had limitations. Land areas covered with varying depths of snow gave unreliable returns, while bodies of water could give reverse images. If ice formed an irregular pattern, it reflected terrain-type features; when smooth, normal land-water contrasts appeared.[44] The navigator, unaware of exact conditions below, had to take great care when using radar returns to determine his position. To complicate his task, he might find land features misplotted on his chart by as much as one degree of longitude.[45]

Celestial observations, when available, offered the most accurate information. But, in northern latitudes, familiar planets and stars are not always available for use; navigators could not observe celestial bodies during the long twilights. During these two- to four-hour periods, dead reckoning became the principal means of navigation. If compass errors and wind shifts developed, the aircraft could deviate far from its intended track without the crew's knowledge. The navigator prepared for this period by acquiring an accurate fix just prior to entering twilight. Clouds, however, could also prevent reliable observations, forcing the aircraft to proceed solely upon dead reckoning. The navigator had to exercise more caution and resourcefulness in the north, yet his usual flying experience did not equip him for Arctic operations.

Nor did stateside training prepare the crews mentally, as SAC soon discovered. In August 1947, the 43rd Bomb Group deployed on short notice to Ladd Field for two weeks of operational training. For the entire period, a representative from SAC's Analysis Branch observed the group and prepared a long evaluation for General McMullen.[46] He described a disorderly deployment, which lacked or left behind the proper equipment. AAC received the group poorly at Ladd Field, although activity scheduled for the 43rd appeared valuable. The observer worried most about crew members' attitudes, noting "the whole unit gave us the impression that they were plain scared of the prospects of going out over the ice." After arriving at Ladd Field, the fliers soon realized that "there might be something in all this arctic poop."

The staff at Ladd Field concluded that stateside training had not prepared the unit for polar operations. Because of the fliers' mental attitudes, the commander cancelled the first flights and instead conducted a ground school simulating polar flight. Finally, when sixteen crews launched training missions for the Arctic Ocean, all but five aborted upon reaching Pt. Barrow and returned to Ladd Field. The men understood polar flying procedures but lacked confidence in their ability. They came to Alaska apprehensive, and when they heard a survival lecture, they were "scared to death." They encountered no cold-weather difficulties, only a mental block about Arctic flying. Before VHB units could routinely deploy and conduct polar operations, the crew members first had to train in the region.

Aviators had some basis for their fears. They knew about the flight of Kee-Bird, a B-29 that had become lost in 1946. The aircraft had begun an eighteen-hour mission to the North Pole; on the return leg to Ladd Field, the crewmen had experienced some common arctic problems. The aircraft first encountered heavy clouds, preventing the navigator from making any celestial observations. The crew, refusing to use the gyro compass, continued on by dead reckoning. Then, when the clouds lifted, they entered a period of twilight and failed to obtain a fix. After several hours, the radar observer noted a land return and, believing it to be Siberia, directed a drastic left turn. Shortly after, he realized his error and the pilot altered right. The bomber soon made radio contact with Pt. Barrow and Ladd Field, but could not determine the signal's direction. Hopelessly lost, the pilot finally advised Ladd Field that he was flying toward the sun, a course over ninety degrees away from their intended destination. After eighteen hours, its fuel supply nearly exhausted, the aircraft crash-landed in northern Greenland. Fortunately, search units found and rescued the men after two days.[47]

Other mishaps had ended more tragically. During the winter of 1946-47, a B-29 from the 28th BW failed to return from a training flight. After more than 900 hours of futile search efforts, the aircraft's exact fate and location remained unknown. During the same period, propeller trouble forced another B-29 crew to bail out, and one flier died on the icy terrain.[48] For aviators suddenly in a strange and unforgiving environment, these incidents loomed large.

Their Alaskan experiences clearly revealed two important facts for SAC and the new air force. First, arctic operations, the central element of the polar strategy, demanded additional manpower and material at great cost. Squadrons could not operate from a single airstrip located in the far north and dependent upon air transport for supply. The AAF had to build complete bases in the Arctic, with supplies and fuel in position.[49] If the AAF could not expand existing facilities, SAC crew members would never gain the experience necessary for deploying and operating in the polar region. Second, the AAF did not have the means to operate at will in the Arctic. Col. George A. Walker, commander of APGC's 616 AAF Base Unit in Alaska, observed, "The extremely low temperatures encountered this season (1946-47) have revealed that AAF equipment is definitely deficient for operation in the arctic."[50] Col. K. E. Tibbets, assistant chief of staff for logistics, agreed and warned, "It will be a great many years before all the problems of full scale round-the clock arctic operations are licked. . . ."[51]

Possibly the AAF could overcome both problems with time and with additional funds for improving northern facilities and developing suitable equipment. During 1947, however, the air arm was already suffering from inadequate funds and had reduced its projected force from seventy to fifty-five groups. Moreover, the executive branch had cut the AAF's research and development budget for the next fiscal year by nearly 20 percent. Air leaders would not have the resources to develop a capability to operate continuously and effectively from the Arctic.

Thus, during 1947, SAC rotated units to three overseas areas to develop and demonstrate its capacity to deploy quickly and to operate from forward bases in time of war. The most critical region presented the greatest problem; the command and AAC were ill equipped to operate reliably in cold weather. Late in the year, one commander privately questioned the value of a polar strategy. In July, McMullen spent several days overflying Ellesmere Island in northern Canada, attempting to find a suitable area to build an operating base. He found none, and confided to Whitehead, "I have practically shed my polar concept."[52] He believed the proper strategic position really centered on Iceland and the British Isles. Although forward bases in temperate climates offered fewer operational problems, foreign governments in Western Europe could easily deny the United States access. Unlike the other two regions, the Pacific bases lay beyond reach of many potential targets. To insure optimum capability and flexibility, SAC had to use forward bases in all three areas.

The AAF had one promising solution to its problem of dependable and usable bases. If aircraft range could be extended by better design, larger fuel-carrying capacity, or aerial refueling, SAC could use the polar routes without operating from the arctic surface. The command would soon receive the B-50, which had greater range than the B-29, and later the B-36, which promised a 10,000-nautical-mile capability. Air leaders also began giving aerial refueling serious consideration. Until this procedure became operational and the new bombers arrived, SAC had to continue its dependence on forward bases, in all three theaters, despite the limitations of each.

NOTES

1. DC/SAC to CG/AAF, subj: Operational Training and Strategic Employment of Units of Strategic Air Command, 25 July 1946, 416.01-46, Albert F. Simpson Historical Research Center, Maxwell Air Force Base, Alabama (hereafter cited as AFSHRC).

2. General McMullen to General Whitehead, 31 May 1947, 168.6008-3-McMullen, AFSHRC.

3. General Spaatz to C/G SAC, subj: Operational Training of SAC VHB Units to Europe, 5 May 1947, 416.01-47, AFSHRC.

4. General Spaatz to C/G SAC, subj: Short Training Flights to Germany, 19 June 1947, 416.01-47, AFSHRC. The AAF had directed SAC to conduct a good-will flight of nine B-29s to Europe and the United Kingdom in response to a similar American visit by the Royal Air Force in 1946. See "History of Strategic Air Command 1947." Typescript history prepared by Hdg. Strategic Air Command, Command, Offutt AFB, Nebr., 1949, pp. 155-56 (hereafter cited as "SAC-1947"), AFSHRC.

5. General Spaatz to C/G SAC, subj: Supplemental Directions on Short Training Flights to Germany, 2 July 1947, 416.01-47, AFSHRC.

6. Message, C/G USAFE to CG/AAF, 25 July 1947, 416.01-47, AFSHRC.

7. Col. William McDonald, Hdq. 97th Bombardment Group to C/G Fifteenth AF, subj: Training Flights to European Theater of Operation, 3 July to 19 July 1947, 24 July 1947, 416.01-47, AFSHRC.

8. "A Five-Year Summary of USAFE 1945-1950." Typescript history, prepared by Historical Division, Hdq. USAFE, Wiesbaden, Germany, 1952, p. 138 (hereafter cited as "USAFE Summary"), AFSHRC.

9. AC/S A-3, SAC to CG/AAF, subj: Training Flights to ETO, 18 September 1947, 416.01-47, AFSHRC.

10. "USAFE Summary," pp. 119-21.

11. "USAFE Summary," p. 138.

12. General LeMay USAFE to General Kenney, 22 December 1947, 416.01-47, AFSHRC.

13. "SAC-1947," pp. 163-64.

14. General McMullen to General Whitehead, 13 December 1947, 168.6008-3-McMullen, AFSHRC.

15. DC/SAC to CG/AAF, subj: Operational Training of Strategic Air Command Very Heavy Bombardment Units in the Pacific Theater, 27 February 1947, 416.01-47, AFSHRC.

16. General Whitehead to General Kenney, 23 May 1947, 168.6008-3-Kenney, AFSHRC.

17. Ibid.

18. "SAC-1947," p. 165.

19. "SAC-1947," pp. 166-67.

20. H. H. Arnold, *Global Mission* (New York: Harper and Brothers, 1949), p. 211.

21. Commander Cold Weather Detachment, APGC to CG/AAF, subj: Future Army Air Forces Low Temperature Development, Testing and Training, 15 January 1946, 168.64-48, AFSHRC.

22. Ibid.

23. Maj. Gen. Donald Wilson to General Carl Spaatz, 31 August 1946, 168.64-48, AFSHRC.

24. Memorandum for the record, General LeMay, DCS Research and Development, subj: Low Temperature Test Program—Winter of 1946-47, 10 October 1946, 168.64-48, AFSHRC. Aircraft included the A-26, B-29, C-47, C-54, C-74, C-97, F-15, P-80, and P-82. See also "SAC-1947," p. 107.

25. Report A1 314.7, Asst. C/S A-1 and Asst. C/S A-3, to CG/15th AF, subj: Report on Visit to 15th AF Units TDY in Alaska, 11 April 1947, p. 4, 416.01-47 (hereafter cited as "15th AF Report"), AFSHRC.

26. 333 (IN-4), Capt. Homer Lear, O & T Inspector to Station Commander, Smoky Hill AAF Field, subj: Report on Polarization Lectures, 4 December 1946. Also reply, Col. G. Whatley, C/Hdq. 3718 AAF Base Unit to Acting AC/S A-3, SAC, 9 January 1947, 416.01-47, AFSHRC.

27. "15th AF Report," p. 13.

28. "15th AF Report," pp. 4-7. A wing contained approximately thirty aircraft.

29. Memorandum, Col. H. R. Sullivan, GSC, to General LeMay, 5 February 1947. 168.64-48.

30. "15th AF Report," pp. 4-7.

31. "15th AF Report," pp. 7-10.

32. "Condensed Briefings on Arctic Activities." Report presented at the 1947 Cold Weather Conference, 24 April 1947, at Eglin Field, Fla., 168.64-48, AFSHRC.

33. Memorandum for the record, Col. Kenneth Bergquist, Deputy

Asst. C/S A-3, subj: Trip to Alaska, 3 February 1947, 168.64-48, AFSHRC.

34. "15th AF Report," p. 13.

35. Col. George Walker, APGC Hdq. to Deputy C/S R&D, 29 January 1947, 168.64-48, AFSHRC.

36. Col. George Walker, AAC Hdq. to Maj. Gen. L. Craigie, Chief Engineering Division, AMC, 13 February 1947, 168.64-48, AFSHRC.

37. "SAC-1947," p. 219.

38. "SAC-1947," p. 147.

39. Memorandum, Requirements Div. AC/AS A-3 to AC/AS-3 and AC/AS-4, subj: Equipment for Strategic Air Command Detachment, Ladd Field, Alaska, 15 November 1946, 168.64-48, AFSHRC.

40. "15th AF Report," p. 8.

41. Department of the Air Force, *Air Navigation*, AF Manual 51-40, vol. 1 (Washington, D.C.: Government Printing Office, 1968), p. 19-1.

42. *Air Navigation*, p. 19-8.

43. Convergence factors on Lambert conformal charts equaled 0.785 of the local meridian, contrasted with polar gnomonic charts, where convergence seldom exceeded 2.5 degrees anywhere above the Arctic Circle.

44. *Air Navigation*, p. 10-14.

45. Operations Analysis Branch AACS to CO AACS, subj: Information from Polaris Operation, 16 January 1947, 168.64-48, AFSHRC.

46. General McMullen to General Ramey, 19 September 1947, 416.01-47, AFSHRC. The letter contains highlights of the report but does not reveal the observer or author.

47. "SAC-1947," pp. 142-44.

48. "15th AF Report," p. 9.

49. Col. K. Tibbets, AC/S A-4 M&S, to AC/S A-4 and AC/S A-5, subj: Logistical Data for A-5 Plan 3, 14 August 1947, 416.01-47, AFSHRC.

50. Col. G. Walker, APGC Hdq. to Maj. Gen. L. Craigie, Chief Engineering Division, AMC, 21 January 1947, 168.64-48, AFSHRC.

51. Col. K. Tibbets, AC/S A-4 M&S, to AC/S A-4 and AC/S A-5, subj: Logistical Data for A-5 Plan 3, 14 August 1947, 416.01-47, AFSHRC.

52. General McMullen to General Whitehead, 1 August 1947, 168.6008-3-McMullen, AFSHRC.

5 THREAT AND RESPONSE

From its inception in March 1946 until the Berlin blockade of 1948, Strategic Air Command was unable to develop a strong force. For over two years following World War II, the United States lacked the aircraft, technicians, and weapons to deliver a strong, concerted attack upon the Soviet Union, one sufficiently powerful to destroy its warmaking capability. Every command of the United States Army Air Forces had encountered difficulties with demobilization and personnel shortages, problems that eroded their strength to a dangerously low level. SAC made limited gains by reorganizing units, but its capability rested on mobility and on reliable overseas stations within reach of enemy targets. In late 1947, SAC enjoyed dependable use of few forward bases and maintained only a few effective bomb groups.[1]

SAC needed to expand its force and improve forward base operations, activities that demanded additional appropriations. During 1946 and 1947, the prospects for gaining increased funds appeared dim. Wartime tax levels, budget surpluses, fear of a new depression, and pent-up consumer demand encouraged the Republican-controlled Eightieth Congress to favor a lowering of tax rates. Each year the House of Representatives offered a tax reduction bill, which President Truman rejected. Like most of his contemporaries, the president believed in balancing the federal budget; he even sought a surplus, to reduce the national debt. Neither the Congress nor the executive branch favored additional defense spending.[2]

Without adequate appropriations the AAF and SAC would fail to achieve two of their primary objectives. The third, unification of equal military branches, was realized in 1947 largely because of the economy it promised. The total military budget for fiscal year 1948, as well as that portion allotted to AAF research and development, fell nearly 20 percent from the 1947 level; funds for new aircraft procurement decreased by 7 percent, to $281 million. Aviators considered these reduced amounts insufficient for building a modern air arm.[3]

Within the fiscal restraints of the 1948 budget the AAF carefully divided its resources among the commands. But, while struggling with demobilization, personnel, and appropriation problems, air leaders were assessing their existing capabilities and immediate wartime potential against those of the USSR in terms of Soviet intentions in Europe and Asia. Military leaders began drawing up basic war plans, but they were handicapped because the United States had not clearly defined its foreign policy objectives. Despite the cold war, United States defense leaders doubted the Soviet Union would undertake an aggressive role in Europe and Asia, but generals had to weigh the enemy's power, and the USSR maintained a massive army within a short distance of Western Europe. Military leaders hoped United States capability and potential would discourage any aggression on those continents, but that capability had limits.

United States generals held no illusions about their military capability between V-J Day and 1948. They had concluded the war with a superior air arm, a rebuilt navy, a modern army, and a monopoly on atomic weapons. The USSR had likewise ended the conflict with a powerful military force. Considering Soviet strength, resources, geographical position, and the devastated condition of Europe, American military leaders understood that their power against the USSR in Europe and Asia had certain limitations. During this period, intelligence and planning leaders agreed that Soviet armies could successfully overrun all of Europe and parts of Asia. They doubted that the Soviets would undertake this effort because of economic and political considerations, but they never forgot the Soviet potential. The military made formal evaluations between late 1945 and 1948 that demonstrated a realistic appraisal of United States capability.

The Joint Strategic Survey Committee (JSSC) of the Joint Chiefs of Staff (JCS) in October 1945 prepared an early study on the effects of atomic bomb warfare and recommended steps that the United States should take. The committee recognized that American security "would be greatly impaired if atomic weapons fell into the hands of other nations," because the United States had concentrated its industry and population in coastal regions, open to attack from the sea.[4] By contrast, the USSR had dispersed its industry and population over a wider area, and its vital targets lay far inland. Therefore, the JSSC made two recommendations. The United States should establish "defensive frontiers well advanced in the Atlantic and Pacific Oceans and to the shores of the Arctic." Second, the nation should accumulate an atomic weapons stockpile to implement any future strategic war plan.

A month later the Joint Intelligence Staff (JIS) of the JCS also examined Soviet objectives and capabilities and found reason for concern. In a November 1945 report the JIS concluded that "the principle immediate aim of Soviet foreign policy is to establish and consolidate Soviet hegemony in peripheral areas."[5] The intelligence advisors believed the Soviets had a high degree of capacity to achieve their objectives over the next two years without resorting to war, but they sounded a warning nonetheless. As an absolute minimum, the report continued, the Soviets maintained 8.6 million men under arms (about half on active duty), including 213 divisions and 3.3 million men in Eastern Europe.[6] Moreover, the satellite nations contained another eighty-four divisions. With such manpower, "the Red Army could probably overrun, initially, most of continental Europe, Turkey, Iran and/or Afghanistan." In the Far East, the USSR held the same capability for overrunning Korea, Manchuria, and North China. In both regions, the American military would be unavailable to stem an invasion.

The future looked bleak. Even after demobilization, the JIS estimated the USSR would maintain approximately 113 divisions, fifty of them in occupied Europe. Without exaggeration the staff warned, "The U.S.S.R. is probably capable of over-running Western Europe now or by 1 January 1948."[7] Their invading army would face Anglo-American air supremacy, but the Soviets had strong air-to-ground support forces. Moreover, the USSR faced no unsolvable problems in producing atomic weapons. Assuming maximum effort, the JIS believed the Soviets could build atomic bombs within five years, or by 1950. With atomic weapons in their arsenal, the Soviets might consider aggression more favorably.

The intelligence staff did offer important consolations. It did not believe the Soviet Union could successfully invade the British Isles, North Africa, Arabia, or India; three of these areas contained forward bases for the United States. Nor did the advisors feel the Soviet economy could support a major war for another five years: about 25 percent of their prewar capital stock had suffered war damage. Finally, their report optimistically suggested, "The immediate objectives of the U.S.S.R. in Europe are already largely accomplished. What remains to be done either does not require or does not warrant resort to international hostilities."[8]

During 1946 the War Department developed a more ominous evaluation of Soviet capability but generally supported the JIS report. On 29 October 1946, Maj. Gen. Lauris Norstad, now assigned to the War Department's Operational Plans Division, prepared a briefing for the president outlining Soviet capability and probable actions in the next five years. The general prefaced his remarks by noting recent political differences between the USSR and the United States; to his mind, "it seems to be an altogether sound conclusion that there exists a fundamental conflict between the aims and purposes of the United States and the Soviet Union."[9] Therefore the War Department anticipated a war with the Soviet Union, Norstad continued, and "at this time, it appears not only the *most* probable, but in fact the *only* probable source of trouble in the foreseeable future."[10]

Norstad found Soviet capabilities disturbing. To date the USSR had demobilized to 4.5 million men, but maintained some 208 divisions and 15,500 combat aircraft, a larger force than projected by the JIS in 1945. Ninety-three divisions and 7,200 aircraft faced allied forces in Europe, with another thirteen divisions in Korea. The Soviets had also regrouped their units in order to integrate tanks and infantry forces below divisional levels. Their armies were becoming more mechanized, and maneuvers were being held to familiarize the men with new tactics and equipment.[11] Satellite nations had increased their military strength to 100 divisions and 3,300 combat aircraft. The War Department Intelligence Division estimated the Soviet Union could mobilize 10.5 million men within a month and 15 million in 150 days. Seemingly, the USSR maintained a more than adequate ground force. Although the Soviets lacked strategic air power, they could have the potential of attacking the United States by 1948, with 1,000 aircraft similar to our B-17 or B-24, augmented by a smaller number of very heavy bombers. We might expect the Soviets, Norstad warned, to have achieved production of atomic bombs by 1949; two years later they could have significant stockpiles. In addition, their guided missiles could have a 3,000-mile range and a one-ton payload by 1951. The War Department discounted any threat to the United States from the Soviet navy or from biological warfare for another fifteen to twenty years, and they considered the USSR incapable of conducting an airborne invasion against the United States. Norstad conceded that Alaska was vulnerable to invasion; however, he believed any Soviet aggression would focus on territory immediately adjacent to the USSR.[12]

If the Soviet Union resorted to force within the next five years, the War Department believed the Soviets would aim to destroy all Western allied forces on the Eurasian and North African land masses. Secondarily, they would attempt to seize and hold those areas of Eurasia and Africa that Allied powers might use as forward areas to strike quickly at the USSR. In

Germany alone, forty-two ground divisions and 2,500 aircraft faced the United States occupation forces. By 1 January 1947, the United States would have in Europe between one and two divisions, with twelve air groups. Norstad pointed out the obvious:

> Simple arithmetic dictates hasty withdrawal in the event of an emergency. It is our estimate that it would require good fortune as well as good management to retain as much as a small bridgehead on the continent of Europe if the Russians should decide to strike.[13]

The United States could only respond with strategic air strikes from forward bases in England, North Africa, and Japan. The offensive would include conventional and atomic bombs, as the army believed that "we must be prepared to use this weapon (atomic) if necessary. This is a basic assumption in all our planning."[14] The United States military would have no alternative if directed to defend Western Europe.

During the briefing Norstad warned the president of another danger. Technology would bring rapid changes in the next five years; by 1951 atomic warfare, guided missiles, biological warfare, and extended airpower capabilities would alter force composition, equipment, and strategy. The United States could not neglect research and development and still remain militarily strong.

General Norstad's presentation contained one note of hope, while pointing out a serious dilemma. The War Department still believed the USSR would not initiate a major war for at least five years, and then only if certain conditions were fulfilled. The United States military, on the other hand, held responsibility for maintaining the security of the nation and furthering national policies and interests.[15] To achieve some of these goals the armed forces had to continue to occupy Germany and Japan; by January 1947, the army alone would require over a million men to carry out these responsibilities. Nevertheless, an invading Soviet army could drive the United States military out of Western Europe. Any hope of stopping this eventuality lay with strategic air power, and SAC's capability had limitations at the moment. Norstad ended his presentation by repeating General Marshall's warning to the Senate Military Affairs Committee in 1945:

> We have come to know through the hard experience of World War II that the future peace of the world will largely depend not only on the international policies of the United States but even more on our practical ability to endow those policies with the strength to command international respect.[16]

The military wanted to ensure that the nation would have such strength.

Civilian leaders agreed that, because of its own internal circumstances, the Soviet Union would not undertake aggressive military action. Russia could more easily obtain her objectives by other means. Both Robert Lovett, assistant secretary for air, and Averell Harriman, then secretary of commerce, held this view. Russia, they advised, worried little about the United States Army; they knew the allies could only offer limited resistance with existing troops and techniques. The United States Navy offered even less threat, as major Soviet cities lay beyond the reach of carrier aircraft. "She [the USSR] is, however, keenly aware of the power of an adequate air force, and recognizes that our position and influence in the world will, as far as she is concerned, be in some direct relation with our supremacy or lack of it, in the air."[17] Both men believed the AAF should press for additional funds; only a strong air arm provided an answer to Soviet threats. The United States Army, however, could not afford to admit this fact, although Lovett believed the president would come to share his view.

George F. Kennan worried less about Soviet intentions because he considered industrial systems in the USSR too vulnerable to risk war with the United States. In Russia, he said, "there are about ten vital points."[18] The Soviets probably had mastered the theory of atom-splitting, he admitted, but they would not develop the know-how for a long time. "They lack the culture of production," he explained. "Unless we teach them, it is not likely they will acquire that know-how for many years."[19] If war were to come, the United States should limit its participation to air combat. Then, internal dissension in the Soviet Union might even bring the Bolshevik government down.

During the following year military advisers continued to give evaluations similar to the previous reports. In 1947, the JCS Joint Strategic Planning Committee and Joint Intelligence Staff prepared more estimates of Soviet intentions and capabilities for the coming decade. Although the intelligence staff believed the Soviets could "overrun Western Europe in rapid order, occupying the Low Countries and the Channel Coast as far as Flushing" within fifteen days, committee planners still considered war within that period militarily inadvisable for the USSR and doubted that any planned war would eventuate before 1957.[20] The planners, however, anticipated no change in Soviet expansion plans, and they believed the strength levels maintained by the Western powers would determine Soviet strategy. The JSPC conceded, of course, that miscalculation in Moscow could bring accidental war. For instance, if Western nations should lapse into an economic recession, the Soviet Union might be tempted to use military force in order to expand quickly in Europe. Generally, though, the JSPC believed that the Soviet economy would offer the principal restraint against war.

Later in the year, the AAF intelligence division (AC/AS-2) prepared a less optimistic briefing for the Air Policy Board, warning against the prevailing theory that "Russia will need ten to fifteen years to lick her wounds, refurbish her economy and gird her loins for more conquest."[21] The USSR had recently toppled the Hungarian and Rumanian governments and could be prepared for more activity. AAF experts believed the Soviet Union had expanded its air arm to 14,000 first-line combat aircraft and that, by January 1948, the Soviets could launch 1,000 very heavy bombers against the United States. Two American B-29s had fallen into Soviet hands in 1944; within two years the USSR had attempted to purchase twenty-five sets of B-29 tires, wheels, and brake assemblies from the Goodyear Tire and Rubber Company. In September 1947 intelligence sources observed fourteen VHB-type aircraft flying near Moscow. Numerically, Soviet armed forces had increased from double that of the United States in 1946 to two and a third times the size a year later. This growing strength and the potential of Soviet aviation disturbed the AAF leaders.

The familiar warning came again. "Almost at will she [Russia] can overrun Western Europe, the Middle East, and China down to the Yellow River,"[22] and the Soviets could subject Britain to missile and conventional air and sea bombardment. Against the United States, any attack would come through the air; the Soviets would need long-range aircraft with atomic weapons. The USSR might have such a fleet by 1948, but the briefers could shed little new light on its progress in developing atomic energy. Air leaders believed the Soviets would have the atomic bomb before 1952, and the intelligence division gave 1949 as its best estimate. When this occurred, the relative strength of the United States would fall dramatically.

After considering the threat, the intelligence advisers discussed American targets critical to the air arm. The United States stored approximately 70 percent of its aviation fuel near Baton Rouge; Seattle and Fort Worth produced all the heavy bomber aircraft; and Indianapolis manufactured four out of five of the new jet engines. Moreover, three-fourths of the nation's iron ore passed through the Sault Ste. Marie, while the Hanford plant in Washington produced and stored all the plutonium for atomic weapons. If the enemy could destroy these targets, United States warmaking capability would suffer severely.

By contrast, critical targets in the USSR lay deep in the interior and would be difficult to reach. The Soviets had concentrated many wartime support functions in the Moscow and Gorki areas, but they had spread many new facilities throughout the Urals. They had developed new industrial centers along the median line of the earth's broadest land mass. Only long-range bombers could attack these targets, and American intelligence knew little about their exact location. SAC would have difficulty eliminating them. No land power could attack these production centers; the Soviets vastly outnumbered our potential land forces, even without counting their 243 reserve divisions. Although the United States and Great Britain sailed over

85 percent of the world's combat vessel tonnage, sea power had severe limitations against the USSR. Military staff papers credited carrier aircraft with a 300-mile radius of action, but only a small area of the Soviet Union would fall within reach of the United States Navy. Moreover, the Soviets defended the Baltic approaches heavily, limiting the accessible area even further. The 1947 AAF briefing contained a greater note of danger than previous staff evaluations, but the military assessment had remained constant since November 1945.[23]

Clear points emerged from each evaluation. The USSR had lost great resources and manpower during World War II but had concluded the conflict with a massive army under arms and with a mushrooming industrial production. Its military force held tremendous potential in Europe and the Far East. If the USSR chose to invade these areas, no existing power could stop them. Advisers and leaders doubted the Soviets would undertake a full-scale military action, because the USSR needed time for a strong recovery from World War II. Instead, the Soviets would direct their efforts toward subversion and toward aiding Communist parties in Western nations. In fact, the Soviet Union pursued the course predicted by the Americans because it carried far less cost. United States military leaders, however, had to prepare for the worst eventuality, and the memory of Pearl Harbor remained vivid in their minds.

Defense leaders began planning a response to potential Soviet aggression in early 1946, but their effort suffered from inadequate guidance; the United States had not clearly defined its foreign policy objectives. The Joint War Plans Committee of the JCS began a special series of studies under the code name PINCHER to provide data for a concept of operations and a joint war plan. Using the assumptions found in PINCHER, the AAF Plans Section (AC/AS-5) drew up a rough outline showing how its force could be committed in a national emergency. After several versions, the AAF developed its own air plan, MAKEFAST. Reflecting the experiences of World War II, this plan considered petroleum to be the most profitable target, given the limited strength of SAC. MAKEFAST concluded that, within four months following the opening of hostilities, only six B-29 groups could be in operation from Cairo and England, but this force could destroy three-fourths of Russia's petroleum producing capacity in nine months and destroy the mobility of the Soviet ground and air arm in one year. A weapons annex was included outlining how the AAF would conduct combat operations, but the plan did little beyond designating available units and deployment locations to be used during hostilities. A revision in February 1947, EARSHOT, reflected combat capabilities and an atomic weapons annex, but it still lacked certain logistical considerations. Though these plans reflected serious planning by the AAF, they did not integrate with army and navy plans. Consequently, the JCS had no detailed plan for executing an atomic attack by mid-1947.[24]

To correct this deficiency, the JCS directed its Joint War Plans Committee to prepare a joint outline war plan in August 1947, based on the assumption that "within three years, war would be forced upon the United States by acts of aggression by the USSR and its satellites."[25] The committee, however, labored under a cloud of uncertainty. It still lacked a definitive statement of the long-range objectives of the United States or reasonable estimates of the nation's industrial and manpower mobilization capabilities. Moreover, America's immediate war aims were not clear. What was the goal? To destroy the Russian people, Soviet industry, or the Communist party and its hierarchy? Equally important, what would be the objectives following victory? The State Department and, after 1947, the National Security Council, held the responsibility for giving direction in these matters. Neither provided the needed guidance.[26]

Nonetheless, the JCS had formulated an "Over-all Strategic Concept," which gave some general direction to planning. In the event of war, the concept held, the will of the USSR had to be destroyed by a main offensive effort in Western Europe and a strategic defense in the Far East. Initially, the United States would launch a powerful offensive against the vital elements of the Soviet warmaking capacity. By exploiting the destructive and psychological power of atomic weapons, the United States could protect the Western Hemisphere, the United Kingdom, and the Bering Sea-Japan Sea-Yellow Sea line. Other efforts employing political, psychological, and underground warfare could reduce the Soviet war potential, but atomic weapons held the key.[27]

In late 1947, the Joint Strategic Plans Committee of the JCS incorporated this concept into plan BROILER, which relied principally upon an atomic attack. The plan presumed an adequate stockpile of atomic bombs would be available at the outset, and more would be produced during hostilities. Given Soviet numerical superiority in manpower and mobilized tactical air power, the best hope for American victory lay in long-range bombing of vital centers of Soviet warmaking capacity. The principal strategic targets would be governmental centers, urban industrial areas, and selected petroleum targets within the USSR.

Clearly the success of the overall strategic concept depended upon the effectiveness of the early air offensive, particularly that of aircraft delivering atomic bombs. Forward base areas from which to launch the campaign, specifically the United Kingdom, Japan-Ryukyus, and the Cairo-Suez area, would be critical. The bases had to be secure enough to permit deployment and operations, suitable for use without extensive construction, and logistically supportable. Lastly, they had to lie within range of vital Soviet targets. Early drafts of BROILER considered the Cairo-Suez region a promising forward base area. It lay within reach of most Soviet targets. But planners soon realized that Egyptian bases could not be developed quickly enough to support strategic bombing operations and could be overrun. In the final analysis, English bases offered the best prospects for launching a massive air offensive, though other areas would be used as available.[28]

The strategic concept and the BROILER plan rested on the critical assumption that atomic weapons would be used in a war with the USSR. Yet Truman had never given defense leaders firm guidelines on future use of atomic weapons. Although he claimed no regrets over his 1945 decision, the president did not want to use the bomb again.[29] Consequently he remained vague in his attitude towards its role. Necessary decisions, he believed, could be made when and if the need arose.

Government leaders hoped atomic weapons would discourage Soviet aggression in Europe and Asia, but in 1946 and 1947 American atomic capability had serious limitations. United States generals and admirals understood these limits; Soviet understanding on these matters at that time is open to question. In particular, Strategic Air Command faced critical shortages in both the number of atomic bombs stockpiled and the number of aircraft and men capable of delivering the weapons to distant targets. Because of these deficiencies, the United States could not maintain a force with sufficient power to deter aggression completely during these years.

At the close of 1946, SAC could only claim one effective VHB group, the 509th Composite Group at Roswell Field, New Mexico. This unit had delivered two atomic bombs against Japan and contained the few military men trained to handle these weapons. As described earlier, SAC gave this unit the best men and equipment available. The AAF used the code name SILVER PLATE for those bombers capable of carrying the twenty-kiloton atomic bomb of the type used against Japan.[30] In August 1945 the 509th had two B-29s so modified, and twenty-seven by 1946.[31] The remaining groups could carry only the conventional TNT weapons. By mid-1947, SAC maintained approximately 160 B-29s (including the twenty-seven from the 509th) on operational status.[32]

Should the United States government direct SAC to attack targets in the Soviet Union or even in Europe, the command would encounter problems of time and geography. During the period in question, the United States did not anticipate using atomic weapons except for counterattack; therefore, the enemy would determine the time for war. As Soviet armies could move through Germany and into France in a week, the amount of time required for response to an attack was critical. After the president issued a strike directive (which might take several days), the 509th needed five or six days to depart Roswell Field, load atomic weapons at a selected storage site, and fly to a forward base, before it could launch an attack.[33] Other

VHB groups, and cargo aircraft supporting the operation, would also require time for deployment. After completing the long logistical movement to the forward area, SAC would face a huge land mass with a very small force, because not all of the available B-29s would leave the United States. More important, few bombers could carry atomic weapons; the vast majority would deliver conventional bombs.

After moving its units into position, SAC would face difficulties in attack. Most Soviet targets lay deep in the interior; and, if the United States dangerously committed half of its bombers to a mass assault, the Soviets would have a great opportunity to inflict heavy damage. Since World War II, the USSR had used primitive radar warning systems and could position these at strategic points well in advance of target areas. The Soviets had also built a creditable defensive fighter force during World War II, and they would have time to prepare carefully for combat. The military would disperse these units at numerous points between Soviet borders and the interior targets. SAC had no fighter with sufficient range to escort the B-29 deep into the Soviet Union; the bombers would have to defend themselves. During penetration, the B-29s would meet superior numbers of fighters; and after arriving at the target area, the crews would face capable anti-aircraft artillery, probably firing shells equipped with proximity fuses.[34] These defenses would take a heavy toll. After delivering their weapons, bombers would face the same obstacles on the homeward leg. Because of the strength of Soviet defenses and the great distances, only part of the B-29 force would return to participate in further assaults.

Those fliers who reached their target area would also suffer from poor intelligence. From captured German photographs and records, Americans had good knowledge of the Russian area once occupied by Hitler's army. To the east of that region, however, where important targets were located, the United States military knew little.[35] Before launching an attack, crew members would need to know the exact target location and description. The atomic bomb of 1946-47, although very powerful, lacked the extraordinary destructive force of later atomic and hydrogen weapons. The bombardier had to drop the bomb within a reasonable distance of the target, a difficult task even when he knew the target's exact location.

Aircrews also struggled with problems of bombing technique. During World War II, the AAF had concentrated on visual bombing during daylight. Now, to avoid Soviet fighter defenses, SAC would attack at night and could therefore place little reliance on visual bomb sighting. For accurate bombing the observer had to know what scope-returns to anticipate in the target area; he needed to know what physical features existed nearby in order to establish an initial point of approach. If an expected return failed to appear, if he misread a reflection (easily done in a strange area), or if the expected return came from a misplotted feature on his chart (because of poor intelligence), he could miss the target by miles and waste his bomb. The Soviets, anticipating an attack, would black out critical areas and transmit electrical signals to disrupt radar transmission.[36] Crews could attack major cities such as Moscow and Gorki with great certainty, but these areas contained only part of the USSR's warmaking industry. The Soviets would defend these important centers heavily, making precise bombing difficult. When the *Enola Gay* dropped the first atomic bomb on Japan, distance, intelligence, and enemy defenses presented few obstacles. If Americans attacked the Soviet Union, these grave difficulties would appear.

The most serious problem SAC faced was the limited number of atomic weapons stockpiled. Officials have not disclosed the exact number of atomic bombs available after World War II; several facts, estimates, and opinions exist, however, which point to a very small quantity.[37] During this period, only the Hanford Plant produced plutonium, and in small amounts; the scarce supply of fissionable material limited the number of atomic weapons manufactured. Some physicists expressed little hope for a future increase in production; one scientist believed bomb makers would soon be out of business. By piecing together information from various sources, columnist Joseph Alsop and the physicist Ralph Lapp estimated the United States could produce about 750 pounds of fissionable material annually. Assuming the production of 50-kiloton bombs after July 1946, they concluded the United States had about a dozen bombs by late 1945, fifty by 1947, and 150 on 1 January 1948.[38] General LeMay, then chief of staff for Research and Development, gave a lower estimate. Deputy Chief of Staff Lt. Gen. Ira Eaker had directed LeMay to prepare a contingency war plan; and, while working on the project, LeMay discovered the AAF could rely on about twenty-five bombs.[39] In 1950 the Joint Intelligence Group (JIG) of the JCS gave an indirect estimate following the first known Soviet detonation of an atomic weapon.[40] Intelligence advisers always used American experiences to help determine enemy capabilities and usually allowed for technical superiority by considering United States figures as an upper limit. The JCS group predicted the Soviets would produce between twenty-five and forty-five atomic bombs by 1951, a date equivalent to 1947 in the United States development of atomic weapons. The JIG estimate fell between that of Alsop and LeMay; together, the three confirmed that the stockpile was limited. More recent scholarship indicates there were no more than twenty-nine atomic weapons in the American arsenal by mid-1947.[41]

In addition to a limited supply of atomic bombs, SAC suffered other shortages during 1947. The JCS believed the military would need approximately 400 atomic bombs if they were to be used in war.[42] General Kenney held that 200 atomic weapons, dropped on Soviet targets, would insure the United States against any concerted enemy attack, yet SAC had only twenty-seven SILVER PLATE aircraft to deliver atomic bombs, and some would not return from the first missions. Moreover, there were not enough assembly teams to permit that scale of operation. The Armed Forces Special Weapons Project, which supplied and controlled the technical teams assembling atomic weapons, did not expect to have enough crews to assemble even 100 bombs simultaneously for another three and a half years. In fact, by mid-1948, the available teams could assemble only *two* bombs per day for combat operations. The AF realized SAC could not deliver even fifty atomic bombs on twenty selected cities in the USSR, the blow necessary to paralyze roughly half of Soviet industry.[43] The American threat carried a hollow ring.

Between World War II and 1948, atomic weapons and strategic bombing offered the United States its strongest military potential. Without doubt, SAC's atomic force had some capability to deter Soviet aggression in Western Europe or even in parts of Asia; but by no means did it have strength enough to dictate political developments in those regions where the Soviets already enjoyed dominance. The United States military understood its limited capability and had advised the president and high civilian leaders of the limits of their capacity to wage war. It is reasonable to assume the Soviets may have recognized United States limitations. Although they did not know the exact size of the American stockpile in atomic weapons, the scarcity of fissionable material was common knowledge.[44] Military advisers and intelligence personnel agreed that Soviet armies could march into Western Europe at will and that war-weary Europeans might offer little resistance. If the USSR could absorb the limited United States atomic attack, they could control most of Europe and might eventually deny Americans use of North Africa and England. Planners and advisers doubted the Soviets would take this step; the USSR needed to recover fully from the long war and could possibly achieve its objectives without open conflict. Americans found this conclusion logical and grew comfortable with their prediction. The approach, however, depended upon the actions of the USSR. When events in early 1948 suddenly suggested Soviet activity in Eastern Europe, United States leaders slowly reviewed their earlier evaluations and carefully looked at the real capability of Strategic Air Command.

NOTES

1. The official history of Strategic Air Command notes that eleven bomb groups were maintained at the close of 1947, but only the 509th and 43rd were effective. Other groups could deploy only for temporary duty for a limited time. See "History of Strategic Air Command 1947." Typescript history prepared by Hdq. Strategic Air Command, Offutt AFB, Nebr., 1949, p. 47 (hereafter cited as "SAC-1947"), Albert F.

Simpson Historical Research Center, Maxwell Air Force Base, Alabama (hereafter cited as AFSHRC).

2. President Truman discussed his fiscal policy approach in *Memoirs*, vol. 2: *Years of Trial and Hope* (Garden City, N.Y.: Doubleday and Company, Inc., 1956), pp. 31-41. For a scholarly analysis of the period's fiscal activity, see Herbert Stein, *The Fiscal Revolution in America* (Chicago: University of Chicago Press, 1969), pp. 197-240.

3. U.S. Congress, House, Committee on Appropriations, *Military Establishment Appropriations Bill of 1948: Hearings before a subcommittee of the Committee on Appropriations*, 80th Cong., 1st sess., 1947, pp. 73, 653-54, 717. See also U.S., Department of Commerce, Bureau of the Census, *Statistical Abstract of the United States, 1950* (Washington, D.C.: Government Printing Office, 1950), p. 309.

4. Joint Strategic Survey Committee, "Over-All Effect of Atomic Bomb on Warfare and Military Organization," 26 October 1945. Fairchild Collection, Library of Congress, Washington, D.C. An early fear was that the enemy could deliver atomic weapons to major United States port cities by submarine or merchant vessels. Dr. Vannevar Bush, who participated in drawing up the report, concurred on this point. In 1949, Bush again discussed the possibility in his book, *Modern Arms and Free Men* (New York: Simon and Schuster, 1949), p. 105. See also Record Group 218, "Records of the United States Joint Chiefs of Staff," CCS 381, 2-18-46 Sec. 3. Recommendation for JCS 1630/19 (circa May 1950), National Archives, Washington, D.C.

5. Record Group 218, "Records of the United States Joint Chiefs of Staff," CCS 092 USSR 3-27-45 Sec. 3. JIC 250/6, 29 November 1945 (hereafter cited as JIC 250/6), National Archives, Washington, D.C.

6. Soviet divisions usually contained between 10,000 and 12,000 men, while United States divisions carried 12,000 to 15,000. The overall size of the Soviet armed forces cannot be conclusively known at this time; most American and European observers estimate between four and five million men, not counting security units. See Thomas W. Wolfe, *Soviet Power and Europe 1945-1970* (Baltimore: Johns Hopkins University Press, 1970), pp. 9-13, and Raymond L. Garthoff, *Soviet Strategy in the Nuclear Age* (New York: Frederick A. Praeger, 1958), p. 150.

7. JIC 250/6.

8. Ibid.

9. "Presentation Given to President by Major General Lauris Norstad on 29 October 1946, 'Postwar Military Establishment,' " Vandenberg Collection (hereafter cited as "Norstad Presentation"), Library of Congress, Washington, D.C.

10. Ibid.

11. The USSR had a total of 12.5 million men under arms at the end of World War II, including 550 ground divisions and 23,500 combat aircraft. See also "Military Summary of Europe, Russia, and the Middle East,"

vol. 1, no. 11, 5 September 1946, p. 68, produced by the Intelligence Division of the War Department General Staff, 170.22770, AFSHRC.

12. "Norstad Presentation."

13. Ibid.

14. Ibid.

15. Specifically, the War Department had broken the mission into nine basic tasks. They were: the occupation of Germany and Japan; provision of United Nations commitment; implementation of United States foreign policy in Northern China and Trieste; provision of forces for liberated areas of Korea and the Philippines; assistance in training and equipping Western Hemisphere forces for mutual defense; development of an adequate and reliable intelligence organization; maintenance of supremacy in research and development; and maintaining forces in being plus the necessary support to permit rapid mobilization.

16. "Norstad Presentation."

17. Robert A. Lovett to General Carl Spaatz, 4 April 1946, Spaatz Collection, Library of Congress, Washington, D.C.

18. Memorandum to General Spaatz from Dr. Bruce Hopper, 20 June 1946, Spaatz Collection, Library of Congress, Washington, D.C.

19. Ibid. In the memorandum, Hopper records the lunchtime conversation between Spaatz and an unnamed visitor. Noel Parrish discovered, from an appointment log, that Spaatz had lunched with George Kennan on that day. See Noel Parrish, "Behind the Sheltering Bomb: Military Indecision from Alamogordo to Korea" (Ph.D. Diss., Rice University, 1968), p. 121.

20. Record Group 218, "Records of the United States Joint Chiefs of Staff," CCS 092 10-9-46, enclosure JSPC 814/3 (circa 1947), and CCS 092-U.S.S.R. 3-27-45 Sec. 19, 18 April 1947, National Archives, Washington, D.C.

21. AAF AC/AS-2, "Air Policy Board Briefing," 16 September 1947, Spaatz Collection, Library of Congress, Washington, D.C.

22. Ibid.

23. Ibid.

24. Record Group 319, "Records of the Army Staff." ABC 381 USSR (2 March 46), Sec. 3, National Archives, Washington, D.C. Memorandum for General Lincoln, subj: Brief of Outline Air Plan "MAKEFAST," from R.W.P., 26 October 1946. Also Record Group 341, "Records of Headquarters, United States Air Force." OPD 381 (5 November 47), National Archives, Washington, D.C. Memorandum for the Secretary of the Air Force, subj: Status of Current Joint War and Mobilization Planning from General Hoyt S. Vandenberg, 5 November 1947. See also John T. Greenwood, "The Emergence of the Postwar Strategic Air Force, 1945-1953," in *Air Power and Warfare*, Proceedings of the Eighth Military History Symposium, USAF Academy (Washington, D.C.: Government Printing Office, 1979), pp. 226-31.

25. Record Group 341, "Records of Headquarters, United States Air Force." OPD 381 (5 November 47), National Archives, Washington, D.C. Memorandum for the Secretary of the Air Force, subj: Status of Current Joint War and Mobilization Planning from General Hoyt S. Vandenberg, 5 November 1947.

26. Ibid.

27. Record Group 218, "Records of the United States Joint Chiefs of Staff." CCS 381 USSR C32-46, Sec. 10. JSPG 496/4, "BROILER," 11 February 1948, National Archives, Washington, D.C.

28. Ibid.

29. Richard F. Haynes, *The Awesome Power* (Baton Rouge: Louisiana State University Press, 1973), p. 60. Haynes and others believe Truman did have some private doubts.

30. Memorandum to C/S from SAC, subj: Minutes of "Silver Plate Training Conference," n.d., 416.01-47, AFSHRC.

31. Memorandum to General Eaker from General Vandenberg, subj: The Establishment of a Strategic Striking Force, 2 January 1946, 416.01-46, AFSHRC.

32. General McMullen to General Whitehead, 31 May 1947, 416.01-46, AFSHRC.

33. Maj. Gen. John B. Montgomery, a private interview held at Los Angeles, Calif., 14 July 1975 (hereafter cited as Montgomery Interview). See also Oral History Interview with Maj. Gen. William C. Kingsbury by Robert M. Kipp, March AFB, Calif., 18 December 1970, Interview no. 733, AFSHRC.

34. See SAC Intelligence Briefs, "Capabilities of the Soviet Air Force to Defend Western Russia Against Air Bombardment," No. 42, 2 April 1948, and "Capabilities of Soviet Anti-Aircraft for Defense Against VHB Operations," No. 44, 12 April 1948 (hereafter cited as SAC Brief No. 44), 416.606, AFSHRC.

35. Montgomery Interview.

36. SAC Brief No. 44.

37. Within the Atomic Energy Commission, the exact figure of weapons stockpiled was omitted from documents and "recorded on separate and detached pieces of paper safeguarded in a special way." See Truman, pp. 301-2. In briefings, the number was given orally. See David E. Lilienthal, *The Journals of David E. Lilienthal*, vol. 2: *The Atomic Energy Years 1945-1950* (New York: Harper & Row, 1964), p. 209.

38. Parrish, pp. 233-34. After the Bikini Tests in July 1946, the size of atomic bombs was increased from twenty to fifty kilotons.

39. General Curtis LeMay, a private interview held at Newport Beach, Calif., 1 October 1975. See also Oral History Interview with General Curtis E. LeMay by John Bohn, March AFB, Calif., 9 March 1971, Interview no. 736, AFSHRC. The exact date of LeMay's survey is not clear; he held the research and development post from January 1946 through September 1947.

40. Record Group 218, "Records of the United States Joint Chiefs

of Staff," CCS 381 2-18-46, Sec. 3. JIC 497/4 (circa May 1950), National Archives, Washington, D.C. See also George H. Quester, *Nuclear Diplomacy* (New York: The Dunellen Company, Inc., 1970), pp. 4-6.

41. David Alan Rosenberg, "American Atomic Strategy and the Hydrogen Bomb Decision," *The Journal of American History* 66 (1979): 65.

42. Record Group 218, "Records of the United States Joint Chiefs of Staff." CCS 471.6 (8-15-45) Sec. 7, National Archives, Washington, D.C. Memorandum for Chairman, Atomic Energy Commission from Admiral William D. Leahy, 29 October 1947.

43. George F. Lemmer, "The Air Force and the Concept of Deterrence 1945-1950." Typescript, unpublished history, prepared by the USAF Historical Division Liaison Office, Washington, D.C., 1963, pp. 36-37. See also memorandum for General Schlatter from Col. William E. Kennedy, Office Ass't/Operations for Atomic Energy, 27 August 1948. AF OPD A/AE 381 (Harrow), National Archives, Washington, D.C.

44. The Soviets may not have known the number of SILVER PLATE aircraft maintained by SAC, but probably assumed enough existed to deliver the United States stockpile of weapons. The AAF did not modify additional B-29s because new B-50s were anticipated for use in 1947, and all the new bombers would have atomic carrying capability. Moreover, the supply of bombs did not promise to outstrip SAC's capability to deliver before the B-50s arrived. The new bombers, however, did not become operational until 1948.

6 A NARROW VICTORY

The Soviet Union blockaded the surface routes between Berlin and Germany's western zones in June 1948, denying the Allied powers free access to the divided city for nearly a year. Initially, American leaders believed the United States could respond in one of two possible ways to the Soviet action: use military force to break the blockade or withdraw slowly from Berlin. President Truman rejected both alternatives and elected to keep American troops in the city for as long as possible. To provide supplies, the United States Air Force (AF) had begun a small airlift from Western Germany through the air corridors leading into Berlin. Soviet officials permitted the airlift because they were unwilling to destroy American cargo planes in flight. Although the United States could delay a withdrawal by using an airlift, no one believed the AF could supply the city's population through the winter. Time, the Soviets reasoned, was on their side and would not alter the outcome of what they considered a low-risk, high-yield strategy in Berlin. The United States, however, expanded the airlift into Operation Vittles, which—to the surprise of both Americans and Russians—was adequately supplying the Allied sectors of Berlin when winter arrived. Largely because of the success of Operation Vittles, the Soviets removed the blockade in May 1949 and ended the crisis.[1]

The United States was unnecessarily surprised by the Soviet action in Germany and was ill-equipped to make a strong response. The government had received indications of possible difficulties in Germany but had not prepared itself for a confrontation. Truman's containment policy of 1947 and his proposed Marshall Plan should have alerted United States leaders to a corollary requirement: a strong, balanced, military capability was needed to support these far-reaching policies. Yet American forces in Europe amounted to less than two divisions. After nearly three years of peace, the United States still lacked a definite policy in Europe and had no clear military plan, except evacuation, should an emergency arise. Until the blockade the State Department had discounted any strong Soviet action in Germany. The successful airlift obscured the nation's shortcomings in foreign policy planning and in its potential for deterring Soviet expansion, but the fact remained: civilian and military leaders were unprepared for a confrontation in Europe.[2]

The limits of United States military capability stemmed from several causes. In addition to previous problems of demobilization, limited appropriations, and personnel shortages, defense leaders lacked direction concerning United States objectives in Europe and therefore could not plan for proper support. During the first months of 1948, the government grew divided over the size and composition of its defense organization. Congress began to modify its position on low defense spending and, along with presidential and defense advisers, recommended a strengthening of the nation's air arm. The president, however, continued his austerity measures, with one exception: he urged the Congress to adopt a universal military training measure for the nation's youth, an action that would actually cost the taxpayer more than an expanded air force and would have questionable impact on the USSR. In addition to shortages, the military also struggled with questions about the control and use of atomic weapons. Defense leaders drew up plans assuming the utilization of the atomic bomb, but President Truman gave no assurance that he would ever use this powerful weapon again. Strategic Air Command, which bore the responsibility for delivering atomic bombs, had very restricted access to the stockpile, and its commanders believed that the harsh restrictions hindered their preparations for responding quickly to Soviet action. Without strong executive leadership and support, the United States military could not build an adequate defense organization or plan for its optimum use in a time of crisis. The events of 1948 clearly demonstrated to government and defense officials that the United States lacked the force necessary for engaging in the cold war.

For three years following the attack on Hiroshima and Nagasaki, military commanders contended with two troublesome matters regarding atomic weapons. Even though the JCS made a bombing offensive including atomic weapons the central part of their war planning, President Truman never gave defense leaders firm guidelines on future use, and military units found their access to the new bombs severely restricted. The first problem stemmed from Truman's deep desire not to use atomic bombs again, although he never regretted his earlier decision.[3] In part, this attitude accounted for his failure to establish specific policies on using atomic weapons. Truman chose instead to make the necessary decisions when and if the need should arise. Quite properly, he wanted maximum attention directed toward peaceful use of atomic energy and therefore preferred strong civilian authority over all atomic energy matters. This included strict physical control of the weapons stockpiled, with military access to them limited.

The issue of control surfaced immediately after V-J Day and led to the establishment of the Atomic Energy Commission (AEC). During World War II, civilian scientists working on the Manhattan Project had developed the first atomic weapon; Maj. Gen. Leslie R. Groves directed the operation for the military. Immediately following the war, Congress proposed the May-Johnson Bill, to provide for a permanent Manhattan District under military direction. Truman opposed this arrangement because he believed that control of atomic energy should reflect its future application, specifically to peaceful uses. In late 1945, Senator Brian McMahon proposed a compromise bill, incorporating Truman's civilian control concept with some modifications to allow for military advisers. Many congressmen and military leaders opposed this measure; but, after months of dispute, Congress passed and Truman signed the McMahon bill on 1 August 1946. The new law provided for a commission of five civilian members to assume responsibility for directing atomic energy development and production. The president appointed David Lilienthal to head the new Atomic Energy Commission.[4]

Defense officials and the military objected to this arrangement because they lacked access to atomic weapons. SAC, the only military organization capable of delivering these bombs, believed quick and effective use depended upon familiarity and immediate availability. The generals fully supported the need for presidential approval before employing atomic bombs, but they found little reason for a civilian agency to control the stockpile physically. The United States had charged the AF with the responsibility of being ready to launch a prompt retaliatory atomic attack, which required a strong, highly trained fighting team. General Spaatz, air force chief of staff, argued that this fighting team should "have available to it for prompt use, when required, such atomic weapons as are available and which are appropriate to its use. It is not clearly evident how this state of immediate readiness can be achieved if atomic weapons remain under the control of the Atomic Energy Commission."[5] Lilienthal, however, shared Truman's position and felt disgusted with military leaders for even assuming the possibility of using the atomic bomb again.[6]

Peace in 1946 and 1947 allowed the president to avoid establishing guidelines for atomic weapons use, but the military needed direction. The new bomb represented its strongest force, and the AF had to assume its potential employment and to plan accordingly. It offered the only deterring force against the Soviet Union in Western Europe. Without access to the stockpile, the AF believed, its ability to handle and deliver these weapons had suffered.[7]

These difficulties aggravated a growing concern among aviators: AF strength did not complement its responsibilities. Admittedly, by 1948 various units had improved from previous years; but aging airplanes, rising procurement costs, and limited resources threatened any further improvement. Before 1948, Congress and the president had generally agreed upon extensive demobilization and a drastically reduced defense budget; after that date, however, Congress grew more aware of military limitations and, along with the aviators, began to differ with Truman over the force levels necessary in the air arm.

The basis for their disagreement came from high-level government reports appearing in early 1948. The president's own Air Policy Commission first released its Finletter Report in January.[8] This commission had emerged six months earlier after business and government leaders expressed alarm over the depressed aviation industry. In response, Truman had appointed five civilian businessmen to examine all aspects of military and civilian aviation, with the hope of establishing a coordinated national aviation policy.[9] The lengthy Finletter Report described America's military air power as inadequate and hopelessly wanting for the future and called for a dramatic increase in procurement funds to build a seventy-group air force.[10] Then, on 1 March 1948, the Congressional Aviation Policy Board, chaired by Senator Owen Brewster, released a similar report on the same subject. This study also adopted the AF position and urged completion of seventy air groups. The Brewster Report conceded that portions of the total budget would have to yield, as congressmen would not support increased taxes and debt financing.[11] Both reports demonstrated strong concern over United States military strength.

These surveys found glaring shortcomings in military and government planning. The Brewster Report strongly criticized the Joint Chiefs of Staff for failing to develop unified plans that would permit better procurement practices among the services. Under the National Security Act of 1947, the JCS held responsibility for preparing such plans, and its failure to do so shocked the congressmen.[12] Likewise, the Finletter Report noted the services had not integrated their future requirements but merely consolidated them.[13]

Years later Finletter elaborated on this deficiency, noting

that the JCS had failed to devise a specific war plan. During the Finletter Commission's proceedings, its members felt obligated to examine the overall war plan; unsuccessfully, they requested appropriate information from the JCS. Finally, the chairman went to Truman, who promised the committee it would receive the war plan. Shortly afterward, Admirals William Leahy and Chester Nimitz and Generals Eisenhower and Vandenberg met with the Finletter group and presented their plan, "pages thick, pages and pages," accompanied by an oral presentation. The group found the briefing very confusing; and after several questions, General Eisenhower apologized, "I'm sorry, I guess my mind is worse than I thought it was; I can't understand what the war plan is." After more fruitless discussion he continued, "Gentlemen, these five civilian gentlemen who are here are just patriotic American citizens trying to do something they've been asked to do by the President. I think we owe it to them to tell them that there is no war plan."[14] The Truman administration had given little guidance to its military leaders, and the JCS had yet to agree upon an integrated war plan, atomic or conventional. Each service had made its own preparation independently and with little coordination.[15]

The two reports convinced most congressmen that the nation's air arm needed a costly expansion, and they began to support the AF goal of seventy groups. Since World War II the flying generals had insisted this figure constituted the minimum needed to perform their mission, and on this point they had stood firm. The president and Secretary of Defense James Forrestal disagreed. Forrestal worried more about a balance among ground, naval, and air forces. In particular, the army had suffered from poor recruits and needed immediate attention.[16] Moreover, Forrestal realized the president's budgetary policies would not support a seventy-group program. These disagreements appeared in early 1948, during appropriation hearings for fiscal year 1949.

While government leaders debated in Washington, events were developing in Europe that made 1948 a pivotal year for the United States, its military, and its Strategic Air Command. After World War II, the USSR had made several expansion attempts, which greatly concerned the United States. None proved more alarming than the fall of the Czechoslovak government to Communist leadership in February 1948. Before that coup, Americans had had some reason for optimism over the cold war. In 1946, Soviet troops had left Iran; and, by late 1947, military aid to Greece and Turkey promised results. The Marshall Plan, designed both to rehabilitate Western economies and to contain Communist expansion, awaited congressional approval. The nation supported the bill's principles, and prospects for passage looked favorable.

This proposed European Recovery Act (ERA), however, threatened the peace by placing the USSR in a difficult position, and American leaders appreciated the Soviet dilemma. If large infusions of economic aid revived the Allied economies, Communist parties in Europe would lose support. The Marshall Plan could force the Soviets to react quickly with their own aid programs and to consider military action before the ERA became a reality. President Truman believed that, after the Marshall Plan began functioning, "the opportunity to communize Western Europe . . . would be lost."[17] Averell Harriman took another view; he believed that time was running out for peace in Europe. Communist demonstrations in France and Italy, he warned, indicated more than a planned tactical maneuver.[18] Military leaders, in particular, grew uncomfortable over possible Soviet reaction. From the Pacific, General Whitehead wrote, "I feel that there is grave danger of war with the U.S.S.R. within a few months. U.S.S.R. has moved so far along the aggression road, that she must continue to move along the same way."[19] In late 1947, a JCS report gave similar warnings. Political events in Europe, it advised, would take one of three courses: the status quo would continue, the Western position would improve, or Soviet influence would increase. Most importantly, the firmness shown by the allies would determine Soviet action in Europe. The JCS evaluation also warned of an increased danger of war once economic aid arrived from the United States. American assistance would weaken Soviet influence, and any delay in their response would work against the Russians. Therefore, some strong Soviet action was likely soon.[20]

During the 1947-48 winter, State Department officials became alarmed when unofficial reports advised them that the Soviet military had sought Stalin's permission to advance troops into Western Europe. Soviet generals wanted to move quickly and to establish themselves before American economic aid arrived in Europe. Reportedly, the Politburo resisted this suggestion and directed internal strikes and revolts throughout Western Europe.[21] Substantiating this intelligence, in December 1947 the USSR established the Cominform to aid such actions. Disorders followed in France, Italy, and Finland; but only the government in Czechoslovakia fell. Described as the "second Munich," that event dramatically confirmed American fears of aggressive Soviet intentions and suggested that more action would follow.[22]

In Germany, General Lucius D. Clay, the United States military governor, had slowly arrived at the same conclusion. Contrary to some characterizations of him as a hard-nosed cold-war general, Clay had earlier expressed strong hope of working with the Soviets. When Assistant Secretary of War for Air Stuart Symington was traveling through Germany in July 1946, he had met with Clay and found him the most sympathetic military man he had met with regard to Soviet positions. Clay had cautioned Symington against inaccurate press reporting of Soviet behavior in the Russian zone of Berlin and regretted that the United States had not followed Eisenhower's policy of giving the Russians access to our zone. He advised Symington, "I am one who believes we can get to know them and they can get to know us. I believe we can, over a period, work out the prevention of that war which so many people think inevitable."[23]

General Clay had always scoffed at the possibility of war with the USSR. Over the months, however, his position began to change, as discussion between the major powers over the future of Germany brought few results. By February 1948, he noticed a serious change in the attitude of every Soviet, "faintly contemptuous, slightly arrogant, and certainly assured."[24] Ten days after the Czech coup, Clay drafted his famous cable to General Omar Bradley, army chief of staff, revealing his growing apprehension:

> For many months, based on logical analysis, I have felt and held that war was unlikely for at least ten years. Within the last few weeks, I have felt a subtle change in Soviet attitude which I cannot define but which gives me a feeling that it may come with dramatic suddenness.[25]

Subsequent events quickly heightened his fears. On 20 March the Control Council which governed Germany concluded its meetings with acrimony and without agreement on major occupation problems. To Clay, the end of these meetings meant that a struggle with the USSR would follow.[26] On 31 March the Soviets advised the Allied powers that, effective 1 April, military passenger trains enroute to Berlin from the West would be stopped and their baggage and passengers checked by Soviet troops. If the United States accepted this new restriction, Clay warned, "it will be only a day or two until one of our people is pulled off on trumped up charges. It is unthinkable."[27] With Washington's support, General Clay continued to move trains eastward, and the Soviets responded by shuttling them onto side tracks. Within days, the trains retreated and the Soviets lifted the restrictions. Some traffic resumed by the end of April, but the issue of United States occupation in Berlin, however, remained volatile.

As the crisis in Germany developed, the AF reviewed its fighting capability and hoped for additional appropriations in order to expand. Air leaders found their prospects competing with President Truman's long-held desire for a universal military training (UMT) program. The president believed UMT offered much to every young man and to the nation. He considered it a program "giving our young people a background in the disciplinary approach of getting along with one another, informing them of their physical makeup and what it means to take care of this temple God gave us."[28] General Marshall supported Truman, realizing Americans would never accept a large standing peacetime army. He considered a small military force capable of rapid expansion to be the best alternative, provided that it had a sufficient supply of trained men. Congress had rejected UMT after 1945; but in 1948 the events in Europe encouraged the president to advocate the program again.

Outside the administration, however, little support existed for UMT. During past wars, most Americans had viewed compulsory military training as necessary only in wartime. After each conflict, they had expected training to cease. Citizens harbored some fear of "the man on horseback," but primarily they questioned the value of training thousands in military camps during peacetime. Even within the Defense Department, leaders gave only qualified support. The navy believed the program offered little to its potential strength, while the AF considered its personnel requirements incompatible with UMT. As elements of the Defense Department, however, the admirals and air generals supported the proposal.[29]

The defense budget and politics posed the primary stumbling blocks for UMT. Funds diverted into a comprehensive training program would allow the AF only fifty-five groups and the navy few ships. Congressmen worried about the cost of UMT in terms of money and votes; consequently, they favored a small, volunteer military force. To the public, the AF seventy-group program had greater appeal than UMT, and the recently released Finletter and Brewster reports justified this alternative.

During the troubled period of February and March 1948, two serious military questions demanded answers. First, how would a newly implemented UMT program aid the U.S. military in Germany? Most supporters conceded that a year would pass before any results appeared. To the AF, the problem proved most vexing; aviators realized that if the Soviets attacked in strength, the Allied occupation forces could not remain in Berlin, in Germany, or perhaps even in Europe. Air power from England and North Africa offered the *only* serious threat to the USSR, yet Truman was focusing on expansion of ground forces rather than air groups. Second, the military did not know what response the United States would offer under such circumstances; the president had offered no guidance on using atomic weapons.

Moreover, the military lacked an integrated war plan, and the specific responsibilities of each service still needed clarification.

A week after General Clay's early March warning, Forrestal assembled the JCS at Key West, Florida, attempting to establish clearly the mission of each branch and to settle interservice differences. In 1947, the military had shelved certain control and responsibilities issues in order to facilitate unification.[30] Unfortunately, the three-day Key West Conference failed to resolve the mission dilemma, but it did address manpower and atomic energy problems. The JCS recommended an immediate reenactment of the draft law because UMT could not strengthen United States forces quickly enough. As the possibility of using atomic weapons had increased, the service chiefs also urged the executive to reconsider the control issue. On 15 March 1948, Forrestal returned to Washington to advise the president.[31]

Truman, meanwhile, took steps to secure passage of UMT. His advisers had convinced him the bill would pass only on the basis of military necessity, and the administration had to present the plan to Americans in dramatic form, perhaps in a speech by Secretary of State George C. Marshall outlining the necessity of UMT as a support for United States foreign policy.[32] Instead, Truman elected to address a joint session of Congress. On 17 March, he laid the groundwork for rearmament by requesting a supplemental defense appropriation. He also asked the Congress for three items: quick passage of the European Recovery Act then before them, a temporary reenactment of the Selective Service Act, and adoption of UMT.[33]

The following week Forrestal presented the president's proposal to the House Armed Services Committee, requesting a three-billion-dollar supplemental budget. Secretary of the Air Force Symington and Spaatz testified later, hardly disguising their negative attitudes toward UMT. Although overruled within the administration, they continued to seek a seventy-group force, and suggested that an additional $800 million would provide that number. Spurred by the Finletter and Brewster reports, congressmen found this proposal more attractive than a four-billion-dollar UMT program already unpopular with voters. The defense secretary, however, argued for balance; he believed the strengths of all the branches should remain relatively equal. Considering the army's very limited response capability, a product of the manpower shortage that had followed the end of the draft in 1947, Forrestal supported Truman's and Marshall's position on UMT. AF leaders, however, deemed this approach unrealistic. They believed air power offered the only response against the Soviet Union; consequently, the air arm should logically receive a disproportionate share of the budget. As problems in Berlin developed, the air-power issue grew even more important, because existing Allied forces in Germany could not stop a strong Soviet action. Congress agreed with the generals; and, along with the supplemental request, it approved an additional $822 million earmarked for aviation and for seventy air groups.[34]

Meanwhile, the United States military watched in Berlin, unsure of the future and of its own response should the Soviets act aggressively. Truman certainly wanted American forces to remain in Berlin, yet the United States lacked the means to keep them there if confronted. Forrestal chafed at the government's lack of planning and urged the National Security Council to define our position in Western Europe. Certainly the Marshall Plan had received attention; but, he warned, "the time has come when it must be studied on a broader basis, such basis to include important military factors."[35] The quality of planning also shocked columnist Joseph Alsop. In May, Alsop had gained access to certain military information (apparently from the AF) while preparing an article for *Life* magazine. He privately advised a friend that there was still no overall, agreed-upon American plan to meet possible Soviet aggression in Europe. Alsop blamed the deficiency on Admiral Leahy, Truman's trusted advisor. Unlike Leahy, other military men believed the United States should include atomic weapons in its war plans. Alsop also uncovered a severe bottleneck in American capability: only three teams were available to assemble atomic bombs.[36] The only hope against Soviet attack in Europe revolved around the AF, but unanswered questions remained concerning American response. Truman clearly guarded his thoughts about using atomic weapons and left military planners on their own.

Spurred by events in Berlin, the JCS finally adopted a short-range emergency war plan called HALFMOON on 19 May. The authors of HALFMOON continued to operate under the assumption that atomic weapons would be used but admitted that no political guidance had been afforded them. The plan contained the same national war objectives adopted by BROILER six months earlier.[37] HALFMOON also acknowledged certain shortcomings. Specifically, the authors recognized the plan did not provide adequate assistance to the countries of Western Europe. In fact, HALFMOON called for Allied forces in Germany to withdraw to the Rhine and offered little support for retaining Middle East bases and oil resources. Planners believed the Mediterranean could be closed off to the Allies after a week of hostilities. Therefore the United Kingdom had to be protected, for its air bases held the key to Allied operations. Like BROILER, the plan called for an early attack against vital elements of the Soviet warmaking capacity. Strategic Air Command would deploy available units to bases in England and to the Khartoum-Cairo areas and would conduct operations from these bases and Okinawa. Atomic weapons and operating bases in Great Britain were the critical elements of the plan.

HALFMOON left important questions unanswered and ignored certain realities. Three weeks after the acceptance of the plan, the Joint Logistics Plans Committee concluded that if war came within the next several months, parts of the planned operation would fail because of logistical deficiencies. The committee doubted adequate personnel with proper qualifications could be provided to the right units to make a balanced force. Moreover, a serious shortage of aircraft existed, and all three services lacked certain supply items. The committee suspected further deficiencies would be uncovered as more detailed planning evolved. Energetic action was needed to correct these problems.[38]

United States leaders wondered about their response to a Russian attack in Europe; most adopted one of two opinions over probable Soviet action. The more optimistic believed the USSR could not afford and did not wish a major war. Barring miscalculation or accidents, these defense leaders felt the United States could maintain its position in Berlin without fighting. This view had originated in previous intelligence reports, and it received further support in 1948. On 1 April, the Joint Intelligence Committee at the American embassy in Moscow dispatched an appraisal reinforcing this interpretation.[39] As late as June, the State Department's Policy Planning Staff concluded that "the Soviet Government is not now planning any deliberate armed action of this nature and is still seeking to achieve its aims predominantly by political means."[40]

For reasons not entirely clear, military leaders expressed more concern. On 9 March 1948, the Chief of Naval Operations, Admiral Louis Denfeld, urged plans for preparing the American people for war, including a partial remobilization.[41] In April, the Army Chief of Staff, General Omar Bradley, advised columnist Alsop that he (Bradley) was one of a small minority who expected war in 1948.[42] Likewise, Col. R. B. Landry, Truman's air aide, believed that "war will begin in a matter of a few months."[43] Regardless of which opinion the president shared, he had only one course: to remain in Berlin and hope the Soviets would not attack.

On 24 June, the Soviets reinstated the Berlin blockade, but the United States military still lacked direction on any offensive response. On 27 June, defense leaders convened in Washington to discuss possible actions. They considered three alternatives: withdrawal, stiff reaction followed by a military response, or the compromise action of remaining firm while still striving for diplomatic recognition of United States rights in Berlin. On the following day, they made their recommendations to the president, who had already selected the third alternative.[44] Truman elected to continue his existing policy of standing pat, without any definite reaction plans except for evacuation.

From this high-level defense meeting came another decision, one that has misled journalists and later historians. In 1951, while editing the *Forrestal Diaries*, Walter Millis highlighted the Berlin crisis, introducing the B-29s as a critical element. According to the *Diaries*, the president "expressed affirmative approval of sending B-29s to Germany."[45] Most observers assumed that the deployment of ninety bombers in July demonstrated United States willingness to use atomic weapons.

It should be noted, however, that in mid-1948 only two SAC

groups could carry atomic weapons, and neither unit was deployed overseas. The command's Eighth AF held responsibility for delivering atomic bombs; and of its four bomb groups only the 509th and the 43rd had programs connected with the AEC and were organized to handle atomic weapons. By contrast, all of SAC's Fifteenth AF groups remained outfitted for conventional weapons only. SAC headquarters directly controlled the one remaining group, the 307th, and it too had only conventional capability.[46] Before the Berlin crisis erupted in June, Fifteenth AF had deployed one B-29 squadron from the 301st to Europe on a normal rotation tour. In July the president sent the remaining two squadrons from the 301st, as well as the 28th (also from Fifteenth AF) and the 307th. Truman did not send to Europe any atomic weapons or any capability to deliver them in July 1948.

Millis and later scholars merely assumed that the B-29 groups dispatched had had atomic capability and believed that Truman had taken a firm action by deciding to use these weapons if the need arose. Certainly the public, reporters, and government observers associated the B-29 with atomic capability. In fact, the deployment actually revealed Truman's great reluctance to take that critical step. It demonstrated that his plans at that point were unclear, as conventional bombing would have had little effect on the USSR.

If President Truman had wanted to rattle his saber, he would have sent at least one squadron from the 509th. No one would have had any doubts about potential action. By deploying groups with conventional capability, Truman indicated hope for a diplomatic settlement; he also gave the Soviets time. Ironically, time was the factor that would make the blockade work and force the Allied powers from Berlin.

SAC generals puzzled over the B-29 deployment and considered the action a strictly political move, not a true show of force.[47] Militarily the deployment left too many questions. What operational plans would follow? Would atomic weapons eventually enter the picture? The commander of the first squadron arriving in Germany did not even know what bomb-loading configuration to expect; thus, he could not position any weapons. He suspected that the B-29s would be used for hauling coal in the airlift and expressed relief when spared this duty.[48] Kenney chafed at the limited leverage offered by the conventional B-29s, complaining, "The Russians may of course be worried about our 90 B-29s now in Europe, but we don't seem to be using them as a club. Perhaps in time, the Russians will figure that as long as we don't mention them around the green table, that they are no good anyhow. How I would like to see Gen. Mac at that conference with Uncle Joe."[49] In Europe, even General LeMay realized that "as far as combat capability was concerned they weren't too much good."[50]

It is not clear how Soviet leaders perceived this deployment. Many American scholars believed the Russians were fearful of atomic weapons and considered the move a strong response. The deployment could be the first step toward a strategic bombing attack, launched from England and Germany against Soviet cities. SAC's true capability and the conventional capacity of the deployed bombers could have been unknown to them. Atomic tests in the Pacific by the United States in 1946 and 1948 might have indicated the Americans held an ample stockpile of awesome weapons. The increased radar protection of the Hanford plant in early 1948 may have suggested increased production. For those so inclined, no doubt, other United States actions could have given the Russians cause for concern. But one fact argues against these considerations; whatever the extent of their fears, the Soviets did not lift their blockade from Berlin following the deployment and they maintained their effort for ten months thereafter. Seemingly, the Russians were not outwardly influenced by the ninety B-29s.

Ironically, it is plausible they held a more accurate assessment of United States capability than did American observers and later scholars. Most historians, who have assumed the deployment was a strong and credible response, have also presumed the Soviets shared that view. It is impossible at this time to determine precisely what perceptions the Soviets held and acted on after July 1948, but there is good reason to suspect the Russians did not consider American atomic capability a serious threat.

A case can be made that the Soviets judged Truman's response a cautious move. It is not certain what information the USSR may have had regarding the three deployed groups; the Russians' knowledge would have depended upon the level of Soviet intelligence within the United States between 1945 and 1948. But enemy order of battle, a basic concern of any military intelligence organization, would have caused the Soviets to focus on the 509th Composite Group. The 509th had bombed Hiroshima and Nagasaki and was now operating from Roswell Field; that much information was commonly available. Because of an unpleasant United States experience in 1944, the Soviets could also surmise that no B-29 configured to carry atomic weapons would operate from bases near Russian-occupied territory or overfly land not controlled by the United States. (During World War II, two B-29 Superfortresses had landed in Siberia, and the Soviets refused to return the aircraft to the Americans. Indeed, United States airmen had become extremely bitter when the USSR subsequently used these bombers as models for its own developing strategic air arm.) The United States would certainly not risk losing a SILVER PLATE B-29 and more valuable information; the Soviets could have confirmed this conclusion by observing the 509th. That unit never left the North American continent except for atomic tests in the Pacific, where they flew from United States-controlled bases and territory.[51] If the Soviets were observing the 509th and 43rd Groups during the summer of 1948, they found the former training in Labrador while the latter was testing and converting to the new B-50. The 301st, the 28th, and the 307th had each rotated units to Europe or Japan during 1947 or 1948, revealing that their capabilities were conventional. It is likely the Soviet leaders did not consider the B-29 deployment a serious threat.

It is also possible the Russians held no firm perceptions of American intentions or capability. Those who would argue this view could point to the Soviet wait-and-see action in Berlin. The fact remains that there is no hard evidence currently available to demonstrate exactly what the Russians believed in the summer of 1948.[52]

If the Soviets were uncertain, they were not alone; the deployment had confused Forrestal as well. He believed it impossible to carry out his responsibilities without resolving certain questions. He wanted objectives set down and plans drawn up, both for the use of atomic weapons and for strictly conventional ones. Forrestal took his problem to the National Security Council, the body established by Truman to draw political and military plans for the United States. In hopes of filling the gap, the secretary of defense initiated action for planning on 10 July. Writing the president, he stated, "I am convinced that the formulation of a sound military program and intelligent decisions concerning the size and character of our future Armed Forces depend upon a prior determination of our basic national objectives, and of the roles which military strength and other non-military activities should play in furthering these objectives."[53] Forrestal was requesting the National Security Council (NSC), at the height of the Berlin Crisis, "to prepare a statement which specifies and evaluates the risks of the future, states our objectives, and outlines the measures to be followed in achieving them."[54] The secretary believed "such a statement is indispensable to the National Military Establishment in determining the level and character of forces which it should maintain."[55] In a memo to the NSC, Forrestal added "I believe it is imperative that a comprehensive statement of national policy be prepared particularly as it relates to Soviet Russia."[56]

These requests revealed flaws in the administration's conduct of affairs. Nearly three years after World War II, American foreign policy in Europe could be summed up by Truman's containment policy and the Marshall Plan. The NSC, in existence for nearly a year, had not established any specific foreign policy objectives. Consequently, the military, with its limited capability, had no detailed responsibilities. Moreover, the generals did not understand the president's exact attitude toward use of the atomic bomb, and the dispatch of conventional B-29s to Europe merely left the hardest questions clouded over.

In searching for more direction, Forrestal and the AF reopened the matter of controlling the atomic weapons stockpile.[57] The president agreed to reconsider the issue. On 21 July, representatives of the AEC, defense officials, and the military met and set forth their respective arguments. Two days later, Truman advised Forrestal that the AEC would continue the control and surveillance of atomic weapons.[58] A major change in the summer of 1948 could have a negative impact on the forthcoming presidential election; he would reconsider the idea after November.[59] Lilienthal considered this a victory, but the AF and Forrestal still lacked guidance on the conditions under which atomic weapons could be used. The best indication they received came six weeks later. During a meeting between Truman and Secretary Forrestal, the president "prayed that he would never have to make such a decision, but that if it became necessary, no one need have a misgiving but what he would do so."[60]

As late as November 1948, however, the AF still had certain unanswered questions about its role in Europe. During August, the United States had promulgated Plan Harrow, which gave additional direction to air force commanders in Europe. But, when Lt. Gen. John K. Cannon assumed command of the USAFE in late 1948, he immediately asked for more specific guidance. In a long letter to the new Air Force Chief of Staff, General Hoyt S. Vandenberg, he outlined his concern over current operational responsibilities.

> Is the basic role of the Air Force in Europe one of occupation or is it one of occupation plus preparation for combat operations on the continent?
>
> The organization as now constituted and as currently disposed, is of very dubious value as a fighting force and cannot be considered adequate even in terms of the broad mission laid down in . . . USAF Plan Harrow. . . .[61]

Cannon wanted to "set up a command capable of combat action in the event of trouble."[62] He had taken preliminary steps, realizing that his action conflicted with the evacuation-of-the-continent concept contained in Plan Harrow but believing it lay along the line previously drawn for him by AF officials in Washington. Although Plan Harrow had accented evacuation, the developing Western Union Defense Plan could soon change the thrust of United States intent, and Cannon wanted clarification.[63] Not until late November did the NSC finally establish peacetime and wartime objectives in Europe, incorporating them into NSC 20/3 and 20/4.[64]

The confrontation with the Soviet Union in 1948 did not shock the United States. As the crisis developed in Germany, both nations made predictable responses. Fearing the Marshall Plan and its possible impact on Europe, the USSR hoped first to force the Allied powers from Berlin. Although the Soviets held military advantage on the ground, they considered fighting unnecessary. By blocking access to Berlin in June, the Soviets had only to wait for insufficient supplies to force the West out by winter. The Americans, however, refused to withdraw, planning instead to remain as long as possible.

Nevertheless, the United States entered the Berlin crisis with little organized preparation and reacted cautiously. Certain events and intelligence sources had alerted the government to possible difficulty, but the president and his National Security Council failed to formulate any specific European objectives or any military plan of action until after the blockade began. The first United States response came with a small airlift from the Western zones into Berlin. Neither nation placed great importance on this small supply effort, and the Soviets permitted the cargo aircraft to pass through the air corridors unchallenged. During the summer, the United States displayed little military strength, and the AF left its atomic capability at home, barely hinting its possible use.

President Truman, an accomplished poker player, held and played a weak hand. He elected to place his hopes in diplomacy—which, however, offered the Soviets time to make the blockade effective. Meanwhile, Operation Vittles expanded and the tonnage delivered increased weekly. The airlift's success surprised both governments; by winter it had rendered the blockade ineffective. Within a year, cargo aircraft, not the threat of atomic destruction, defeated the Soviet strategy and brought the United States its narrow victory. Fortunately, President Truman's hand was never called.

NOTES

1. For an excellent discussion of deterrent capability during the Berlin crisis, see Alexander L. George and Richard Smoke, *Deterrence in American Foreign Policy: Theory and Practice* (New York: Columbia University Press, 1974), pp. 107-36. See also W. Phillips Davison, *The Berlin Blockade* (Princeton: Princeton University Press, 1958).

2. A review of the State Department's 1948 Policy Planning Papers demonstrates these points. PPS 27 (March 23) noted the president's words to Congress a week earlier indicating the United States should assure the free European nations of " 'the [military] support which the situation requires.' " Truman was urging a commitment without fully understanding American capability. At the same time, the United States had no clear position with regard to Russia, PPS 38 (August 18). The papers recognized the need for a strong United States force but PPS 43 (November 24) took heed of a JCS warning; the discrepancy between commitment and military resources was increasing. Policy Planning Staff Papers, Diplomatic Branch, National Archives, Washington, D.C. (hereafter cited as PPS).

3. Richard R. Haynes, *The Awesome Power* (Baton Rouge: Louisiana State University Press, 1973), p. 60. Haynes and others believe that Truman did have some private doubts.

4. Harry S. Truman, *Memoirs*, vol. 2: *Years of Trial and Hope* (Garden City, N.Y.: Doubleday and Company, Inc., 1956), pp. 2-5. See also Richard G. Hewlett and Oscar E. Anderson, Jr., *A History of the United States Atomic Energy Commission*, vol. 1: *The New World, 1939-1946* (University Park: Pennsylvania State University Press, 1962), pp. 482-530.

5. Memorandum, General Spaatz to General Lewis Brereton, Chairman, Military Liaison Committee to the Atomic Energy Commission, subj: Delivery of Atomic Weapons to the Armed Forces, 31 October 1947. Spaatz Collection, Library of Congress, Washington, D.C. At the time, the Armed Forces Special Weapons Project was responsible for the storage of such atomic weapons as the president might direct the AEC to transfer to the military.

6. David E. Lilienthal, *The Journals of David E. Lilienthal*, vol. 2: *The Atomic Energy Years 1945-1950* (New York: Harper & Row, 1964), pp. 374-75.

7. Lilienthal, p. 391.

8. President's Air Policy Commission, *Survival in an Air Age* (Washington, D.C.: Government Printing Office, 1948), pp. 24-25 (hereafter cited as *Finletter Report*).

9. *Public Papers of the Presidents, Harry S. Truman, 1947* (Washington, D.C.: Government Printing Office, 1963), pp. 344-45.

10. *Finletter Report*, pp. 24-25.

11. Congressional Aviation Policy Board, *National Aviation Policy*

(Washington, D.C.: Government Printing Office, 1948), pp. 7-8 (hereafter cited as *Brewster Report*).

12. *Brewster Report*, p. 6.

13. *Finletter Report*, pp. 29-30.

14. Oral History Interview with Thomas K. Finletter by Col. Marvin Stanley, February 1967, pp. 35-37, Interview no. 760, Albert F. Simpson Historical Research Center, Maxwell Air Force Base, Alabama (hereafter cited as AFSHRC).

15. Although legal unification had taken effect in 1947, the services had not begun to operate in that manner. The National Security Act of 1947 limited the authority of the defense secretary, and Forrestal was unable to bring about the necessary degree of unified planning and cooperation. See Arnold A. Rogow, *James Forrestal* (New York: The Macmillan Company, 1963), pp. 304-5.

16. Walter Millis, ed., *The Forrestal Diaries* (New York: Viking Press, 1951), pp. 374-75, 401-2.

17. Truman, p. 120.

18. Memorandum, Bruce Hopper to General Spaatz, 22 November 1947, Spaatz Collection, Library of Congress, Washington, D.C.

19. General Whitehead to General Spaatz, 9 December 1947, 168.6008-3-Spaatz, AFSHRC.

20. Record Group 218, "Records of the United States Joint Chiefs of Staff," CCS 092 10-9-46. Enclosure JSPC 814/3 (circa 1947), National Archives, Washington, D.C.

21. Robert F. Futrell, *Ideas, Concepts, Doctrine: A History of Basic Thinking in the United States Air Force 1907-1964* (Montgomery: Aerospace Studies Institute, 1971), pp. 213-14. Futrell referred to a lecture given by A. Berle, "The Democracies Face the Post War Problem," given at the Air War College, 8 October 1952.

22. See "The Battlefields of Peace," *Time*, 8 March 1948, p. 26.

23. Memorandum for the record, "Interview with General Clay, July 25, 29, 30, 1946," by Secretary Symington, Spaatz Collection, Library of Congress, Washington, D.C.

24. Lucius D. Clay, *Decision in Germany* (Garden City, N.Y.: Doubleday and Company, Inc., 1950), p. 354.

25. Jean Edward Smith, ed., *The Papers of General Lucius Clay*, vol. 2 (Bloomington: Indiana University Press, 1974), pp. 568-69. Some scholars now believe Clay's dramatic words were intended to help the military secure larger appropriations from Congress.

26. Clay, pp. 356-57.

27. Smith, pp. 602-3.

28. Truman, p. 54.

29. See Rogow, pp. 298-99, and Haynes, pp. 80-86.

30. For an excellent treatment of unification difficulties, see Herman S. Wolk, "The Defense Unification Battle, 1947-50: The Air Force," *Prologue*, Spring 1975, pp. 18-26.

31. Millis, pp. 390-94.

32. Millis, pp. 369, 384-85.

33. *Papers of the Presidents*, pp. 182-86.

34. U.S. Congress, House, Committee on Armed Services, *Selective Service: Hearings before the Committee on Armed Services*, 80th Cong., 2d sess., 1948, pp. 6079-6161, specifically 6098 and 6161. See also Millis, p. 415.

35. Memorandum, James Forrestal to The Executive Secretary, National Security Council, 18 March 1948, Spaatz Collection, Library of Congress, Washington, D.C.

36. Noel Parrish, "Behind the Sheltering Bomb: Military Indecision from Alamogordo to Korea" (Ph.D. Diss., Rice University, 1968), pp. 263-64. Parrish quoted from a letter Alsop had sent to Martin Sommers, 8 June 1948.

37. HALFMOON did not contain the "Overall-Strategic Concept," but the concept was inserted in a late July revision (1844/13). It was probably omitted to facilitate acceptance by the three service chiefs, which may suggest that one or two chiefs were troubled by the concept. Because of security compromises, the HALFMOON code name was changed to FLEETWOOD and later DOUBLESTAR.

38. Record Group 218, "Records of the United States Joint Chiefs of Staff," CCS 381 U.S.S.R. (3-2-46), Sec. 16, "The Logistic Feasibility of Operations Planned, 'HALFMOON'," JLPC 84/16, 15 June 1948, National Archives, Washington, D.C.

39. Record Group 319, "Records of the Army Staff," NSC 20/2 P & O 092 TS (25 August 1948), case 116/5, National Archives, Washington, D.C.

40. Ibid. The CIA, however, guessed the Soviets would resume their efforts to force a western withdrawal from Berlin. Central Intelligence Agency, "Review of the World Situation as It Relates to the Security of the United States," CIA 4-48, April 1948. Annadel Wile, ed., *The Declassified Documents Quarterly Catalog*, vol. 3, no. 4, January-December 1977 (Washington, D.C.: Carrollton Press Inc., 1978), p. 179C.

41. Record Group 218, "Records of the United States Joint Chiefs of Staff," CCS 334 12-2-47, Sec. 1. Memorandum, Admiral Louis Denfield to the Secretary of Defense, subj: Evaluation of Current Strategic Air Offensive Plans, 9 March 1948, National Archives, Washington, D.C.

42. Parrish, p. 249.

43. Memorandum, Col. R. B. Landry to Admiral Leahy, 16 July 1948, Vandenberg Collection, Library of Congress, Washington, D.C.

44. Millis, pp. 452-55.

45. Millis, pp. 456-58. At first Millis advises his readers only that "The B-29s were known throughout the world as the atomic bombers. . . ." Several pages later, he automatically assumes they had the capability: "However the decision to send the atomic bomb carriers. . . ." Five years later, Millis acknowledged, "it has never been made clear whether they

actually carried atomic weapons in their bomb bays or not." Still, Millis believed it quite possible. See Walter Millis, *Arms and Men* (New York: G. P. Putnam's Sons, 1956), p. 289.

Later historians, perhaps influenced by his comments in the *Forrestal Diaries,* have also assumed atomic capability was sent to Europe. See Gaddis Smith, "Visions and Revisions of the Cold War," *New York Times,* Section 6, 29 April 1973, p. 55.

46. "History of Strategic Air Command 1948." Typescript history prepared by Headquarters Strategic Air Command, Offutt AFB, Nebr., 1949, pp. 54-55 (hereafter cited as "SAC-1948"), AFSHRC. See Exhibit no. 35, Appendix no. 1 (509th Bombardment Wing), and Appendix no. 2 (43rd Bombardment Wing), n.p.

47. Memorandum, General J. B. Montgomery, SAC Director of Operations to SAC Historical Section, 18 August 1949, 416.0-48, AFSHRC. NSC Action 77, 15 July 1948, supports this view. While approving of the B-29 deployment, that group reserved its decision on increasing the airlift to Berlin.

48. Comments cited from letter, General Leon Johnson, C/G Fifteenth AF to General McMullen, 13 July 1948, 416.01-48, AFSHRC.

49. General Kenney to General Whitehead, 9 August 1948, 168.6008-3-Kenney, AFSHRC.

50. Oral History Interview with General Curtis E. LeMay by John Bohn, March AFB, Calif., 9 March 1971, Interview no. 736, AFSHRC.

51. One exception occurred in February 1948, but during the time of an atomic test in the Pacific. A squadron of the 509th visited Japan for two weeks and conducted training and other classified work. See "SAC-1948," pp. 182-87.

52. Because the Soviets could not directly threaten North American territory, they probably considered their large armies in East Europe their best deterrent against Western expansion. See Malcolm Mackintosh, *Juggernaut* (New York: The Macmillian Company, 1967), pp. 270-71, and Thomas W. Wolfe, *Soviet Power and Europe 1945-1970* (Baltimore: Johns Hopkins University Press, 1970), pp. 33-38. Wolfe also suggests (pp. 19-20) that Stalin may have viewed the Berlin blockade as a good test of American resolve to remain in West Europe.

53. Record Group 319, "Records of the Army Staff," NSC P & O 092 TS (12 July 1948), case 116/2, National Archives, Washington, D.C. Ltr., Secretary Forrestal to President Truman, 10 July 1948.

54. Ibid.

55. Ibid.

56. Ibid. Memorandum, Secretary Forrestal to the Executive Secretary, National Security Council, subj: Appraisal of the Degree and Character of Military Preparedness Required by the World Situation, 10 July 1948.

57. In late April, Senator Kenneth Wherry of Nebraska had unsuccessfully proposed legislation to return atomic bomb production to the

military during the world crisis. He felt the move would have great effect upon the Soviets. See *New York Times,* 26 April, p. 1.

58. Millis, p. 461. For a detailed narrative of this meeting, see Lilienthal, pp. 387-92.

59. George Elsey, "Will We Use the Bomb?" Manuscript (circa fall 1948). Annadel Wile, ed., *The Declassified Documents Retrospective Collection* (Washington, D.C.: Carrollton Press Inc., 1976), p. 304A.

60. Millis, p. 487.

61. General John Cannon to General Hoyt Vandenberg, 16 November 1948, Vandenberg Collection, Library of Congress, Washington, D.C.

62. Ibid.

63. The Western Union Defense Plan emerged from the Brussels Pact of January 1948, which included the Benelux countries, England, and France. The United States did not actively consider joining until July, in part because it did not want to provoke the USSR. Participating nations finally resolved organizational problems by October, although the United States did not sign the treaty until April 1949. See Truman, pp. 243-51.

64. Record Group 319, "Records of the Army Staff,"NSC 20/3 and 20/4, P & O 092 TS (2 November and 23 November 1948), case 116/10 and 116/13, National Archives, Washington, D.C.

7 COMMAND CHANGES

Political events in Eastern Europe, along with the Berlin blockades of 1948, forced the air force to examine the capability of Strategic Air Command to conduct offensive operations. General Hoyt Vandenberg, the new AF chief of staff, made unexpected and disturbing discoveries: SAC was improperly prepared for combat and had less capability to deter aggression than was previously believed by military leaders. In preceding years, SAC had focused on three central problems: obtaining new personnel and training them in basic skills, reorganizing for efficiency and economy, and rotating combat groups to forward bases and the Arctic. Demobilization and shortages in funds, personnel, and equipment had made training difficult to complete properly; but, after General McMullen instituted his cross-training program in late 1947, existing capability quickly deteriorated.[1] After nine months of this program, there were some leaders who doubted the command could perform its mission. With a potential conflict unfolding in Europe, the AF carefully reviewed SAC's combat capability and determined that new leadership was required. Consequently, General Vandenberg appointed Lt. Gen. Curtis LeMay as SAC's new commander.

General LeMay immediately set out to build a force that

could deter Soviet aggression. After the Berlin blockade developed, government leaders began giving more consideration to the concept of deterrence; and, in November 1948, the National Security Council formally adopted that policy in its defense planning. The nation, the NSC concluded, must "develop a level of military readiness which can be maintained as long as necessary as a deterrent to Soviet aggression."[2] After the Czech coup in February 1948, the United States expanded its production schedule of atomic weapons, thus increasing the possibility of building a stockpile sufficient to deter. Unfortunately LeMay found the force responsible for delivering these weapons to be inadequate, ill-trained, and lacking the military capability to support NSC goals and aims. The new commander carefully examined every aspect of his organization and realized he would first require increased support from government and AF officials before SAC's capability could improve. Within the constraints of a low defense budget, LeMay needed to acquire more equipment, increase manpower, and extend the combat range of his bombers. In late 1948, however, President Truman had begun scaling down United States defenses from the summer level, forcing the AF to reduce its strength from a projected sixty-six to forty-eight groups. If SAC wanted additional resources, it would have to compete with other military branches and AF commands. LeMay considered this initial battle for increased support critical for building a deterrent force.

The Berlin crisis dramatically reminded government officials of their limited military options with the Soviet Union in Europe. The public realized the airlift had saved the Western position in Berlin and had averted war, but only a few understood that Operation Vittles had also cloaked the inadequate offensive capability of the United States. As 1948 ended, national leaders realized that, on the Eurasian land mass, only air power and atomic weaponry could deter future Soviet expansion and hold promise of real United States military influence. The United States strategic force, however, required vast improvement and growth; and the greatest burden fell on General LeMay.

When General Vandenberg appointed a new SAC commander

in September 1948, most AF generals believed he was acting on two considerations. Primarily, the AF had found SAC's combat readiness wanting; that demanded a leadership change. Other aviators, however, believed the reassignments also stemmed from Vandenberg's desire to place his own appointees in critical positions, and the personality of General Kenney had played an important part in his decision. Evidence indicates the first consideration alone would have justified Vandenberg's action, but the latter belief is difficult to ignore. To some degree, certainly, the personality of General Kenney, as well as his relationship with AF leadership, was instrumental in SAC's early development and must be considered in any analysis of Vandenberg's final decision to change commanders.

General Kenney's most important career assignment had come in March 1942 when General Arnold ordered him to lead the Pacific Air Forces. His performance in that role catapulted him to success, fame, and four stars. He worked well with General MacArthur and quickly became a favorite. With MacArthur's support Kenney could hope for the highest AAF position after Arnold retired. If that hope failed, there were other possibilities. Should MacArthur win high political office after the war, Kenney's military career would go forward. That awareness developed as early as March 1943 when Kenney and General Richard Sutherland, MacArthur's chief of staff, journeyed to New York and met Senator Arthur H. Vandenberg of Michigan. Their discussion focused on MacArthur's potential as a Republican presidential candidate in 1944.[3] Little support developed for MacArthur, however, and the Republicans looked elsewhere; Kenney remained loyal to MacArthur.

In 1945, the length of the Pacific war indirectly began to affect Kenney's future career. The fighting in Europe ended four months before the Japanese surrendered, and AAF posts in Washington fell to airmen returning first from England. Generals in the Pacific stayed at their posts; and, when the war ended, General MacArthur wanted Kenney and Whitehead to remain in the Far East. Poor health forced General Arnold to retire; as his successor he chose his trusted associate,

General Carl Spaatz. Like Kenney, Spaatz had proven himself a superior wartime commander. But with independence a primary goal, Spaatz's diplomatic manner made him a logical choice to command the AAF. Given Arnold's preference for Spaatz, Kenney remained in the Pacific.

In late 1945 a new high-level air position developed; the recently established United Nations required ranking military advisers, and the War Department appointed Kenney, one of AAF's four full generals, as a military air adviser to the United States delegation. Initially, the position appealed to Kenney, because provisions existed for a United Nations military force and he considered himself a logical commander of any future U.N. air arm.[4] That force never evolved.

Instead, Kenney began finding himself at odds with his superiors. In January 1946, he and the civilian members of the American delegation publicly expressed divergent views on trusteeships in the Pacific, Kenney suggesting the United States should annex certain Pacific islands. Moreover, he voiced his belief that the United States should make its army and navy available to the U.N. Security Council. Embarrassed by these comments, the War Department quickly advised Kenney to limit his advice to military matters.[5]

Two months later the *New York Herald Tribune* carried remarks from an interview given by General Kenney.[6] He had predicted the United Nations would soon have land, sea, and air forces, in accordance with Article 45 of the U.N. Charter. Again the War Department complained to General Spaatz about Kenney's statements. When Spaatz criticized him, Kenney promptly defended himself. He believed greater problems had developed recently from security leaks within the United States delegation. Kenney correctly advised Spaatz that his interview contained nothing new and, "Instead of hopping on me for saying nothing, I'd like to see some action on the ones who are really messing things up by giving secret information."[7] The AAF, however, worried about the image Kenney projected, not just about the content of his remarks.

General Kenney quickly grew disillusioned with his new post and, as Spaatz had recently appointed him commanding general of the newly formed SAC, he wished to leave the United Nations. In a telephone conversation with Spaatz, Kenney asked when he could expect relief from his current assignment. Spaatz replied that General Eisenhower had no other full general to replace him.[8] Kenney remained at the United Nations until November 1946, when Lt. Gen. Harold L. George assumed the post and allowed him to take full-time responsibility for SAC.

Even then, Kenney did not give his new command full attention. He was an outgoing, loquacious man who excelled at public speaking and enjoyed such appearances. His wartime reputation placed him in demand, and he accepted many invitations to address groups. Again the quest for independence played a part. Many air leaders believed with Secretary Symington that the AAF needed positive public exposure and that Kenney could help the drive for autonomy by his many appearances. Yet these numerous activities forced Kenney away from his command and accounted for a growing opinion that SAC was not progressing far during its first year. Deputy Chief of Staff Lt. Gen. Ira Eaker felt, "TAC is making the greatest strides in reorganizing, training, and administrative matters and on all these matters, is surpassing the other commands at the present writing."[9]

In late 1946, Kenney obtained General McMullen as his deputy and promptly gave him great latitude in running the command in his absence. McMullen embarked on the reorganization experiments and efficiency moves already described. Parts of his program encountered opposition from the AAF. With Kenney's support, the deputy commander wanted to reduce the number of higher-ranking and nonrated officers in SAC. General Spaatz correctly recognized that McMullen's pre-World War II attitudes were no longer appropriate and urged all his commanders to use the AF's many well-qualified technical officers. SAC continued to transfer as many nonflying officers as possible to other commands and balked at taking its proportion of ranking officers. At one point the command stated it had no requirements for quartermaster colonels, but Spaatz termed that contention "absurd" and tartly advised Kenney, "I have made an effort to explain to you in a staff conference for that purpose my personnel plan. If it is not clear to you at this time, come to me, so report, and I will endeavor again to make it clear. I expect that you and your staff will become familiar with the Air Force policies and plans and will carry them out promptly and loyally."[10]

In early 1947 the AAF continued to seek a positive image and publicity, but certain efforts became counterproductive. Kenney believed a huge demonstration of airpower might prove beneficial and directed his staff to plan an en-masse overfly of New York City with every available B-29 in the United States. On 17 May 1947, SAC conducted the demonstration, but citizens and the press expressed negative reactions. Shortly afterward Spaatz strongly discouraged Kenney from undertaking any future mass flights over major cities.[11] At the same time Secretary Symington wrote Kenney from Missouri, advising him against leading a proposed long-range global flight. Concerned about unification hearings in the Senate, Symington did not want a "war hero engaged in any saber rattling movements." He too expressed dismay at the adverse publicity coming from the New York demonstration and noted, "with people in very high places, the AF has a reputation for popping off."[12] He and General Spaatz wanted to end this feeling and avoid negative publicity.

Adverse feelings increased as Kenney openly opposed the B-36 bomber in his most serious disagreement with AF leadership. The AAC had requested the huge, eight-engine bomber in 1941 while England was waging the Battle of Britain. If the island nation fell, long-range B-36s could attack Germany from North America. When Hitler abandoned his British efforts and turned on the Soviet Union, interest in the bomber lagged; but after the war, range became important again and the AAF reconsidered the B-36. General Kenney opposed development of the large aircraft, urging concentration on a new jet bomber. His contemporaries considered jet engines too unreliable at that point, preferring to develop a long-range propeller-driven aircraft for the next five years. Shortly after leaving his U.N. duties, Kenney wrote Spaatz, explaining his many objections to the developing B-36. He considered it too slow and unsuitable for its mission; he worried about engines and structural problems. Spaatz defended the new bomber and discussed the dangers of abandoning development. Admittedly, major problems existed, but, he added, "We could never have bought a single type including the B-17, if we had waited for a better type we knew was just around the corner. If we stumble into that pitfall, at one stage of three to five years, your strategic air forces will be without equipment."[13] General Nathan F. Twining, commander of Air Materiel Command, supported Spaatz's position, warning that experimental models could not be equated with future performances. Moreover, the B-52 would not arrive until 1953-54.[14] Kenney remained unconvinced.

In late 1947 opinions again clashed when Kenney testified before the important USAF Aircraft and Weapons Board, made up of the top AF leaders. At this point, his opposition had become quite annoying; however, the B-36 production program had lagged. By April 1948, General Norstad, now deputy chief of staff, operations, and others considered curtailing the program at a level below even that which Kenney had accepted. Nevertheless, after several months the manufacturer began correcting major problems and the program revived.[15]

General Kenney's persistent opposition proved annoying and may have estranged him from AF leadership; but by the spring of 1948, many others, including Secretary Symington, had also developed grave misgivings about the B-36.[16] Some historians and aviators have considered this difference instrumental in Kenney's later removal from SAC, but air leaders objected more to Kenney's manner of opposition than to his argument.[17]

Another difference with AF leaders had far greater effect on General Kenney's future. Kenney believed the air force chief of staff should have greater authority over aviation matters, with less interferences from the civilian secretary. Kenney believed the secretary's role consisted of defending the AF budget before Congress and fighting for resources. He admired the past relationship between former Assistant Secretary of War Lovett and General Arnold, noting that Lovett limited himself to appropriation battles.

That this concept found little favor with Symington and

other leaders became evident in September 1947. When the AF finally achieved independence, many generals received new assignments. General Spaatz had wanted to retire soon after unification, as had his deputy, General Eaker. Spaatz remained, however, to direct the AF transition. Reorganization and retirements followed, bringing about numerous command changes, which were to determine AF leadership in the coming years. Some officers believed Kenney, by virtue of his experience and rank, would succeed Spaatz. General Whitehead, for one, even sent Kenney two personal memos: one listing primary objectives he should pursue as chief of staff, and the other recommending future command reassignments for top AF generals.[18] For his own part Kenney doubted he would become the next chief of staff because of the attitudes he had expressed about that post. His feelings proved correct.

When the new assignments appeared, General Vandenberg received a fourth star and became deputy chief of staff under Spaatz, an excellent position for the grooming of a new AF chief. The appointment bypassed several older officers who now considered their future limited. Symington believed Vandenberg would do well with congressional leaders, and perhaps President Truman saw political value in this appointment. The chief executive needed to build support for a bipartisan foreign policy and the Marshall Plan. The new deputy's uncle, Senator Arthur Vandenberg, held a key position in the Republican-controlled Congress and chaired the Foreign Relations Committee. In the following months Truman was able to obtain the support needed from the senator, while General Vandenberg assumed an active role as vice chief of staff. On 31 March 1948, Truman called General Vandenberg to the White House. In one month Spaatz would retire; the president had selected Vandenberg as the next chief of staff, USAF.[19]

The new commander inherited the burden of the crisis in Berlin. When the military first grew concerned over possible Soviet aggression in early 1948, Spaatz and Vandenberg had taken a close look at AF capability and made preparations for a conflict. Spaatz ordered all radar units to operate continuously in the Pacific-Seattle area (to protect the Hanford

Plant) and directed all overseas commands to update and refine their war plans—particularly their evacuation procedures.[20]

In addition, the air leaders examined SAC's group expansion and cross-training activity; by March 1948, General Spaatz suspected there were problems within the command. In a routine letter to his commanders, Spaatz reviewed the status of each command, noting that all had had difficulty maintaining aircraft in operational condition. To General Kenney, however, he suggested, "SAC's low index of aircraft in commission may be symptomatic of other difficulties such as below standard organizational training."[21] SAC's cross-training program also received scrutiny. The AF had approved the program in late 1947 but soon began to question its effect; if crew members trained in new skills for extended periods, their proficiency in primary duties would certainly suffer.[22] General McMullen, however, "intended to ride herd" enthusiastically on cross-training and even asked permission to award additional aeronautical ratings to crewmen who met SAC's qualifying standards.[23] General Spaatz rejected his request, indicating concern over the additional training burden placed on fliers.[24]

To detect specific problem areas, the AF asked Charles A. Lindbergh to examine AF combat capability, specifically that of the atomic squadrons, and to offer recommendations for improvement. In the spring of 1948, the famed aviator met several times with General Vandenberg and expressed disappointment with what he had discovered; he urged the new chief of staff to visit an Eighth AF group personally.[25] After months of observation and flying with SAC aircrews, Lindbergh submitted his final report to General Vandenberg in September 1948. His conclusions supported the apprehensions of certain AF leaders.

Lindbergh hit hard at personnel and training problems. "It is obvious," his report began, "that the standards of performance, experience, and skill which were satisfactory for the 'mass' air forces of World War II are inadequate for the specialized atomic forces we have today."[26] Lindbergh added, "I have come to the conclusion that a great and almost immediate improvement in the striking power of our atomic forces can be made through attention to personnel." Moreover, he believed, "the personnel for atomic squadrons were not carefully enough selected, the average pilots [*sic*] proficiency is unsatisfactory, teamwork is not properly developed, and maintenance of aircraft and equipment is inadequate. In general, personnel are not sufficiently experienced in their mission."[27] Lindbergh largely blamed these problems on

> numerous assignments to temporary duty, an intensive cross-training program, and extracurricular flying activities [which] have seriously interfered with training in the primary mission of the atomic squadrons. Resulting absences and frequent changes in home location have had a bad effect on family relationships and on overall morale. Line crews, as well as flight crews are over worked.[28]

Lindbergh concluded by offering recommendations. He urged the command to stabilize its personnel, strengthening aircrews by limiting replacements. He recommended that the AF "eliminate or greatly moderate cross-training until high proficiency is attained in the primary mission." Moreover, commanders should "simulate probable wartime missions to [the] greatest practicable degree." Finally, he suggested the AF "create conditions of responsibility, work, pay, housing, etc. which will draw highest quality personnel." Lindbergh further advised, "This report is not written in criticism of a job well done. It is written to suggest improvements. . . ."[29] Indeed SAC had struggled under disadvantages and shortages, but the findings still reflected poorly on Kenney's and McMullen's leadership.

General Norstad, deputy chief of staff, operations was equally concerned and directed Maj. Gen. F. H. Smith, Jr., to evaluate the impact of SAC's self-imposed personnel ceiling. At Weaver Air Force Base, South Dakota, the 28th Bomb Group had recently departed on the famed B-29 deployment to Europe. Smith found the movement was hindered by shortages of airmen, a condition he blamed on the low ceilings, aggravated by the cross-training program. He found the staff at Castle Air Force Base, California, struggling with their reduced allotment of men; at Roswell, Smith discovered one-fourth of the non-flying officers had been reassigned during June and July. Given the responsibilities of the 509th, especially during the Berlin crisis, this turnover seemed dangerous and well exceeded the recommended changeover of no more than one-third *per year.* Smith concluded that the command's ceiling had hurt morale and mobility. He found the cross-training program had been a "diluted effort, dangerous to our national security."[30] After reporting to Norstad, Smith shared his evaluation with Kenney. In his judgment, SAC had incorrectly focused on economy and broad training, normal concerns of a peacetime military. Given the international conditions, he advised, "within the Strategic Air Command, we must think in terms of a wartime Air Force."[31]

Certain AF generals believed that SAC's problems stemmed from two related problems: General Kenney had made a poor choice in selecting General McMullen as his deputy, and neither commander really understood strategic bombing. Without doubt, McMullen had proven himself a superior maintenance and supply officer, but he had never commanded a large combat organization. Moreover, the AAF had essentially fought a tactical war in the Pacific until General LeMay launched strategic missions against Japan. To close observers, this lack of experience in conducting strategic operations accounted for the poor training given SAC units.[32]

Furthermore, General McMullen had erred in trying to re-establish a pre-World War II organization, a low-manned, cross-trained, all-rated force. The AAC had cross-trained crew members at multiple positions before 1941, but the practice had simply grown impractical thereafter. Most airmen realized this; unfortunately, for reasons not clear, McMullen refused to believe it. While trying to restore the old system, he and Kenney had neglected a basic consideration: to achieve and maintain proficiency, crew members must practice realistically and regularly. If other duties or training should interrupt, primary skills deteriorate dramatically. Despite his good motives, McMullen courted disaster when he reinstituted multiple training and additional duties for his flying officers. Hoping for economy, he undermanned his groups and lost efficiency; the subsequently low capability caused Lindbergh and Smith to make their negative reports.

SAC's commanders had grown concerned over their poor bombing capability by April 1948.[33] During the preceding year, crew members had not dropped nearly their allotted number of bombs, and scoring results demonstrated decreased proficiency.[34] General Kenney quickly ordered intensive practices for different groups at an AF bombing range in Utah and also ordered a command bombing competition for the end of June in order to stimulate improvement.[35] The meet's bombing scores confirmed the need for far more practice and evaluation.[36] Meanwhile the Soviets were preparing to blockade the routes to Berlin.

To help improve bombing capability, Lt. Gen. Muir S. Fairchild, AF vice chief of staff, assembled a board of officers and civilians to study every aspect of past and present bombing methods and to suggest new actions and procedures. On 1 November 1948, after nearly two months of study, the board conferred at Maxwell AFB and offered the commands a wide range of criticism and recommendation. Its members concluded that SAC crew members had not trained sufficiently or under realistic conditions. Moreover, crews had given much attention to visual bombing, at the expense of radar practice. Finally, the members described the reflecting targets used on radar runs as "completely unrealistic."[37] Their report merely echoed Lindbergh's summary: the command needed more and better practice.

The revelation of SAC's low level of capability, alarming at a time of crisis, reflected poorly on AF leadership. Unification battles, reorganization problems, and the quest for additional funds, groups, and aircraft appeared to have overshadowed fundamentals. The value of a strategic force depended upon its ability to launch aircraft, arrive at target areas, and drop bombs accurately. Without this capability, supporting activities meant little.

The inevitable change in SAC leadership occurred in October. According to one eye-witness, the decision began to emerge at a high-level meeting in mid-1948. Secretary Forrestal had assembled top military leaders from the services; each major commander gave a short briefing on his organization. When General Kenney addressed the group, his presentation rambled, embarrassing the air generals before the other military leaders. After the meeting, General Norstad insisted that Vandenberg name a new SAC commander. Vandenberg asked whom he would recommend, and Norstad responded with a question: Who would you want in command of SAC if war broke out tomorrow? The chief of staff quickly replied: LeMay.[38]

Late in August, Vandenberg and Symington visited Europe and met with General LeMay. They found his organization, USAFE, ready for the emergency facing them in Germany, and the air leaders returned to the United States impressed with the job LeMay had done. After the decision came to appoint LeMay as SAC's new commander, Secretary Symington wrote President Truman about the forthcoming change, "It appears advisable in the national interest to reassign certain Air Force general officers. These include General George C. Kenney. . . ."[39] Kenney became the commander of the newly formed Air University at Maxwell AFB. In Europe, General LeMay learned of his new assignment and prepared to return.[40]

The change of leadership at Strategic Air Command came principally out of one consideration: after two and one-half years, the organization still lacked the combat capability expected of the nation's most crucial military force. The difficulties lay beyond shortages of resources and men; the responsibility rested also on the command's top leadership. The personalities of the commanders involved may have played some role, although the human element cannot be measured with accuracy. Air leaders can and did, however, closely evaluate bombing scores and combat capability. On this basis, the command changed.

General LeMay assumed command of SAC on 19 October 1948, with support never enjoyed by General Kenney. Because of the Berlin crisis, the AF, JCS, Congress, and the president wanted to strengthen the nation's atomic deterrent force, and the NSC adopted that policy in its defense planning. With this high-level support, the new commander began building an offensive force that could deter.

In late 1948, however, the Department of Defense encountered two financial problems that threatened LeMay's efforts. First, President Truman had impounded the additional $822 million appropriated by Congress in April for building a seventy-group air force. The supplemental budget, approved at the same time, only permitted limited expansion beyond forty-eight groups.[41] Second, the chief executive reduced the ceiling for military spending in fiscal year 1950. To build a strong, capable, deterrent force, LeMay had to obtain additional funds for SAC while the total defense budget declined, a feat requiring the full support of other AF commanders and service branches.

The prospects for changing Truman's mind appeared dim; executive leaders had argued over the 1950 budget since May 1948. At that time the Bureau of the Budget Director James Webb had advised Forrestal that his 1950 proposal should not exceed $15.3 billion. Forrestal appealed to the president, but Truman announced a defense ceiling of $15.0 billion for the coming year. Even after the USSR imposed the June blockade on Berlin, the president resisted pressure to increase spending. Forrestal sympathized with his service chiefs, who considered the administration's figure wholly inadequate to sustain necessary forces, but the secretary had no choice but to carry out the president's directive.[42]

As military leaders had initially estimated a need for $23.6 billion for 1950, they faced a major effort in trimming their requests. By October the service chiefs had still not agreed on a defense budget, and Forrestal found himself at an impasse with his planners. He elected to submit two plans to the president, one totaling $14.4 billion, the other $16.9.[43] For the lower budget he urged the service chiefs to allot $4.8, $4.6, and $5.0 billion for the army, navy, and AF respectively. This smaller budget only permitted a bomb-from-Britain war plan; but the larger one of $16.9 billion would give the navy greater assistance and allow the United States to conduct military operations from the Mediterranean. On 1 December, Forrestal sent both plans to Truman; and, eight days later, the service secretaries and chiefs met with Webb and the president. In an hour-long presentation, Forrestal urged adoption of the larger proposal. Truman, however, insisted on $14.4 billion, limiting the military to 60 percent of its original request.[44]

The smaller amount forced the AF to reduce its strength to forty-eight groups and to reconsider its organization and areas of emphasis. Accordingly, General Vandenberg convened a USAF Senior Officers Board in Washington to examine and suggest appropriate AF actions with respect to the force's future composition.[45] Fortunately, a recent JCS paper had determined a strategic concept of operations against the Soviet Union and gave the senior officers some basis for their recommendations. The board quickly determined that "the launching of an atomic offensive and defense of the Western Hemisphere and the essential areas from which to launch the atomic offensive must be considered as the primary mission of the Air Force and must be given the greatest consideration and priority."[46] Before SAC could expand its deterrent force, however, other commands would have to suffer additional cuts.

Having established the primacy of SAC's mission, the board called for General LeMay's opinion on group composition. The new commander addressed the members on 3 January 1949; he began by stating as his basic belief, "the fundamental goal of the Air Force should be the creation of a strategic atomic striking force capable of attacking any target in Eurasia from bases in the United States and returning to the points of take-off."[47] LeMay outlined SAC's needs and described the equipment required, including additional B-36 bombers. Four B-36 groups could deliver the nation's limited stockpile of atomic weapons, yet the AF had programmed only two for SAC.[48] LeMay asked for two more, plus a B-36 reconnaissance group. His request stemmed solely from calculations of capability; the B-36 possessed greater range and payload capacity than any other existing bomber.

The new commander worried most about bomber range. Existing war plans relied heavily on forward staging bases because the B-29 and B-50 each had a limited radius of action.

This reliance bothered LeMay because foreign governments could easily deny SAC the use of North African and Middle East facilities. Moreover, if the Soviets could damage English airdromes, the United States would lose its most critical staging fields. Most AF leaders believed the United Kingdom lay vulnerable to Soviet attack, even without a land invasion. They were concerned that, under pressure, the British might refuse SAC bombers on their soil or seek conciliation with the Soviet Union. The Joint Chiefs of Staff advised: "In the event of major war within the next few years the United States will not have the active support of any of the European nations, with the exception of Spain which if attacked, will ally with the U.S."[49] Arctic bases presented too many obstacles. As deputy chief of staff for Research and Development (1946-47), LeMay had dealt closely with cold-weather operations and understood the problems. The budget could not support the facilities required in a cold climate. For the immediate future, SAC had to depend on foreign facilities to avoid range problems.

General LeMay could build the force described to the Senior Officers Board in two ways. He could obtain bombers possessing a 10,000-mile range, or he could develop aerial refueling techniques in order to extend the range of existing aircraft.

Work on both alternatives had preceded LeMay's command. General Kenney had always advocated aerial refueling and had realized some progress toward that end during his last year at SAC. Aviators had determined that a standard B-29 with maximum loading could fly approximately 4,200 miles; by refueling 2,000 miles after take-off and again at the same point en route home, the bomber could cover 7,000 nautical miles.[50] The procedure would extend B-50 range equally well. Only by launching from forward bases could SAC bombers reach Soviet targets and safely recover without refueling. Therefore, in late 1947, SAC joined with Air Materiel Command to perfect a refueling system for U.S. aircraft.

In January 1948, the Aircraft and Weapons Board met and urged the AF to upgrade aerial refueling to a 1-A priority.[51] Rather than develop its own system for B-29 tankers and receivers, the AF elected to adopt one designed by an English firm, British Refueling Limited; in March, AMC purchased forty refueling sets.[52] The British method involved trailing hoses, grapple hooks, and reels; but these soon proved unreliable, difficult to use, and incapable of transferring fuel rapidly enough. Meanwhile, the Boeing Company was struggling to improve the range of its new B-47 jet bomber. Late in the summer, Boeing developed the idea of a flying boom for aerial refueling. The boom was a simple rigid tube that telescoped from the tanker to the receiver and eliminated the problems posed by the hose-and-reel system.[53] When General LeMay and his staff arrived at SAC in October, they immediately recognized the flying boom as a superior system and decided to adopt the boom as SAC's future method of inflight refueling.

As aerial refueling promised a timely solution to range problems, General LeMay dramatized its potential by preparing two demonstration flights, still using the British system. In both instances, planners and airmen worked in secret until each flight neared completion. SAC scheduled the first to coincide with the AF Commanders Conference held at Maxwell AFB, Alabama, during 7-9 December 1948. At that conference, AF officials were considering future AF development plans; they concluded by approving increased emphasis upon improving SAC's deterrent capability. At one point during the meeting LeMay reportedly told his fellow commanders that a B-50 had just passed overhead, completing a mission of nearly 10,000 miles with a bomb-drop at midpoint. Three aerial refuelings by KB-29s had made the flight possible.[54]

Three months later a SAC crew completed a more dramatic mission by flying another B-50, the "Lucky Lady II," nonstop around the world. In planning the mission SAC secretly positioned tankers at four points: the Azores, Saudi Arabia, the Philippines, and Hawaii. After departing on 26 February 1949, the "Lucky Lady" encountered typical mechanical and weather problems, but circled the globe in ninety-four hours. AF leaders and the press, notified hours earlier about the flight, met the aircraft as it landed in Arizona. By these two flights SAC dramatized for the public, government officials, and all military leaders the achievements and potential of aerial refueling, supporting General Vandenberg's emphasis on developing SAC forces.[55]

When General LeMay assumed command of SAC, two points concerning aerial refueling stood out. First, his current force of medium-range bombers, including the newer B-50s, required a refueling capability to be effective. To complement his existing bomber force, he had to create a tanker fleet by converting stored B-29s. Conversion required funding; and, by dramatizing the value of aerial refueling, he could more easily request the necessary resources. Second, until the flying boom became fully operational (projected at first for late 1949), SAC had to tolerate the hose-and-reel system. Therefore, LeMay now turned his attention to the other solution to the range problem.

Although engineering, design, and such flying techniques as cruise control could extend the range of the B-29 and B-50, only the B-36 could operate from the United States against the USSR and recover in safe territory.[56] As Consolidated Aircraft Corporation had recently solved certain developmental problems on the B-36s and improved its performance, LeMay believed SAC should replace its shorter-range B-29s with the new bombers. In January 1949, the Senior Officers Board unanimously agreed with LeMay's request and so advised General Vandenberg.

The following month, Consolidated successfully experimented with jet pods attached to the B-36 wing, again improving the aircraft's capability. Impressed with this new modification, General LeMay wrote Vandenberg, urging the AF to revise future aircraft procurement plans.[57] At LeMay's suggestion, the AF convened another Senior Officers Board on 21 February, and SAC's commander then outlined his latest impressions and opinions. Existing plans called for procuring the new B-54, an improved version of the B-50C. While seeking to expand the plane's capability, however, the manufacturer had burdened the B-54 with certain unfavorable features, such as outrigger wheels beneath the wings. Given the increased performance of the B-36 with attached jet pods, LeMay advised cancelling the entire B-54 order and applying the remaining funds toward more B-36 groups.

General LeMay offered several other suggestions for expanding and improving the force. At that time, each group contained eighteen bombers; however, that number could increase without requiring a proportionate expansion of the support organizations. LeMay therefore asked to enlarge each B-36 group to thirty aircraft. In addition, he urged accelerated production and procurement of B-47s. The jet bombers could operate only from forward bases, but their speed would offer additional capability to SAC as the Soviets improved their jet fighters. LeMay presented a forceful case to the board, and again, after a week's deliberation, they accepted his recommendations unanimously.[58] The AF, struggling with limited funds and dim prospects for fiscal year 1951, strongly supported LeMay's request to improve SAC and ordered more B-36s.

SAC's expansion plans proceeded smoothly until spring. In March 1949, Louis Johnson replaced Forrestal as secretary of defense and shortly afterward cancelled construction of the huge supercarrier *United States* on grounds of economy. Stunned, the navy publicly questioned the decision. The admirals blamed the reliance on strategic bombing and attacked the B-36 program. From April through August 1949, charges and countercharges appeared within the Defense Department and in the nation's press, charges that challenged strategic bombing concepts, B-36 capability, and transactions involved in procurement of the huge bomber.

This turmoil disturbed the Congress and brought about two investigations by the House Committee on Armed Services. The first began in August 1949 and carefully examined the issue of B-36 procurement. The second followed immediately and considered service unification, B-36 capability, and the JCS decision to rely heavily on strategic bombing. The final results emerged in October, when the committee exonerated AF leaders of all charges involving procurement irregularities, supporting as well the AF decision to expand the B-36 force.[59]

During General LeMay's first year at SAC, he received strong support from his immediate superiors and even from the president. Truman began placing more reliance on the deterrent power of atomic weapons as the Berlin blockade continued into

1949. In early February, he admitted to AEC Chairman Lilienthal that "the atomic bomb was the mainstay and all he had; that the Russians would have probably taken over Europe a long time ago if it were not for that."[60] The JCS was placing greater importance on atomic weapons; when they developed United States war plans in early 1949, they found it necessary to recommend a further expansion of the atomic stockpile. Lilienthal had a foreboding when he met with the Military Liaison Committee and learned that these revised war plans had "substantially increased atomic weapons requirements."[61] Naturally, the growing reliance on atomic weapons automatically increased SAC's priority for military resources.

Taking a cue from Lindbergh's report, the AF assisted General LeMay in the critical area of personnel assignments. Before 1949, SAC had received many newly trained technicians from specialty schools; but, after serving for twelve to eighteen months, these men would often be reassigned by the AF to overseas posts. To replace them, SAC would receive more inexperienced airmen directly from technical schools. This process prevented the command from developing a strong core of experienced specialists. LeMay successfully drew attention to SAC's problem, and the AF agreed to limit the number of technicians taken from SAC each month for overseas assignments. Reduction of this drain permitted the command to upgrade and sustain its operations, particularly in the areas of maintenance and supply.[62]

Strategic Air Command received additional personnel, even while the AF was reducing its total manpower. Previously the 509th had enjoyed high priority for men and equipment; now preference extended to the entire command. Manpower, including officers, airmen, and civilians, rose from 52,000 in late 1948 to more than 71,000 by the following December. Seldom had a United States peacetime force grown by over a third in one year.[63]

In summary, the events of 1948 proved critical to Strategic Air Command. After the Czech coup in February, the AF had begun to examine its total combat capability, particularly that of SAC. All reports indicated the command had a lower capability than defense leaders could reasonably expect, and its capacity to conduct strategic bombing operations was called into question. Vandenberg, as the newly appointed chief of staff, believed the problem stemmed from SAC's leadership, and appointed a new commander with extensive experience in strategic bombing operations.

General LeMay began his first year as SAC commander with the mission of building an atomic deterrent force. Because of Soviet activity in Germany, the United States government had begun placing greater emphasis on establishing a deterrent air arm. The AF, Defense Department, JCS, and NSC supported LeMay's efforts to an extent never known by General Kenney. The new commander recognized the obstacles presented by limited budgets, but he carefully demonstrated to his military superiors SAC's potential and its needs for new equipment and more resources. Within a year, LeMay had expanded his force, gained approval for additional B-36 bombers, pursued development of aerial refueling, and increased the recognition of SAC's importance to the nation's defense.

NOTES

1. See Chapter 3, pp. 58-60.
2. Record Group 319, "Records of the Army Staff," NSC 20/4 P & O 092 TS (23 November 1948), case 116/13, National Archives, Washington D.C.
3. Arthur H. Vandenberg, Jr., ed., *The Private Papers of Senator Vandenberg* (Boston: Houghton-Mifflin Company, 1952), pp. 77-78.
4. Oral History Interview with Brig. Gen. Noel Parrish by James C. Hasdorff, San Antonio, Texas, 10-14 June 1974, pp. 253-54, Interview no. 744, Albert F. Simpson Historical Research Center, Maxwell Air Force Base, Alabama (hereafter cited as AFSHRC).
5. Message WAR 93198, Generals Eisenhower and Spaatz to Generals Kenney and Ridgway, 16 January 1946, Spaatz Collection, Library of Congress, Washington, D.C.
6. Robert J. Donovan, "World Air Force Expected to Be First Organized," *New York Herald Tribune*, 27 March 1946.
7. General Kenney to General Spaatz, 4 April 1946, Spaatz Collection, Library of Congress, Washington, D.C.
8. Memorandum for the record, subj: Telephone conversation between Generals Spaatz and Kenney, 11 June 1946, Spaatz Collection, Library of Congress, Washington, D.C.

9. General Eaker to General Elwood Quesada, 8 January 1947, Quesada Collection, Library of Congress, Washington, D.C.

10. General Spaatz to General Kenney, 6 May 1947, Spaatz Collection, Library of Congress, Washington, D.C.

11. General Spaatz to General Kenney, 30 May 1947, Spaatz Collection, Library of Congress, Washington, D.C.

12. Secretary Symington to General Kenney, 30 May 1947, Spaatz Collection, Library of Congress, Washington, D.C.

13. General Spaatz to General Kenney, 16 January 1947, Spaatz Collection, Library of Congress, Washington, D.C.

14. Maj. Gen. F. H. Smith, Jr., "History of B-36 Procurement," unpublished typescript report prepared for presentation to the House Armed Services Committee, 1949, pp. 8-1 and 8-2, AFSHRC.

15. Murray Green, "Stuart Symington and the B-36" (Ph.D. Diss., American University, 1960), pp. 82-98.

16. Green, p. 95. On 25 June, Generals Vandenberg, Norstad, Kenney, and Wolfe, along with Symington, agreed to complete development of the ninety-five B-36s ordered. Kenney claimed no objection to the building of approximately a hundred, a number less than had been first proposed by the AF.

17. Green, p. 79.

18. Memorandum, General Whitehead to General Kenney (circa 1947), and memorandum, General Whitehead to General Kenney, 4 September 1947, 168.6008-3-Kenney, AFSHRC.

19. Appointment Log of General Vandenberg, 31 March 1948, Vandenberg Collection, Library of Congress, Washington, D.C.

20. Message WARX 98510, General Spaatz to C/G Air Defense Command, 27 March 1948. Also WARK 97474, General Spaatz to Generals Twining, LeMay, Whitehead, Wooten, and Hale, 12 March 1948, Spaatz Collection, Library of Congress, Washington, D.C.

21. General Spaatz to General Kenney, 2 March 1948, Spaatz Collection, Library of Congress, Washington, D.C.

22. Cross-training has remained closely identified with General McMullen; however, Spaatz's early support has been largely overlooked. In a letter to his Fifteenth AF Commander, General Leon Johnson, McMullen quoted part of a letter sent to General Kenney from Spaatz on 22 January 1948: "The importance of cross-training among our combat crews cannot be over-emphasized." 670-01-1948, pt. 1, AFSHRC.

23. General McMullen to General Whitehead, 6 January 1948, 168.6008-3-McMullen, AFSHRC.

24. C/S USAF to C/G SAC, subj: Aeronautical Rating, 28 May 1948, 416.01-48, AFSHRC.

25. Vandenberg Appointment Log for 9 April, 13 and 18 May 1948, Vandenberg Collection, Library of Congress, Washington, D.C.

26. Charles A. Lindbergh, "Report to General Vandenberg," 14 Sep-

tember 1948 (hereafter cited as "Lindbergh Report,"), p. 1. For access to Lindbergh's personal copy of the report, I am indebted to Raymond H. Fredette, a Lindbergh biographer.

27. "Lindbergh Report," p. 2.

28. Ibid.

29. Ibid., p. 3.

30. Memorandum for General Norstad, subj: Orientation Visit to Strategic Air Command Medium Bomb from Maj. Gen. F. H. Smith, Jr., 9 August 1948. Record Group 341, "Records of Headquarters United States Air Force," DCS/OPNS, Admin Off, 452.1 "Programing General," National Archives, Washington, D.C.

31. Memorandum for General Kenney from Maj. Gen. F. H. Smith, Jr., 11 August 1948. Record Group 341, "Records of Headquarters United States Air Force," DCS/OPNS, Admin Off, 452.1 "Programing General," National Archives, Washington, D.C.

32. Oral History Interview with Maj. Gen. C. S. Irvine by Robert M. Kipp, March AFB, Calif., 17 December 1970, Interview no. 734, AFSHRC. Irvine served in SAC under both Kenney and LeMay. Also Maj. Gen. John B. Montgomery, a private interview held at Los Angeles, Calif., 14 July 1975.

33. General McMullen to General Hutchinson, AC/S, A-3, 26 May 1948, 416.01-48, AFSHRC.

34. General Hutchinson, AC/S, A-3, to C/G Eighth AF, subj: Bombing and Gunnery Training, 2 July 1948, 416.01-48, AFSHRC.

35. Lieutenant Colonel Hamilton, Asst. Adjutant General 15th AF to C/O Wendover AFB, subj: Squadron Training Maneuvers at Wendover AFB, 22 April 1948, 416.01-48. Also C/G SAC to C/G 8th AF, 15th AF, and 307th BW, subj: Competitive Bombing Maneuvers, Castle AFB, 27 May 1948, 416.01-48, AFSHRC.

36. Hdq. 8th AF to C/G SAC, subj: Unit and Individual Standings in Strategic Air Command Bombing Competition, 9 July 1948, 416.01-48, AFSHRC. See also "Bombing Data, by Groups of the Strategic Air Command, for Month of July 1948," which showed radar bombing errors four times larger than visual, 1375 ft. versus 329 ft. Fairchild Collection, Library of Congress, Washington, D.C.

37. "Report of Bombing Accuracy Confererrnce," at Headquarters Air University, 1-2 November 1948, K239-4709Q, AFSHRC.

38. Montgomery Interview. On two occasions, Lindbergh privately claimed a major role in LeMay's appointment as SAC Commander. Personal letter, Raymond Fredette, to the writer, 18 February 1976.

39. Secretary S. Symington to President Truman, 5 October 1948, Vandenberg Collection, Library of Congress, Washington, D.C. The actual decision was announced on 21 September; however, the president had to approve this reassignment. The post of C/G, SAC, required a four-star general, under the provisions of Public Law 381, Officer Personnel Act

of 1947. LeMay's appointment required a redesignation of rank for that post. The only other transfers involved LeMay's replacement and Kenney's new assignment.

40. To the best of his recollection, General LeMay did not learn of his assignment while Vandenberg and Symington toured Europe in August. As he recalled, his notification came later, in the normal manner. General Curtis E. LeMay, a private interview held at Newport Beach, Calif., 1 October 1975.

41. See Chapter 6, pp. 120-23.

42. Walter Millis, ed., *The Forrestal Diaries* (New York: Viking Press, 1951), pp. 430, 435-38. Forrestal's difficulties in meeting the president's ceiling caused Truman to lose faith in his defense secretary and contributed to Forrestal's resignation in March 1949. An excellent treatment of the 1950 budget preparations is found in Warner R. Schilling, Paul Y. Hammond, and Glenn H. Snyder, *Strategy, Politics and Defense Budgets* (New York: Columbia University Press, 1962), pp. 28-213. In particular see pp. 135-43 and 174-99. For a more personal interpretation of Forrestal, his problems as defense secretary, and his tragic suicide, see Arnold Rogow's sympathetic *Victim of Duty* (London: Rupert Hart-Davis, 1966), especially pp. 251-82.

43. The $15.0 billion ceiling contained $14.4 for the armed forces; $600 million was earmarked for a stockpiling program. See Schilling et al., p. 46.

44. Schilling et al., pp. 197-99.

45. This five-man board, headed by General Fairchild, replaced the larger but unwieldy AF Weapons Evaluation Group. The AF established both bodies to survey research and development programs constantly and to insure that proper emphasis fell on new weapons for carrying out the AF mission. Moreover, they recommended the type and number of weapons each combat unit should maintain. See U.S. Congress, House, Committee on Armed Services, *Investigation of the B-36 Bomber Program: Hearings before Committee on Armed Services on H.R. 234*, 80th Cong., 1st sess., 1949, pp. 141 (hereafter cited as "Hearings, B-36").

46. Quoted by Robert Futrell, *Ideas, Concepts, Doctrine: A History of Basic Thinking in the United States Air Force, 1907-1964* (Montgomery: Aerospace Studies Institute, 1971), pp. 223-24.

47. Quoted by Futrell, p. 224.

48. Futrell, p. 224.

49. Record Group 218, "Records of the United States Joint Chiefs of Staff," CCS 381 2-18-46, Sec. 2. JCS 1630/11, 6 April 1948, National Archives, Washington, D.C.

50. Various distances are given for potential B-29 range, both with and without refueling. Experience against Japan in 1945 yielded a 3,000-mile average. Bombers flying between Guam and Japan, however, frequently flew into the jet stream, which moves southward during the

spring and summer months. Boeing provided a more optimistic figure of 5,000 miles with a single refueling. By using cruise control and refueling on both outbound and inbound legs, SAC believed the B-29 could fly nearly 8,700 miles.

51. Routing and Record Sheet to Research and Development, DCS/M from Requirements Division, subj: Air-to-Air Refueling Program, 17 February 1948, 202.2, vol. 2, AFSHRC.

52. DC/S Material, General H. Craig to Under Secretary of the AF, subj: Foreign Procurement-Inflight Refueling Equipment, 15 March 1948, 202.2-59, vol. 2, AFSHRC.

53. Harold Mansfield, *Vision* (New York: Duell, Sloan and Pearce, 1956), pp. 292-93, 297-98.

54. "Strategic Air Command 1949." Typescript history prepared by SAC Historical Section, Offutt AFB, Nebr., 1950, p. 53 (hereafter cited as "SAC-1950"), AFSHRC. See also James Eastman, "Flight of the Lucky Lady II," *Aerospace Historian,* Winter 1969, pp. 9-10.

55. Eastman, pp. 10-11, 33-35. Also "SAC-1949," pp. 54-64.

56. Crew members applied cruise control by continually changing altitude, engine settings, and airspeed as the aircraft burned fuel and thus reduced its weight in flight. Always flying at optimum efficiency extended range greatly. In 1945, then-Col. C. S. Irvine began experiments with cruise control techniques; SAC adopted his procedures in 1947.

57. General LeMay to General Vandenberg, 2 February 1949, 416.01-49, AFSHRC.

58. See "Hearings, B-36," pp. 142-55. In late 1947, General Spaatz had directed Vandenberg to investigate the possibility of increasing the number of aircraft in each group. No apparent results came from this effort, probably because of economic reasons. Memorandum, General Spaatz to General Vandenberg, subj: Increasing Number of VHB Aircraft per Group, 27 December 1947, Spaatz Collection, Library of Congress, Washington, D.C.

59. A thorough treatment of the B-36 controversy is found in Murray Green's "Stuart Symington and the B-36," (Ph.D. Diss., American University, 1960). For a study including many press reports on the dispute, see Elliott Johnson, "The B-36 Controversy: A History of the Air Force-Navy Rivalry Over Strategic Bombardment" (Master's Thesis, University of Wisconsin, 1961). See also Keith D. McFarland, "The 1949 Revolt of the Admirals," *Parameters* 11 (1981): 53-63.

60. David E. Lilienthal, *The Journals of David E. Lilienthal,* vol. 2: *The Atomic Energy Years, 1945-1950* (New York: Harper & Row, 1964), p. 464.

61. Lilienthal, pp. 502-3.

62. General Thomas Power to C/S, USAF, subj: Strategic Air Command Development Program, 16 November 1948; General Lauris Norstad, C/CS Operations to C/G SAC, subj: Strategic Air Command Develop-

ment Program, 22 December 1948; General LeMay to General Idwal Edwards, D/CS Personnel, 22 January 1949; and General Edwards to General LeMay, 10 February 1949, 416-01-49, AFSHRC.

63. "The Development of Strategic Air Command 1946-1973." A typescript summary of SAC histories, prepared by Headquarters Strategic Air Command, Offutt AFB, Nebr., 1974, pp. 9, 13.

8 LeMAY THE ARCHITECT

When Vandenberg appointed LeMay as commander, Strategic Air Command, he must have discussed the contents of Lindbergh's report with its emphasis on the need for training. The chief of staff gave only general instruction to his new commander, but left no doubt about SAC's objectives. LeMay was to take the organization, prepare it for combat, and provide the nation with a deterrent force. LeMay wholeheartedly supported his mission, believing, "no one would dare attack the United States" if SAC became efficient and powerful.[1] Although his effort to secure and retain high-level support for SAC's increased needs was critical, LeMay realized the command would succeed only through effective leadership.

As an experienced combat commander, General LeMay chose to stress two elements Lindbergh had found wanting in SAC. The Lindbergh report had criticized the command's training program, and General LeMay understood that any effective fighting organization first had to undertake rigorous and meaningful training. As his command would probably have to enter war without a mobilization period, he introduced a concept new to the United States military: that of preparing and maintaining offensive forces ready to enter combat immediately. These "forces in being" would require a different type of training; therefore, LeMay and his staff successfully developed a program emphasizing close supervision, realistic flying missions, and continual evaluation of all command activities.

Lindbergh had also noted a morale problem within SAC. LeMay and his commanders paid greater attention to the personal needs of their officers and men in order to motivate them and retain their services. The training necessary for building and maintaining a ready force placed heavy demands upon each individual; yet SAC could offer its men little in terms of material reward. Private industry, on the other hand, offered these same trained specialists better pay and working conditions. LeMay and his commanders had to compete constantly for the men they and the AF had trained. They never achieved the desired retention level, but their innovative approaches to personnel management succeeded in forming the nucleus for SAC's future development.

General LeMay never forgot that, above all, people make an organization successful. His success in rapidly improving the capability of Strategic Air Command rested largely on his personal leadership, his ability to develop the proper environment for realistic training, and his recognition of personal needs.

General LeMay's pre-World War II experiences had burned into his mind the importance of preparation and convinced him that proper training offered the key to successful operations. Before the war, LeMay had served as operations officer for the 34th Bomb Group and then commanded the 305th Group. The AAC generals had warned their combat commanders that, as the United States might enter the war soon, they would have to prepare for fighting. The warning disturbed LeMay; he did not know what preparation to give his men or how to obtain sufficient flying time, practice bombs, or aircraft for conducting any worthwhile training. After war had been declared, LeMay's inexperienced unit deployed to England, unprepared for combat operations. His group faced the highly efficient German Luftwaffe, which had dominated European skies for nearly two years, and the Americans suffered severely in the early months. Crewmen found combat missions a totally alien experience; groups even had difficulty in flying formation. LeMay and other air generals never forgot how weak and unprepared they had been in 1942; they recognized this condition as a by-product of isolationism and the nation's neglect of its military during the 1930s. When LeMay assumed command of SAC, his pre-World War II experiences heavily affected his thoughts and plans.[2]

To prepare SAC crewmen, LeMay replaced the prevailing peacetime atmosphere with a keen awareness that war could erupt suddenly; aircrews must expect to fly critical combat missions with atomic weapons on a few days' notice. Throughout World War II, LeMay had found that whenever crews performed new or different missions, confusion always attended and effectiveness fell. Therefore his crews would fly realistic practice missions frequently, carefully simulating wartime conditions. LeMay would expect accurate and consistent performances, day after day, to insure that capability existed whenever it might be required. At the same time, constant pressure to meet high standards would dispel the complacency usually found in peacetime operations.

General LeMay began by building a dependable staff. He wanted generals with World War II experiences similar to his own and aviators who had proven their ability to complete difficult tasks in combat operations. This led the new commander to choose key advisers from his old 20th Air Force staff, which had operated from the Marianas during World War II. He asked for Brig. Gen. Thomas S. Power, who had commanded the 314th Bomb Group in 1945, and appointed him SAC vice commander. He obtained Brig. Gen. John B. Montgomery and Brig. Gen. Walter "Cam" Sweeney to direct SAC's all-important Operations and Plans divisions. Both Montgomery and Sweeney had served with LeMay in the Pacific, and he knew they possessed the experience and talent needed to direct a combat command. From his old USAFE Command he secured Brig. Gen. August W. Kissner, another veteran of the Marianas operation, to become SAC's chief of staff.[3]

In November 1948, LeMay and his staff moved SAC Headquarters to Crook Field near Omaha, Nebraska, and began to work on two major tasks.[4] First, SAC had to distribute its available resources effectively within the command. Prior to LeMay's appointment, the command had divided its meager allotments of men and material among all groups, with the result that none had a strong organization. To correct this deficiency, LeMay and staff instituted the first Strategic Air Command Developmental Program, establishing goals they wished to attain by 1 January 1949. Rather than upgrading all groups simultaneously, the program established a priority for each group, headed by the 509th. The command directed total attention and effort to that unit until its equipment, manpower, and performances rose to acceptable standards. Under this plan, the necessary resources were taken from other groups to strengthen priority units. Once an organization was upgraded, attention fell on the next priority group. By repeating the process and obtaining additional resources, the command could strengthen all its groups and achieve an overall offensive capability.[5] After meeting the 1 January goals, SAC established a second development plan for the following six months, striving to upgrade three more medium wings and one heavy bomb wing. A third plan followed in July. All three programs distributed and concentrated SAC's limited but growing resources for optimum use.[6]

The second task, improving combat proficiency, first required a test of the flying crews. In his memoirs, LeMay has described the force he received: "We didn't have one crew, not one crew, in the entire command who could do a professional job. Not one of the outfits was up to strength—neither in airplanes nor in people nor anything else."[7] Even more disheartening, crew members did not realize their limited capability. LeMay's staff found the command's bombing scores acceptable but questioned their relevancy. The crews had conducted missions at low altitudes and had bombed against reflector targets over water or on desert ranges. This training lacked realistic features and permitted crew members to deceive themselves about their capability.

Before any realistic training could begin, General LeMay felt it necessary to show the crew members how poor was their ability. He directed Montgomery to plan a mass practice bombing mission, choosing Wright Field at Dayton for the training target. Crew members received a 1938 photograph of Dayton. This outdated information approximated the kind of available intelligence crew members might have to use in approaching Soviet targets. Then in January 1949, every bomb group in the command participated in a simulated wartime assault against the city. SAC directed the crews to fly at 30,000 feet and to bomb industrial and military targets; they used no unrealistic reflector targets.[8] LeMay's expectation proved accurate: the practice mission was a complete failure.

SAC had previously operated its aircraft at low altitudes to avoid equipment failure. When the bombers climbed to higher altitudes, engine trouble developed and radar sets malfunctioned, forcing many aircraft to abort before reaching Ohio. Moreover, scope returns from Dayton confused the inexperienced radar observers, accustomed to prominent or bright reflector targets. To complicate matters, thunderstorms in the area made local weather poor. The typical bombing score on this mission ranged between 5,000 and 11,000 feet from the target, an unacceptable margin of error. Without doubt, the negative effects of cross-training still lingered in SAC. According to LeMay, "You might call that just about the darkest night in American aviation history. Not one airplane finished that mission as briefed. *Not one.*"[9]

The Dayton exercise dramatically revealed SAC's poor bombing capability; but, more important, it exposed other problems. The type of training SAC had performed did not relate to its mission; it had stressed only the mechanics of flying, navigating, and bombing.[10] General Montgomery suspected this when he took over as SAC's new operations chief in late 1948. He directed aides to deliver SAC's combat plan to him for review and recalled, "the officer who brought it to him, had it in his pocket!"[11] Not only had the command practiced unrealistically, they had also failed to develop a coordinated attack plan against the probable enemy. SAC had not established a strong correlation between its training and the real mission—a situation resembling the AAC days of 1941 and 1942.

Nor had the command stressed target study and analysis, which are critical for successful radar-bombing. SAC had selected important enemy targets, with JCS approval, but did not assign them to specific aircrews. Apparently the staff had planned to use World War II procedures, whereby crews received their specific target assignments shortly before launching the attack. This method would fail, using radar-bombing, because each observer would lack familiarity with his assigned target and with the way it would look on his scope. The Dayton exercise had demonstrated the danger of such a lack of preparation; with a limited number of atomic weapons available, this procedure lacked justification.

General LeMay pressed Montgomery to build quickly a coordinated combat plan to insure greater chance of successful execution. In early 1949, Montgomery finally completed a detailed attack plan (SAC Emergency War Plan 1-49), with specific targets for each aircraft and crew. Thus, definite targets and objectives were assigned, and SAC could now begin to make training more realistic and worthwhile.[12]

The command rightly stressed target study and analysis. To insure the most accurate bomb drop, the radar observer must know in advance how the target area will appear on his scope. By carefully studying physical features around the target, he can determine what objects will display best, and he can reference his bomb runs on these returns. The intensity of radar returns differs with the composition of matter and grows weaker as aircraft altitude increases. Bodies of water, which return no signal, appear as blackened areas; land, forests, mountains, and roads appear in varying degrees of brightness, depending upon their surface angle to the aircraft and their material composition. Upright, concrete, or steel objects, for instance, give greater returns than do flat or wooden structures. Therefore, to find his target, the observer must have good knowledge of the area. If his objective lies in or adjacent to a city, the scope would display one large, bright return, with specific targets indistinguishable. The radar unit can be adjusted, next, by mechanically reducing the intensity of returns on all objects; the observer then has to know with certainty what features would still display. By knowing the objects located in the target area, he can predict what returns would appear under various circumstances, and he can prepare his bombing approach according to one or more dependable reference points.

This kind of knowledge would result from good intelligence of enemy territory, information the United States needed badly. The command's knowledge of Soviet cities and target areas came from scattered sources; primarily it was based on captured photographs taken by the German military during its Soviet invasion of 1941-42. The area lying east of the occupied region remained less well known, and the exact locations of certain targets proved difficult to pinpoint.[13]

SAC's planning staffs and crew members studied the available intelligence, then reconstructed on paper and film the probable radar returns of Soviet targets. They looked for objects most certain to appear (waterways, steel bridges, massive buildings, converging highways, or railroad patterns) in order to provide dependable reference points for bombing runs. SAC assigned crew members only a few targets, but they studied each one diligently until they could draw it and the surrounding area from memory. Whenever intelligence personnel learned more about a given target, from eyewitnesses, international publications, or other sources, crew members upgraded their knowledge and improved their capability.

General LeMay's next effort focused on making peacetime training more realistic. Crews began practicing their bombing on United States targets similar to those found in the USSR; SAC intelligence concluded that Baltimore, Maryland, more closely resembled European and Soviet cities than any other urban area in America. Reconnaissance aircraft then overflew the city from every angle, photographing hundreds of scope presentations.[14] From these photos, crew members could determine how objects would appear in either peacetime or wartime operations. For training, they studied similar photographs of other United States cities and planned bombing attacks against a variety of targets. Then, simulating wartime conditions, the crews flew their aircraft and practiced their bombing. Radio scoring units below, or photographs taken from the bomber at release time, measured the accuracy of their drops. After each landing, the crews would carefully reexamine their run, the problems encountered, and the accuracy of their approach and release.

To improve preparation for Soviet targets, SAC also employed a new electronic trainer. From the information gathered on United States cities as they appeared on radar scopes, artists re-created the probable images a crew member would view when approaching each Soviet target. On the ground, the trainer displayed the appropriate Soviet terrain on a scope; then, by manipulating various controls, observers and bombardiers could simulate an attack on the assigned target. Thus, using both ground simulators and inflight training over United States cities, SAC's crew members improved their chances of successfully bombing enemy targets.[15]

The stress on realistic training and improved bombing led SAC into an operating system that appealed to ambitious and competitive crewmen. In late 1948, LeMay instituted the lead-crew concept, whereby each wing placed the most highly qualified fliers together to form specially designated crews. Their performance standards then became a goal for other crews. In addition to normal flying duties, lead crews instructed other fliers on techniques and procedures; thus, they held great responsibility for upgrading the proficiency of the entire group.

In 1949, SAC decided to standardize flying operations further and established a lead-crew school at Walker AFB, New Mexico. Each group sent one or two of its best crews to the lead-crew school, where airmen learned the standard flying procedures that SAC had determined to be the most efficient. Graduates of this school returned to their home units and instructed other fliers in these procedures. New crews achieving a certain proficiency level could earn the lead-crew designation, while those working to attain that level carried a Class Two label. Later in the year, SAC reclassified crews as either combat-ready or non-combat-ready, still retaining the lead-crew concept.[16] Being a lead crew member enhanced promotion chances and, in later years, became the basis for immediate advancement to higher rank.[17] As a result of the standards and motivation provided by the lead-crew system, all SAC combat units performed in the most effective manner then known.

Standardized flying procedures proved successful, and the idea spread to other aspects of operations. On the basis of past and ongoing experiences, the command soon developed standard procedures for every task, from repairing engines to handling weapons. SAC recorded these procedures in a series of working manuals, so that each man had a complete reference outlining the best method for completing his duties. This plan had some flexibility: if an airman believed another method superior to the standard procedure, he could submit a recommendation for change. If Headquarters SAC found his suggestion valid, it would become the new method. SAC was constantly reexamining and changing its procedures while continuing to outline in working manuals the most effective methods known for completing any task. Some considered this standardization too rigid, but SAC's rapidly growing force included men drawn from all walks of life, with varying aptitudes and skill levels. In the face of such diversity, standard methods for each task proved worthwhile.[18]

Standardizing its operations and comparing the performances of its men and crews logically led SAC into a system of evaluating combat-group potential, served to keep command capability high. This system, beginning in 1949 with operational readiness tests (already common in the AF), in time became known as the SAC rating system. To determine the potential capability of each group, LeMay's staff first determined the relative importance of each factor necessary for the group to accomplish its mission, assigning that factor a numerical weight. For instance, bombing comprised one-third of the total points possible, while various support functions counted less. When inspectors visited a group, they examined every aspect of its operations, allotting points to each according to previously established criteria. The point-total indicated a wing's combat capability level. SAC could uncover weaknesses by reviewing those areas receiving fewest points and could direct corrective measures.

As all groups became combat-ready under SAC's three development plans, LeMay could compare the scores of each unit and could determine which wing commanders practiced effective leadership. Admittedly, certain units possessed better facilities or newer aircraft, but these qualifications made no difference in terms of combat potential. The primary question remained: if war came, could a given wing, with the equipment and resources available to it, perform its assigned mission? With facilities and equipment taken into consideration, the rating system functioned as a yardstick for measuring a wing's capability, thus giving commanders a standard by which to evaluate themselves.

Initially, wing commanders reacted negatively; but the rating system prevailed, compelling each commander to improve his unit's performance. The system brought proper and balanced attention to each operating and training activity and dramatically revealed any weakness. It also provided a means of evaluating leaders objectively; those who succeeded gained promotion. Those who failed often lost their positions to more promising officers. The ability to train and maintain a highly ready and capable combat group became the criteria for success in SAC, and the most able commanders stood out clearly under the rating system.[19]

General LeMay's leadership extended well beyond the mechanics of training and organizing combat groups; he recognized the importance of motivating people. By demonstrating genuine concern for his men, the new SAC commander was able to elicit greater efforts. When LeMay introduced new and higher standards of excellence and proficiency, he forced many airmen to reexamine their desires for a military career. Industrial salaries for those trained in aviation were dramatically outpacing military compensation, and even the less skilled enjoyed good earning potential out of uniform. In contrast to a forty-hour civilian work week with extra pay for overtime, military duty could include seventy to ninety hours per week, and the compensation was set. Moreover, airmen had to perform temporary duty away from their home stations, causing additional hardships for their families. Still further, the quality of military life suffered from poor and inadequate housing, frequent transfers, and limited recognition for individual achievements and needs. In the face of these negative features, and even while setting higher performance standards for his men, LeMay nevertheless inspired many to remain with SAC.[20]

LeMay approached leadership with three basic principles in mind regarding men, simple but important considerations he had developed during his military career. He believed, first, that supervisors and associates must recognize the importance of each man's job or task, as well as of the man himself. Second, some progress, however small, must be made toward an established goal; otherwise, serious dissatisfaction will develop. Lastly, commanders and supervisors must recognize and demonstrate real appreciation to those who have accomplished their assigned tasks. With all three of these elements present and working, an organization could produce dramatic results even when facing severe difficulties.[21]

These principles were closely related and mutually supporting. The Berlin blockade, a growing fear of future warfare, and the government's solid support of the deterrence concept made every man in SAC realize his importance. To make this understanding more credible, SAC adopted realistic operating procedures, constantly reminding airmen that they might fly combat missions tomorrow. To measure progress, the command established acceptable standards for every operational activity. For crewmen, flying proficiency and bombing capability provided criteria for evaluation; for maintenance men, a decline in aircraft out of commission; for wing commanders, the overall weaknesses and later improvements revealed by the rating system. In the third area, recognition and support of his people, General LeMay excelled. Airmen needed and received appreciation for the long hours and difficult tasks they faced. LeMay believed loyalty among commanders and men must travel a two-way street, and he knew his men would perform better if SAC helped them meet their needs and improve their personal circumstances.

One of General LeMay's strongest efforts focused on SAC's critical housing shortage. When the AF received its allotment of bases from the army in 1947, it gained many newer but temporary and incomplete installations, designed essentially for training. Family housing on these bases and in surrounding communities could not support a growing peacetime force that included dependents. When married airmen moved to certain SAC bases, they waited in line to rent attics, chicken coops, garages, and other substandard housing, in order to bring their families.[22] Naturally, a man working under pressure, on the flight line or away from home, needed acceptable housing and living standards; otherwise, he would leave the military, taking his badly needed skills to industry. Nonetheless, President Truman's tight fiscal budget for 1950 provided little money for housing construction.

Consequently, LeMay attempted to alleviate the housing problem within SAC. On 14 January 1949, he wrote Vandenberg about the deplorable housing conditions facing married airmen and officers at nearly every SAC station.[23] He wanted to organize a Strategic Air Command Association, which would construct new houses on sites leased from military installations, land with streets and utilities installed. The plan envisioned airmen joining the association with a $300 returnable deposit or loan. The organization would obtain loan commitments from private or government lending agencies and would purchase low-cost, prefabricated housing packages. Volunteers would erect the houses during off-duty hours, with some assistance from the manufacturers. The houses would then serve as security for the loans while occupants surrendered their monthly military allowances to the association for debt retirement. Initial plans called for a housing package costing $2,000, a sum repayable in less than five years. After that period the association would grant the debt-free homes to the government. LeMay proposed to help the men of his command at no expense to the taxpayers.[24]

With tentative approval from the AF, SAC quickly set to work. The Federal Housing Administration doubted it could guarantee the association loans, but the Reconstruction Finance Corporation approved the idea and promised support. SAC first decided to erect 2,600 units at eleven selected bases; it invited more than sixty companies to submit housing bids. In late April it altered the original plans and selected a larger, more practical house sold by the Lustrom Corporation. The command decided to eliminate membership fees for the association, but elected to retain sizable portions of each housing allowance for upkeep, insurance, and other expenses. With the new changes, the total cost would now require twenty years to amortize. In late June, SAC legally formed the association and tentatively drew up contracts to purchase 2,657 two- and three-bedroom homes from several firms, principally from Lustrom.

At this point LeMay encountered difficulties. During the preceding months SAC's proposal had found general acceptance by the AF, the Bureau of the Budget, and other government agencies; however, SAC could obtain neither final approval for the project nor the funds necessary to install streets and utilities on selected sites. The indecision at higher levels stemmed from several causes. The AF could not determine with certainty which bases would remain open while budgets continued low. Then, several legal questions required answers: Could the government subsidize the association? Could housing allowances be surrendered by men living in nongovernment quarters? Moreover, a bill pending in Congress promised to provide more military housing.

The Congress recognized that the government required approximately 261,000 housing units for military and civilian personnel. A recent AF study had revealed a high correlation between the quality of area housing and the level of reenlistment and civilian retention. Obviously, the Defense Department and Congress lacked the funds to provide that number of units; therefore, they were considering enticements to attract private construction investments.

On 21 February 1949, Senator Kenneth Wherry of Nebraska introduced a housing bill designed to encourage private construction of houses on or near military installations, with mortgages to be guaranteed by the Federal Housing Administration. Military bases would lease the necessary land, or even sell portions to private contractors. General LeMay considered Wherry's proposal sound but too expensive in the end. If the cost rose too high, such housing would be placed out of the reach of airmen with low quarters-allowances. In order to prevent this, the private contractors might, LeMay feared, reduce the size or quality of the home, and the airman would receive less for his money than under the association's plan. After debating the Wherry bill, Congress finally accepted a compromise version in late July, and President Truman signed the measure on 8 August 1949.[25]

The prospect of the Wherry proposal, however, accounted for LeMay's trouble in getting final AF and government approval, and its passage caused the association to dissolve. The SAC commander could not secure funds to install utilities or obtain final permission to proceed until the Wherry bill either passed or failed. After its passage, the new law threatened the association's plans. Who would now have first choice of land at selected military sites, private contractors or the association? LeMay pressed for a decision in mid-August and received a disappointing reply: the government would permit the association to construct a mere 750 units at two or three bases. However, private contractors would have priority for selecting housing sites on the bases. In effect, the association would be allowed only to build a few homes in areas unattractive to private contractors.[26] LeMay suffered great disappointment and rejected the proposal, considering the small authorization hardly worthwhile.[27] He advised Vandenberg that the association would abandon its earlier plans and, in effect, allow the Wherry bill alone to stimulate housing construction in demand areas.

SAC lost this battle but won its war. Many in the command felt the pressure and attention brought about by the association accounted for the Wherry measure passing through Congress unscathed. General LeMay, however, believed his airmen would receive smaller and poorer-quality houses, and he resented the extra cost to be paid by the government for these units (amortization of the debt now required thirty years). But he succeeded on another point: every SAC airman knew of his efforts. They understood the lengths their commander had gone to provide for their needs. The conviction began to develop that SAC took care of its people. Meanwhile, the Wherry provisions began to encourage home construction at nearly all military installations and aided the military in retaining personnel.

General LeMay insisted his commanders demonstrate concern for the needs of their men and show appreciation for jobs well done. In notes intended for dissemination to all his top commanders, he reasserted the importance of recognition.[28] The Hook Commission, appointed by Forrestal to examine military organization, had focused on the problems of enlisted men. Referring to their findings, LeMay wrote, "The commission stressed the importance of sympathetic understanding of their problems by officers as one of the most important elements in personnel relations." Moreover, "cash compensation did not figure as prominently as the interest of the administrative echelon in their comfort, health, and advancement." Airmen, the commission found, "asked for due respect for the dignity of the individual, irrespective of rank; attention to personal family hopes and problems; provision for adequate housing and medical care, . . . and above all, fair dealing."[29] LeMay stressed this point by advising his commanders that "junior and senior officers who cannot or will not recognize the requirement to provide incentives other than pay for personnel under their command will not be promoted to higher grade."[30] In writing this to his commanders, he wanted to "emphasize the basic truth that people are and will always remain, the heart of any undertaking."[31]

Placing an emphasis on people led General LeMay to instigate and support related activities. The command's mission required men to perform duties away from home station frequently for extended periods (TDY). While an airman was away, problems often developed for his family; therefore, LeMay encouraged his commanders to reestablish personal-affairs sections to assist these families. In the past, he noted, the program had "proven beyond doubt to be of utmost importance to all officers and airmen," and he stressed that "priority goes to the families of men absent on TDY and unit rotation."[32] Later, wives of military personnel grouped together to assist those whose husbands had departed on TDY. Together they possessed a wealth of talent and ability and provided support to families in need.

General LeMay worried about his young single airmen, recognizing that adequate housing and meals played a critical role in their performance and retention. He discounted the notion that a military mess could not serve quality meals. Given the demands upon them, airmen could rightly expect quality in such requirements. LeMay found SAC's dining halls poorly organized and the young cooks lacking in culinary knowledge. He began sending his chefs to one of Omaha's best hotels to learn food preparation. The local unions looked askance at this move, but the airmen worked as free apprentices while learning the trade. The food service improved. The attention LeMay gave the dining halls resulted in all of SAC's stations improving their kitchens.[33]

General LeMay demanded clean and comfortable barracks, not for the sake of military appearance but because his men deserved proper rest and relaxation. He avoided the old, open-bay barracks used by the army, gradually providing dormitory-style buildings, with two people per room. The open barracks had prevented men from obtaining rest because duty hours ran around the clock and some men required sleep while others were active.[34]

If SAC could satisfy personal needs, airmen would perform better and would be more likely to reenlist. When the command inspected a wing, the living quarters and dining halls for unmarried airmen received close attention. Proper recreation, particularly for single men or those in remote areas, strongly affected an airman's attitude toward himself and his job. Therefore, the command established recreation centers at remote sites (such as Matagorda Island Bombing and Gunnery Range, off the Texas coast) and provided additional facilities for golf, tennis, and baseball. These first-year efforts to improve recreation were modest, but later the command was able to establish many worthwhile hobby shops and activity clubs. Each effort, however small, worked to make military life more attractive to SAC's airmen.[35]

LeMay placed renewed emphasis on motivation and on individual contributions. He believed each man had to understand the value of his task and the total mission in order to exert the greatest and best effort. Keeping everyone informed involved extra staff work, but it made the sense of mission more real. LeMay reminded his staff organizations that they existed to help men in the field perform their duties better. Too often, staff personnel adopted a superior attitude toward crew members and flight-line personnel, burdening them with questionable requirements rather than assisting them in achieving greater proficiency. LeMay warned against this tendency, insisting that supervisors pay more attention to the opinions voiced by crew members and support personnel. A better operation would result, and people would take interest in their work.[36]

SAC's commander quickly modified or adopted other policies to motivate men in their jobs. He found unwise and wasteful SAC's old practice of using only pilots in command positions. SAC now encouraged nonrated officers to excel by permitting them to command nonflying units on the strength of their own leadership and technical ability.[37] General LeMay personally encouraged aircrew members by promoting men early when their skills and proficiency justified advancement. In October 1949 he realized that many aircraft commanders were only lieutenants, although they performed in the most critical role and had demonstrated ability. As SAC commander, he could use a number of temporary promotion positions, and he recommended advancement for 243 well-qualified pilots.[38] In following months the concept expanded to include other crew positions; later, it became the spot promotion system. LeMay's willingness to promote effective officers early offered great incentive to every crewman, particularly important at a time when the AF was reducing its total force.

LeMay brought a simple but effective approach to command, and he incorporated his convictions into solid leadership practices. He placed premiums on hard work and cooperation; primarily, though, he stressed integrity. "Discipline takes care of itself," he remarked, "if you pick people with integrity."[39] This belief allowed LeMay to delegate authority properly; and, in turn, his subordinates hated to disappoint him. He expected each man always to be on the job and to put forth whatever effort was necessary to accomplish each task. LeMay wisely avoided building an organization or staff around a single man, preferring teamwork. Most important, LeMay never forgot his mission: to train and prepare his men for immediate combat.

During his first year at SAC, LeMay and his staff brought changes to all operational and training areas. They instilled in airmen a constant awareness of their mission: to develop the capability of launching the bomber force and of successfully attacking enemy targets. Only when they achieved that capability would the United States possess the deterrent force considered necessary for future defense. Under the new leadership, SAC first developed plans for redistributing command resources and wisely upgraded groups to proficiency one by one. LeMay's staff developed a detailed war plan and implemented training that better prepared aircrews for their wartime tasks. Realistic and purposeful flying, target analysis, and ground simulation all contributed to greater crew capability. SAC established procedural and proficiency standards in all areas of operation, standards that provided both direction and motivation. Selected airmen were given responsibilities for upgrading fellow crewmen, and their lead-crew status encouraged others to achieve similar levels of performance. The command continually evaluated every aspect of group training and operations to determine strengths and weaknesses. SAC made a great effort to improve the well-being and material comforts of every airman, and the men in turn recognized their commanders' efforts and interest. Each man understood SAC's importance and that of his own contribution to the total mission; each realized that the command's success, and his own, rested on one criterion: completing the assigned task.[40] LeMay's new policies were not radical, but simply reflected practical approaches to meeting SAC's mission requirements.

General LeMay's early efforts took on a new importance in September 1949. At that time, President Truman received word that the USSR had unlocked the secret of atomic weaponry and had detonated an atomic blast in Central Asia. Now, even greater attention fell on LeMay and his men; but SAC had a solid foundation and a growing capability.

NOTES

1. Oral History Interview with General Curtis E. LeMay by John Bohn, March AFB, Calif., 9 March 1971, p. 24, Interview no. 736 (here-

after cited as LeMay-Bohn Interview), Albert F. Simpson Historical Research Center, Maxwell Air Force Base, Alabama (hereafter cited as AFSHRC).

2. LeMay-Bohn Interview, pp. 24-29. Generals Arnold and Spaatz also believed that America's weak military strength had enticed the Axis nations to undertake World War II. See Carl Spaatz, "Strategic Air Power," *Foreign Affairs* 24 (1946): 394-95. See also General Hap *Arnold's Third Report of the Commanding General of the AAF to the Secretary of War* (Washington, D.C.: Army Air Forces, 1946), p. 61.

3. General Curtis LeMay, a private interview held at Newport Beach, Calif., 1 October 1975. Hereafter cited as LeMay Interview.

4. LeMay played no part in the decision to move SAC Headquarters to Omaha; General Vandenberg made that determination in the spring of 1948, perhaps at the urging of Senator Kenneth Wherry of Nebraska. Wherry had heard of AF plans to move ADC and SAC Headquarters inland and, on 23 January 1948, asked Vandenberg to consider Omaha. Wherry reminded Vandenberg that, as a member of the Appropriations Committee, he (Wherry) had always supported the AF; if reelected, he planned to give further support. Representatives of the Topeka Chamber of Commerce also traveled to Washington and urged Vandenberg to select their city for SAC's new headquarters. After 15 April, the Omaha site was selected, although it had previously been low on the list of AF preferences. See Appointment Log, 23 January and 15 April 1948, Vandenberg Collection, Library of Congress, Washington, D.C. See also General Kenney to General Vandenberg, subj: Relocation of Headquarters Strategic Air Command, 15 January 1948, and General Vandenberg to General Kenney, subj: Relocation of Headquarters Strategic Air Command, 3 June 1948, Vandenberg Collection, Library of Congress, Washington, D.C.

5. General Power to C/S USAF, subj: Strategic Air Command Development Program, 16 November 1948, AFSHRC. Also LeMay Interview and General John B. Montgomery, a private interview held at Los Angeles, Calif., 14 July 1975 (hereafter cited as Montgomery Interview), 416.01-48, AFSHRC.

6. "History of Strategic Air Command 1949." Typescript history prepared by SAC Historical Section, Offutt AFB, Nebr., 1950, pp. 20-24 (hereafter cited as "SAC-1949"), AFSHRC.

7. General Curtis E. LeMay, *Mission with LeMay* (Garden City, N.Y.: Doubleday and Company, Inc., 1965), pp. 429-30.

8. "SAC 1949," pp. 140-41. Lt. Col. William Perry, an untitled report labeled "A Research Paper Submitted to the Faculty of the Air Command and Staff School of the Air University, Regular Course Code Number 342," Maxwell AFB, Alabama, 1949, pp. 5-6, M-32984-C, P 465s, AFSHRC. Perry's background is not known; but he wrote this report within four months of the exercise, and his paper suggests he had direct knowledge of its planning and results. When LeMay wrote his memoirs in 1965, he found the official AF report on the Dayton mission still

classified. See LeMay, p. 433. See also Oral History Interview with General Thomas Power by Kenneth Leish, July 1960, Oral Interview no. 81, AFSHRC.

9. LeMay, p. 433.

10. Oral History Interview with Maj. Gen. William Kingsbury by Robert Kipp, March AFB, Calif., 18 December 1970, pp. 17-18, Interview no. 733, AFSHRC.

11. Montgomery Interview. While Montgomery may have been guilty of hyperbole with his statement, the plan was clearly inadequate to the task.

12. LeMay-Bohn Interview, pp. 34-35. While LeMay concentrated on building a viable attack force, concern lingered among defense leaders over SAC's capability to deliver an effective strategic bombing offensive against the Soviet Union. Based on discoveries stemming from the Berlin crisis, Forrestal had asked the JCS for two evaluations: (1) "the chances of success of delivering the strategic air offensive contemplated in current war plans" and (2) the effect of this air offensive on the Soviet war effort, "to include an appraisal of the psychological effect of atomic bombing on the Soviet will to wage war." (Record Group 218, Records of the United States Joint Chiefs of Staff, CCS 373, 10-23-48, Sec. 1, National Archives, Washington, D.C. Memorandum for the Joint Chiefs of Staff, subj: Evaluation of Effect on Soviet War Effort Resulting from Strategic Air Offensive, from James Forrestal, 25 October, 1948). The JCS submitted the first problem to the Weapons Evaluation Group, which did not present its findings until February 1950. The second question went to an ad hoc committee headed by Lt. Gen. H. R. Harmon of the AF. Harmon's committee received its charge on 12 January 1949 and rendered an evaluation just four months later. (Record Group 218, Records of the United States Joint Chiefs of Staff, J.C.S. 1953/1. 12 May 1949. CCS 373, 10-23-48, Bulky Package no. 1, National Archives, Washington, D.C.). Based on the current joint war plan, TROJAN, which had designated seventy target areas to be attacked during the first thirty days of fighting, the Harmon Report concluded that "complete and successful execution of the initial atomic offensive against the U.S.S.R. as planned, would probably affect the war effort and produce psychological effects upon the Soviet will to wage war," but cautiously warned its conclusions would change if more or fewer bombs were actually delivered. The committee estimated that "physical damage to installation, personal casualties concentrated in industrial communities, and other direct or indirect cumulative effects would result in a 30-40 per cent reduction of Soviet industrial capacity." This loss, however, would not be permanent and "could either be alleviated by Soviet recuperative action or augmented depending upon the weight and effectiveness of follow-up attacks."

This less than optimistic report came while interservice fighting between the air force and navy was intensifying. Naval leaders argued the report supported their position; United States war plans placed too much dependence on strategic bombing with atomic weapons. Proponents of strategic bombing, however, could point to a key conclusion in the Harmon Report. "The atomic bomb would be a major element of allied military strength in any war with the U.S.S.R., and would constitute the *only* [my emphasis] means of rapidly inflicting shock and serious damage to vital elements of the Soviet war-making capacity." Nevertheless, the attack had to be followed by other military and psychological operations. In short, strategic bombing with atomic weapons was not a complete solution for winning a war against the Soviet Union, but it would be the key ingredient to any success.

Apprehension mounted within military circles in 1949 over the logistical problems associated with the planned strategic offensive. This concern figured prominently in the Weapons Evaluation Group's report. (Record Group 218, Records of the United States Joint Chiefs of Staff, J.C.S. 1952/11, 10 February 1950. C.C.S. 373, 20-23-48 Bulky Package part 2C, National Archives, Washington, D.C.). After qualifying its findings because of limited intelligence on Soviet air defenses, the report concluded that logistical deficiencies and expected bomber attrition rates would preclude an offensive on the scale then contemplated in the latest war plan, OFFTACKLE. It estimated "that about 70 to 85 per cent of the atomic bomb sortied will drop their bombs in the intended target area" and on the average, one-half to two-thirds of the single industry installations bombed would be damaged beyond repair. Bombing accuracy would be a key consideration in the final analysis; and while LeMay was limited in what he could do about logistical problems, he focused on improved bombing capability during 1949.

For a useful discussion of the reports cited, see David Alan Rosenberg's "American Strategy and the Hydrogen Bomb Decision," *The Journal of American History* 66 (1979): 71-84.

13. LeMay Interview and Montgomery Interview.

14. LeMay Interview.

15. Montgomery Interview. From January to December 1949, the average circular error dropped from 3,700 feet to 2,900 and 2,300 for medium and heavy bomb groups. See "SAC-1949," p. 141. In October, SAC held a bombing competition at Davis Monthan AFB, Arizona, and LeMay felt satisfaction at the command's improvement, especially when the winning B-36 crew had an average circular error of only 1,053 feet. See General LeMay to General Vandenberg, 11 October 1949, Vandenberg Collection, Library of Congress, Washington, D.C.

16. "SAC-1949," pp. 132-38.

17. The spot promotion system, which came about in mid-1950, automatically promoted a man to a certain rank if he and his crew members earned lead-crew status, regardless of their time in grade. Conversely, SAC removed the rank whenever a man lost lead-crew status by poor performance.

18. Montgomery Interview.

19. LeMay, pp. 443-45.

20. The percentage of airmen reenlisting provides the best measure of LeMay's success. The rate for 1949 averaged 52.9 percent; however, figures for each month showed no real trend until the last quarter. A high of 76.6 was reached in December. Slightly more than 13 percent of those leaving were ineligible for reenlistment. "General Data Sheet for Airmen, 1 January 1949 to 1 January 1950," a typescript, command paper, 416.01-49, AFSHRC.

21. LeMay-Bohn Interview, p. 39.

22. LeMay, pp. 468-70.

23. General LeMay to General Vandenberg, 14 January 1949, Vandenberg Collection, Library of Congress, Washington, D.C.

24. Information on LeMay's housing efforts is taken largely from "History of Strategic Air Command Housing Plan," a short, undated paper prepared by the Historical Office, Strategic Air Command, 416.01-49, AFSHRC.

25. *Congressional Quarterly Almanac, Vol. V, 1949* (Washington, D.C.: Congressional Quarterly News Features, 1949), p. 486.

26. Message, Assistant Secretary of the AF to C/G, SAC, 22 August 1949, 416.01-49, AFSHRC.

27. Message, C/G SAC to C/S USAF, 30 August 1949, 416.01-49, AFSHRC.

28. General LeMay, "Commanding General's Notes," unpaged summary of information to give commanders, 416.01-49, AFSHRC.

29. Ibid. This quote came from the U.S. Advisory Commission on Service Pay, *Career Compensation for the Uniformed Forces,* vol. 1 (Washington, D.C.: Government Printing Office, December 1949), p. 52. Also known as the Hook Report.

30. General LeMay to General Vandenberg, 9 February 1949, 416.01-49, AFSHRC.

31. General LeMay to General O'Donnell, C/G 15th AF, 9 February 1949, 416.01-49, AFSHRC.

32. LeMay, "General's Notes."

33. SAC Message 353 to C/G 15th AF, subj: Hotel Training for Food Service Personnel, 28 December 1949, 416.01-49, AFSHRC. See also LeMay, *Mission,* pp. 437-39.

34. LeMay, *Mission,* p. 467.

35. "SAC-1949," p. 53.

36. LeMay-Bohn Interview, p. 36.

37. LeMay, "General's Notes." This policy had been urged by General Spaatz as early as 1947, but SAC's leadership at the time disagreed with the concept. See Chapter 3, pp. 57-59. Vandenberg continued to press for nonrated commanders in a letter to General LeMay, subj: Command by Nonrated Officers, 30 December 1948, 416.01-49, AFSHRC.

38. General LeMay to Generals Ramey, O'Donnell, and Atkinson, 18

October 1949. The officers were promoted by SO Number 103, 21 December 1949, 416.01-49, AFSHRC.

39. Oral History Interview with General Curtis LeMay by unidentified interviewer, March 1965, Interview no. 785, AFSHRC.

40. In addition to the oral interviews already cited, two by Robert Kipp give good insight into LeMay's approach to leadership. See Oral History Interview with Lt. Gen. Francis Griswold, April 1970, Interview no. 732, and Oral History Interview with Lt. Gen. C. S. Irvine, March AFB, Calif., December 1970, Interview no. 734, AFSHRC.

9 PRELUDE TO CONFLICT

Just as Strategic Air Command began to achieve a measure of deterrent capability, the USSR detonated its first detected atomic explosion in August 1949. The Soviet advance immediately affected current United States policy and plans, which had come to rely upon the assumption of an American atomic monopoly. At the same time, every foreign government studied the visible American responses to the Soviet achievement.

United States reactions appeared modest. Between September 1949 and June 1950, airmen directed greater attention toward continental air defense, but the nation did not expand or appreciably alter its military establishment; in fact, defense spending declined. President Truman announced his decision to develop thermonuclear (TN) weapons, but SAC received little additional attention or resources. The United States had just expanded its atomic-weapons production and had demonstrated a resolve to defend Western Europe by supporting and signing the North Atlantic Treaty in early 1949. The American government, however, had begun and continued to remove its military force from South Korea, and took other actions which hinted of a declining interest in the Asian mainland. These responses strongly suggested the United States would continue to stress atomic deterrence as its dominant military defense, and that it was placing greater emphasis on Western Europe.

Less visible was the alarm felt by the State Department and Defense Department over the weakness of United States programs designed to contain communism and to support American foreign policy. That concern culminated in the first complete review of the nation's foreign policy objectives and of the military means needed to achieve them. This study, NSC 68, recommended a dramatic strengthening of conventional military forces in Western Europe and the United States. It suggested increases in military spending, which Truman had successfully fought to limit since World War II. As the government was analyzing the cost of these proposals, the Korean War erupted, forcing Truman to make an immediate decision on containment in Asia. When he elected to respond militarily, he removed the lid from defense spending.

North Korean leaders most certainly considered recent American decisions while planning their invasion, and they were not deterred from attacking. While the United States military had made progress in developing a strong strategic force for deterring general war, its capability failed to discourage aggression in Korea, and the nuclear deterrence concept has been the target of strong criticism since. Most criticism, however, has not included an examination of how the United States proposed to use its atomic capability. When the North Koreans studied this matter, they easily miscalculated America's position on containing communism on the Asian mainland; Truman's administration had scarcely projected a firm resolve. His decision to intervene even surprised many United States leaders. The military, economic, and diplomatic actions taken by the United States between September 1949 and 25 June 1950 did not suggest the nation was prepared to use its atomic capability in Asia or would intervene otherwise in Korea.[1]

Following World War II, scientific and intelligence experts began to analyze Soviet potential for developing atomic weapons and to predict probable achievement dates. Differing evaluations emerged during the next four years, but one belief became widely accepted: the Soviet Union lacked the technical capability to develop atomic weapons quickly. As time passed without producing evidence of Soviet progress, the assumption grew stronger. Typical estimates in late 1945 concluded the Soviets would need five years. In 1947, the Army Intelligence Division still suggested late 1949 or 1950; and a year later the JCS Joint Intelligence Committee estimated mid-1950.[2] The Finletter Report projected 1952 as a reasonable date, and the JCS adopted the same year for its own planning purposes in 1949.[3] Also in 1949, Vannevar Bush, former chairman of the Research and Development Board, noted that United States experts had overestimated Soviet capability to develop atomic weapons.[4]

Fortunately several men had held more realistic views. General LeMay, deputy chief of staff, Research and Development, urged the AAF in August 1946 to develop a capability to detect an atomic explosion occurring anywhere on the globe. He considered this need to be of utmost importance and recommended a concerted effort by all the services, the Manhattan Engineering District (which controlled atomic energy development), and the State Department.[5] LeMay's recommendation, however, found little support and did not emerge again until April 1947. At that time a member of the newly formed Atomic Energy Commission, Lewis Strauss, discovered the United States lacked any detection capability. He approached then Secretary of the Navy Forrestal and Secretary of War Kenneth Royall, urging them to assume responsibility for a detection program. Both were shocked that no capability existed.[6] Months later, the government finally gave the AF primary responsibility for the detection mission, and active planning began.

By April 1948, the AF had developed a system that they tested in Operation Sandstone, an atomic exercise in the Pacific. Although the results proved favorable, the project still lacked total government support. For instance, in mid-1949, the Research and Development Board's Committee on Atomic Energy described the $8 million expended for detection as an excessive boondoggle and recommended a partial transfer of the remaining $12 million to other programs. The board's advice reflected the low regard in which many officials held Soviet technology.

Within a month, however, the "boondoggle" proved its worth.[7] On 3 September 1949 a weather reconnaissance aircraft collected radioactive particles while flying off the Kamchatka Peninsula. The AF tracked the contaminated clouds across the North Pacific and east as far as the British Isles, while a special committee, including Bush and Dr. J. R. Oppenheimer, studied the sample material and data. The committee concluded that, beyond doubt, an atomic explosion had occurred on the Asian mainland during the last week in August, and the president was so advised on 21 September.[8] At first, Truman considered withholding the information from the public until other critical world events had subsided. He outlined his plan to AEC Chairman Lilienthal, who promptly disagreed, urging an immediate release to the nation. Truman concurred, and he announced the AF discovery two days later, on 23 September.[9]

In weeks following, government officials denied any surprise at the Soviet detonation and claimed they had always anticipated this event.[10] Evidence, however, refutes this contention, because the government suddenly and extensively reevaluated its military capability and national objectives after the Soviet detonation. Moreover, the planning which developed during the next nine months demonstrated that the government had made little preparation for Soviet advances in atomic technology, and the recommendations that followed reflected more surprise than anticipation. One week after Truman's announcement, top AF leaders met with the Vice Chief of Staff, General Muir Fairchild, to consider the AF position "in view of the accelerated time table imposed by the Russian atomic bomb."[11] Fairchild acknowledged that Americans had underestimated Soviet capability by one to three years and urged the AF to update its military posture. His immediate concern fell on United States continental air defenses. Any hope for effective defense would require a full, seventy-group program and a radar screen network monitoring the northern boundaries of Alaska and the United States. Congress had previously authorized the latter project but had appropriated no funds. Now a warning system seemed imperative. Fairchild ordered General Norstad, deputy chief of staff, Operations, to develop a package proposal for the JCS that would outline the means, budgetary authorizations, and authority necessary to expedite AF plans for United States air defense.

American air defense, neglected since World War II, certainly needed strengthening. Limited budgets had allowed meager resources for air defense and, in 1948, had forced the merger of Air Defense Command and Tactical Air Command. As low funding continued, the AF placed greater emphasis on SAC and on developing a deterrent capability. Air defense received only minimal attention because most planners discounted the possibility of any Soviet invasion while the United States enjoyed an atomic weapons monopoly. As early as 1948 the AF believed the Soviets had at least fifty or more "B-29 type" aircraft, but until they could combine this fleet with atomic weapons the United States would not need an established defense system.[12] When the atomic balance suddenly altered, the Soviet Union's capability appeared ominous—all the more so because it was largely unknown. Assuming the existence of a Russian stockpile of atomic weapons, an attack suddenly seemed possible—and the United States had an abysmal air defense.

In November 1949, Vandenberg took the defense problem to the JCS. He believed the United States had probably underestimated other production figures in the USSR and realized that other blasts might have preceded the August explosion. Vandenberg argued that air defense demanded immediate attention in order to protect SAC's deterrent capability. In two world wars, he reasoned, the United States had intervened in Europe and, because of America's enormous industrial capability, turned the tide of each conflict. Consequently, he argued, the Soviets would not undertake any expansion by force without first attempting to destroy our warmaking capacity. In his opinion, the Russians could, within the next five years, easily stockpile enough atomic weapons to wreck this capability. The Soviets would attack with "a full all-out offensive effort, designed to take the United States out of the war with one blow through concentrated destructive power of the A-bomb." If the Russians destroyed fifty specific United States cities and SAC bases, Vandenberg doubted "that the United States would be able to gather itself together to fight for a period of years." During an attack, "our atomic offensive force becomes a primary enemy target. It must be protected and preserved as our greatest deterrent to aggressive action, as well as our reliance to redress the balance if the attack should be made." Therefore the United States must place its primary defensive effort not on the Rhine, but at the United States boundaries to protect the nation's warmaking capability.[13]

Sadly, Vandenberg described United States air defenses, observing that "almost any number of Soviet bombers could cross our borders and fly to most of the targets in the United States without a shot being fired at them and without being challenged in any way." Moreover, even if the AF completed the approved air defense program, these shortcomings would still remain. The conviction that no enemy defense could withstand a well-planned and executed bomber attack applied equally to assaults against the United States. Even England, with its small area, advanced warning system, and experienced combat airmen, had stopped only 20 percent of the German bombers from reaching their target areas during World War II. To Vandenberg, this made our air defense all the more critical, and he urged the service chiefs to support a strong project, "with a priority and an urgency similar to that of the Manhattan Project in the last war."[14] The AF had expanded its strategic bombing force after the Berlin blockade; now Soviet developments in atomic energy added another burden to the small military budget. Convinced the nation needed an air defense system to protect its strategic capability and its population, the Bureau of the Budget quickly authorized the transfer of $50 million from other AF projects to begin construction of an air defense system.[15] The atomic deterrent force, however, still held top priority.

But while SAC had made progress since the Berlin crisis, it still lacked a strong capability. By 1950, the command operated 225 atomic bomb carrying aircraft (including B-29s, B-50s, and thirty-four B-36s), flew 263 combat ready crews, and was training forty-nine more. Eighteen bomb assembly teams were fully qualified, and four would be added by June. But conventional capability had suffered.[16] Maj. Gen. S. E. Anderson, director of Plans and Operations, advised Symington in April 1950 that in the event of war, the AF could complete only the atomic phase of the planned strategic air offensive. Air defense of the United States would be inadequate.[17] To compound the problem, planning at the JCS level had not gone smoothly since the chiefs first agreed on a joint war plan in May 1948. Though they had implemented several directives to the war plan series, proposed bombing operations continually suffered from logistical problems ranging from short supplies to inadequate forward bases. In fact, each revised proposal was deemed "infeasible" by committees of the JCS.[18] SAC faced serious problems beyond the control of General LeMay.

The most noteworthy response to the Soviet achievement in atomic weapons came with the move to develop a thermonuclear weapon. Immediately following the detection announcement, the Joint Congressional Committee on Atomic Energy began urging the government to pursue fusion research. Partly in response to this pressure, Lewis Strauss sent a memorandum to his fellow AEC commissioners in early October, recommending "an intensive effort to get ahead with the super."[19] The AEC referred the suggestion to its General Advisory Committee (GAC), which included such former participants of the Manhattan Project as Edward Teller and J. R. Oppenheimer. Within this scientific committee, discussion on thermonuclear weapons began in earnest.

The GAC members had limited background for their debate. They had no assurance the new bomb could be built and, assuming its development, could only speculate about its effect. While building the fission bomb in 1945, scientists had considered the possibility of fusing lighter elements to make thermonuclear weapons, but the procedure appeared far more difficult than splitting heavier elements and would require a costly, long-term effort. At that time, Teller had encouraged fusion research, and Oppenheimer had recommended feasibility studies, at least, on thermonuclear weapons. But the Manhattan Project had rejected these proposals and elected to concentrate solely on the atomic bomb. However, after the United States had increased its atomic weapons production schedule several times between 1946 and mid-1949, some consideration did arise for developing a thermonuclear bomb, as SAC's attack pla and target list expanded. In July 1949, the AF intelligence division suggested the new weapon to Headquarters USAF, but received a noncommital reply.[20] Thus, until the Soviet detonation occurred, the United States had ignored fusion research; consequently, the GAC had little experience on which to base its recommendations.

During late October, the GAC carefully considered and then rejected Strauss's proposal.[21] Initially, the four other AEC mem bers agreed, but Commissioner Gordon Dean soon began supporting Strauss's position. Nevertheless, the AEC adopted the GAC recommendations and opposed development of thermonuclear weapons.

Within other government agencies, support for the new weapon was mixed. Led by the AF, military pressures for thermonuclear weapons grew slowly. The army and navy remained skeptical, while Secretary of Defense Johnson supported development. Secretary of State Dean Acheson, however, took no immediate position. Meanwhile, congressional leaders—particularly Senator Brian McMahon—were urging the executive branch to undertake the project as quickly as possible.[22] Faced with conflicting advice, Truman appointed a three-man committee (Acheson, Johnson, and Lilienthal) to aid him in reaching a final decision.

On 10 November, the three men and their advisers began deliberations on the desirability of developing thermonuclear weapons. The Department of Defense (DoD) worried about depleting the stockpile of fissionable material; this would threaten future atomic capability. Therefore the DoD insisted the feasibility of manufacturing and using the hydrogen bomb be examined first. The JCS, having adopted deterrence as its primary defense, was reluctant to abandon or neglect its strongest military weapon in the face of new Soviet capability.[23] Lilienthal did not feel the H-bomb offered any solution to the United States defense problems and feared that, in fact, its development would confuse and impede future efforts toward peace. The idea of outlawing powerful nuclear weapons still appealed to him.[24] Acheson shared Lilienthal's concern, but as deliberations continued he concluded the nation had no choice but to proceed. A delay, reasoned the secretary of state, would not discourage any postponement based on the hope of reaching an accommodation with the Soviets. After four months of discussion, the committee reached a decision.

On 31 January 1950, the three men delivered a unanimous report to the president supporting development of thermonuclear weapons. Lilienthal, however, had reserved the right to dissent orally, and he outlined to the president his own objections. But Truman interrupted Lilienthal and accepted the committee recommendations; apparently he had already made up his mind. The president directed the AEC to expand its research and development for thermonuclear weapons.[25]

Strategic Air Command, the organization that would have responsibility for delivering the proposed H-bomb, did not undertake any extraordinary measures between September 1949 and the time of the Korean War. The new Soviet capability did not alter SAC's mission, although it strongly reinforced the concern for constant preparedness and real capability.

SAC worked internally to enhance its capability. General LeMay directed certain reorganizations in order to provide more efficiency and flexibility. Previously, SAC had formed its three air forces according to function: the Second had sole responsibility for reconnaissance, the Fifteenth maintained most of the medium or B-29 groups, and the Eighth concentrated on the B-50 and heavier bombers. In April 1950, SAC integrated each force with both types of bombers and with separate reconnaissance units, making each a balanced and self-contained combat force.[26] In the months preceding the Korean War, the command continued to refine procedures established in the previous year. Commanders gave particular attention to improving bomb-dropping accuracy and realized better use of their various trainers.[27] Flight training suffered some disruption in early 1950, when SAC temporarily grounded many B-29s for engine modification and imposed altitude restrictions on B-50s.[28] By mid-1950, however, the command had solved most of the aircraft operating problems, had achieved higher bombing scores, and was enjoying a better-balanced organization.[29]

During this period, new and improved equipment offered bright hope for SAC's continued development, although its benefits were not realized until late 1950. The B-36 entered the SAC inventory and received extensive operational testing. Progress permitted SAC to incorporate the huge bomber into its war plan in July 1950.[30] Reconnaissance groups gained new RB-50s, RB-45s, and RB-36s; however, modifications and outfittings did not advance far until the summer.[31] SAC also received B-29s specially equipped with the new flying boom, and B-50 receivers modified for this refueling system. Nonetheless, technical problems prevented any extensive training with the new equipment until mid-1950.[32]

Thus, the United States responded to the Soviet advance in atomic technology principally by expanding atomic bomb production and by moving to develop thermonuclear weapons. Air defense attracted new attention, but little was done to strengthen SAC or the AF's conventional forces beyond previous plans. Clearly the nation would adhere more strongly than ever to nuclear deterrence.

In the eighteen months preceding the Korean War, the Truman administration pursued related government policies that affected the military. The United States increased its commitment to support and defend Western Europe and programmed over a billion dollars of military assistance for North Atlantic Treaty members. The president also continued to emphasize an economy-first defense plan by reducing the United States military budget for the third consecutive year; specifically, he cut spending by 10 percent. Finally, both because of its increased emphasis upon Western Europe and because of declining defense funds, the United States diminished its political and military influence in the Far East. These related policies certainly did not discourage the North Korean invasion in June 1950, nor did they hint of later United States intervention.

Foreign military assistance had begun modestly in 1947 and

by 1949 was seriously competing with Defense Department programs for appropriations. While evaluating military assistance programs in 1947, the JCS numerically ranked various nations according to their strategic importance to the United States and to the amount of aid each would be likely to require. Not surprisingly, combining both factors, the military placed greatest stress on aid to Western Europe and the United Kingdom. The Far East offered the least degree of strategic importance, behind that of the Middle East, Northwest Africa, and Latin America. More specifically, Korea and the Philippines ranked at the bottom of United States concerns.[33] After the Brussels Pact took shape in 1948, military planners grew concerned over the impact that military assistance to Europe would have on the defense budget. Commenting on a report of the State and Defense Departments' Coordinating Subcommittee on Rearmament, the JCS expressed alarm at the number of nations the committee considered worthy of aid and questioned the impact of such assistance on the United States economy. Once military aid began, the JCS warned, it would be difficult to limit. Referring to its own needs and requirements, the JCS insisted that "approval of foreign aid proposals should be secondary to the minimum procurement and training requirements of our own services."[34] The generals and admirals realized that tight fiscal policies had already reduced the United States defense budget, and they feared foreign military assistance would bring further reduction.

Another committee of the JCS undertook a thorough examination of military assistance programs in early 1949. In its report, the committee raised the usual alarm over Soviet potential. Forces of Western Europe, as now constituted, could not adequately meet existing Soviet capabilities; therefore, the committee concluded, Western Europe should ultimately "develop a military posture which will deter Soviet aggression and may eventually provide the Western Union with forces which when employed in conjunction with the U.S. . . . will prevent the overrunning of Western Europe."[35] The committee did not specify atomic deterrence, only the machinery and training for a conventional capability. They believed that building an adequate force to withstand Soviet ground attack would require several years. The JCS recognized the United States commitment to a "free and independent Korea" but felt the military "has no strategic interest in maintaining troops and bases in Korea."[36] Therefore, the JCS urged a rapid reduction of the United States commitments of men and money to Korea, leaving that nation with token aid only. America should concentrate its assistance on Western Europe; however, defense leaders viewed even this aid with concern—it could easily decrease their own resources.

Indeed, apprehension in the Defense Department grew after the United States formally signed the North Atlantic Treaty on 4 April 1949. President Truman then assigned principal authority for administering military assistance to the State Department.[37] This aroused consternation in the Pentagon. Secretary Johnson hurriedly wrote the president, reminding him of the close coordination necessary between the two departments for this program.[38] Johnson, who administered the Defense Department with a stronger hand than had Forrestal, worried about his department losing influence in military assistance matters, but he also felt pressures from another direction. Within days, Edwin Nourse, chairman of the Council of Economic Advisers, warned the Defense Department that military aid should not constitute a mere addition to total spending; military leaders should expect corresponding reductions in their own budgets to provide the needed funds. Nourse considered foreign assistance a long-term investment. Money directed to the European military would yield greater defense returns than if left entirely to the United States military.[39]

Secretary Johnson and his chiefs did not quarrel with long-term benefits, but they worried about immediate effects. Johnson privately stressed to the president that the low 1950 budget could not absorb additional cuts without accompanying danger. Furthermore, he did not expect military aid in Western Europe to yield any benefits until 1952; therefore, if funds for military assistance reduced the United States defense budget, a grave deficiency would evolve. Johnson directed General Lyman Lemnitzer, of the JCS, to stress this point also to the Bureau of the Budget. The Defense Department would support whatever level of assistance the State Department recommended, but the Pentagon could not find "a justification for a reduction in our own military budget."[40] The secretary carried the same message to the Senate Foreign Relations Committee, advising that, at some future time, the Military Assistance Program could "permit us to reduce the investment in our armed forces, but not yet." In fact, the United States now had reasons to "increase our investment in military security."[41] By July the politically ambitious defense secretary had abandoned his earlier position, as Truman continued to emphasize economy and the time for finalizing the 1951 budget drew closer.[42] The problem now fell heavily on the service chiefs.

Defense planners knew the president had always wanted to stabilize annual military spending, and in mid-1949 they believed the 1951 estimate should approximate the 1950 proposal. As usual, the Defense Department had previously directed the JCS to submit its minimum requirements to aid the president in determining a tentative budget ceiling.[43] The JCS undertook this initial evaluation with great concern; despite an apparent easing of international tensions, especially with the lifting of the Berlin blockade, the service chiefs believed Soviet objectives and intentions remained unchanged. Therefore, they felt any decrease from the 1950 level of $14.4 billion would seriously threaten United States capability.[44] Prior to submitting their initial recommendations, General Eisenhower, now acting chairman, Joint Chiefs of Staff, handed a private memorandum to Secretary Johnson outlining their reasoning and their concern. The JCS, he explained, had set out to build an agreed strategic plan in harmony with probable budget ceilings. Eisenhower advised that a very real measure of success had come through "securing unanimous approval of a strategic concept . . . ," and he found among the chiefs "a considerable degree of unanimity in allocating under the strategic concept, tactical forces to various strategic areas of the world."[45] But Eisenhower and the JCS were shocked when they learned the president planned a $1.5 to $2.0 billion reduction from 1950. With such restrictions, the JCS could not devise a military program to complement its agreed strategic concept. As funds fell, overhead and fixed costs would dominate the budget, leaving less for combat capability.

Eisenhower considered strategic bombing the key consideration and reminded Johnson that the JCS and the Defense Department had always stressed the value of military preparation as a deterrent. Given our emphasis on the atomic bomb, he reasoned, "we cannot and must not fail to provide a respectable long range strategic bombing force."[46] Eisenhower wanted to preserve this capability and even suggested "cutting into other features of our program more than we believe desirable or wise."[47] Moreover, the current strategic concept predated any hint of further budget restrictions, and now serious differences would arise between the services. Eisenhower realized "we cannot have everything we want," but he urged Johnson to keep the strategic concept in mind when he reviewed their recommendations.[48] His personal suggestion was, "if we are erring in any direction, it is in failure to allocate sufficient parts of the budget to our strategic bombing capability."[49]

Days later, the Senate ratified the North Atlantic Treaty, and Truman abruptly asked Congress to provide $1.4 billion in military assistance to the member nations. Supported by his economic advisers, the president believed this sum should come largely from the defense budget because military assistance abroad would permit reduced spending in the United States. Specifically, Truman wanted Western Europe to develop a conventional capability that the United States lacked, one the nation could not build given America's negative position on large peacetime forces.[50] The earlier fears of defense leaders proved justified: the president's $1.4 billion aid program coincided with a $1.4 billion reduction in the military budget.

The proposed cuts led the JCS to conclude,

> From this point on, there will be continued lessening in our military capability, accompanied by increases in our strategic deficiencies, such that by July 1952, our strategic plans will need to be radically reduced in scope and a general and very marked increase in war risks and difficulties will develop.[51]

The JCS also surmised that, by 1952, the USSR would possess a limited number of atomic weapons. Within a month of their warning, the Soviets detonated their first known atomic explosion.

Despite the Russian success, Truman felt no need to alter his defense ceiling of $13.0 billion. Military leaders met repeatedly with the Bureau of the Budget, earnestly striving for a balance between defense requirements and resources. Frank Pace, the new bureau director, found merit in the defense arguments and commended the military for its appreciation of economic limitations. But Pace feared for the nation's economy under continued deficit spending. He supported the president's reductions and suggested greater efficiency in military operations, planning, and research to effect savings for other uses.[52]

Military and administration officials appeared before the Congressional Subcommittee on Appropriations in early 1950 to defend the $13.0 billion budget. General Vandenberg, gravely disappointed with the AF portion, sent his vice chief of staff, General Fairchild, to represent the AF.[53] These hearings of February 1950 differed only slightly from previous years, except the congressmen heard an increased emphasis upon economy. Secretary Johnson advised the committee of "our common goal of providing a sufficiency of defense for the minimum dollars required to be appropriated by the Congress."[54] But the committee demurred at this statement, because in previous months Truman had again impounded funds appropriated for defense. The committee expressed grave doubts about an economy-first approach to defense but initially heard few reservations from the Department of Defense.

Later, the AF clearly expressed its own objections while answering specific questions on force levels. General Fairchild again explained the priority placed upon SAC, cautioning the committee that United States "tactical forces are not adequate for a large scale effort."[55] Under further questioning, the AF admitted it would require $650 million more to keep its forty-eight groups modern. Lacking that amount, 20 percent of the force would reach obsolescence by 1952. Concerning the AF budget, Secretary Symington candidly explained, "Some of the decisions on dollar limitations were arbitrary and are based upon a willingness to accept specific risks."[56] Assumption of these risks permitted a 10 percent reduction in the 1950 AF budget but also placed additional strain on the relationship between Symington and the president.

The relationship worsened. Fearful of the low defense budget, the Congress voted 305-1 to expand the AF to at least fifty-eight groups. With this support, Symington made one last appeal to Johnson, urging the president to expand the defense proposal.[57] Johnson, now supporting economy even more than was Truman, argued that the budget adequately provided for forty-eight groups and that Symington was simply fighting for more units. Johnson then asked the JCS if the AF portion could support forty-eight modern groups.[58] A week later, the JCS replied that the AF sum did "not make that provision."[59] After Johnson and the president had refused any change in early April 1950, Symington felt compelled to resign from office.

The government's first two policies, granting military assistance to Western Europe and reducing United States defense spending, dictated the third policy formulated during 1949 and early 1950. Resources would no longer be available to maintain a strong position in the Far East. Moreover, political events in China suggested the United States would have even less influence in this region.

Early in the postwar period, United States interests in the Far East focused on China; but by mid-1948 the United States realized Chiang Kai-shek's government would probably fall. The specter of a Communist China, conceded Kennan, would not present "any intolerable threat to U.S. security," but would require examination of the United States position in the Far East.[60] Meanwhile, Soviet and American troops withdrew from Korea in December 1948 and June 1949. With a new Chinese government and this withdrawal from Korea, the United States shifted its Far East interests to Japan and to a defense perimeter stretching to the Ryukyu and Philippine Islands. While events were thus unfolding in Asia, the Berlin blockade captured United States attention. To support the airlift, the Defense Department moved military units from the

Far East, the Caribbean, and the United States to Europe. In October 1948, the AF made plans to redeploy roughly half of its medium bombers—along with large segments of fighter, reconnaissance, and troop carrier units, totalling twenty-one squadrons—from the Far East.

The Commander in Chief, Far East, General Douglas MacArthur, strongly objected to these reductions, stressing this action precluded implementation of the existing emergency war plan. In a November 1948 communiqué, MacArthur acknowledged that, by early 1950, Communist forces in China could control that nation as far south as the Yangtze River. The Soviets had 4,150 aircraft in the Far East; and, if the Chinese made their bases available to the Russians, the Soviet air arm could easily reach the United States defense line. MacArthur believed, "It no longer appears realistic to consider the Far East as a static and secure flank in the military contest with communism."[61] He could not understand the JCS decision to reduce military strength in the Far East. Army strength, he noted, had already reached "a hazardous minimum," and he termed the naval forces assigned to his theater "negligible."[62] Any reduction now, he advised, would jeopardize the United States' position in the Far East beyond the acceptable point of a "calculated risk."[63] Despite his warnings, redeployment from the Far East followed.

The matter of force levels in the Far East arose again in mid-1949. On 23 July, a devastating typhoon damaged Okinawan air facilities so severely that the AF could not continue operations without extensive reconstruction. General Vandenberg estimated the cost would range between $32 million and $45 million; and, given other AF needs, he opposed a request to Congress for this sum. Instead, he wanted to use Okinawa as a forward staging base, with minimum personnel and operations. Units located on the island would move to Japan, Guam, or back to the United States.[64]

The army objected, and its chief of staff questioned the plan, noting the recent piecemeal redeployments from the Far East. These moves, he warned, would no doubt have military implications for the American mission and objectives in that area. Therefore, he suggested a thorough reexamination of our position in the Far East before adopting Vandenberg's plan of redeployment.[65] General MacArthur opposed the plan even more strongly and immediately wired the army to protest further redeployment of AF units. In a six-page message, MacArthur reminded the JCS that AF capabilities in the Far East had fallen by 46 percent since 1 January 1949, and this reduction cast serious questions on United States capability to secure Japan and the Ryukyu Islands in a general emergency. Vandenberg's plan would leave Okinawa defenseless against attack, while exposing southern Japan and the communication lines to the Philippines. With available air transportation already reduced, the United States could not count on reaching Okinawa to operate its units if needed. Under Vandenberg's proposal, the islands would offer little value. MacArthur believed it necessary to demonstrate United States interest in the Far East by remaining in the Ryukyus, and he felt the containment policy applied equally in the Far East. Therefore, MacArthur urged the JCS to avoid further redeployment of military units by securing the funds needed to reconstruct the facilities on Okinawa.[66]

In urging strategic and economic consideration, MacArthur won a victory. He recognized the importance of budget restrictions, but he believed the expense required to remain on Okinawa constituted a small price for keeping a solid defense perimeter close to the Asian mainland. If the United States made only a half-hearted effort, that line would easily fall. Only three weeks earlier, he continued, the JCS had warned against any weakening of the overall United States position with respect to the Philippines, the Ryukyus, and Japan. Yet the JCS had also considered abandoning the Marianas and redeploying the only medium bomb group available to the Far East Air Force. He could not reconcile the two proposals and feared that the United States would retreat eastward to the 180th meridian.[67]

The JCS Planning Committee finally adopted the army position and recommended a military request of $72 million to reconstruct facilities on Okinawa.[68] Congress approved a measure for over $50 million, and in late October President Truman signed the appropriation bill for Okinawa.

The United States, however, continued to demonstrate a declining interest in the Far East. Despite CIA warnings that "withdrawal of U.S. Forces from Korea would probably in time be followed by an invasion," no strong support developed within Washington for that troubled nation.[69] Nor did an impassioned plea for continued aid from President Syngman Rhee to Truman have any apparent effect.[70] In January 1950, Congress considered a small supplemental appropriations bill to aid the South Korean government in its transition to military independence. At the time, some five hundred United States advisers worked in South Korea attempting to bolster the military organization. Lacking strong executive support for it, the Congress rejected this modest request, and Truman's subsequent efforts to obtain funds from other sources carried no sense of urgency. The American unwillingness to grant this small sum for Korean defense reflected little interest in that nation.[71] This trend continued into May 1950, when General Vandenberg advised the JCS that the 31st Strategic Reconnaissance Squadron would redeploy from the theater, leaving only six aircraft to accomplish the reconnaissance work required by the Far East Command.[72] Equally important, the government's defense spending policy gave no hint the military would ever return to the Far East.

Western scholars have debated the reasons that prompted the North Koreans to attack in 1950; but, without access to their government papers, the matter remains open to interpretation. Increased emphasis upon military assistance to Europe, continued economy in defense spending, and a declining United States role in the Far East, however, gave the North Koreans little reason to expect American intervention in Korea. Certainly these policies failed to deter war; indeed, they may have encouraged the invasion.

The Soviet Union's early success in unlocking the secret of atomic energy stimulated in the United States a serious review of global objectives, international difficulties, and the capability available to meet the challenges confronting the nation.

In December 1949, the National Security Council noted the need for a more detailed and updated appraisal of the United States strategic position; the only existing document directly addressing this matter, NSC 20, considered the Soviet threat as it existed in 1948. Russian achievements in atomic technology had suddenly placed the deterrent-force concept in a different light and forced a reexamination. On 5 January 1950, the NSC decided to undertake a formal appraisal of existing United States commitments, goals, and supporting military forces.[73]

The NSC had already started its review when President Truman issued his 31 January directive initiating the H-bomb program. On that day, the president directed the secretary of defense and secretary of state to review American foreign policy, weighing Soviet achievements in nuclear science, the new Communist government in China, and the future effect of the H-bomb. An ad hoc committee of representatives and staff from the Defense Department and State Department was formed, which merely continued the study initiated by the NSC.

Paul Nitze of the State Department's Policy Planning Staff and General Truman H. Landon of the Joint Strategic Survey Committee, JCS, took on the primary burdens for each department. Fortunately Landon and his staff were able to act independently of any official JCS and Defense Department endorsements of positions they might advance. Nitze, however, continually collaborated with Secretary Acheson during the entire review and presented only ideas supported by the State Department.[74]

From the outset, both men considered the United States responses to recent Soviet advancement inadequate. For this reason Nitze and his State Department staff wanted to concentrate solely on corrective recommendations. Defense officials, on the other hand, accustomed to working under spending ceilings, prepared to study the problem within a framework of realistic appropriations. Because the latter approach would prove limiting, the State Department contingent rejected any economic restrictions in the planning, and this approach eventually prevailed. Very early in the discussions, the ad hoc committee elected to disregard the usual Defense Department procedure and concentrate on proposing recommendations irrespective of budgetary considerations.[75]

The committee completed its work in April and reaffirmed the initial pessimism. Its report, soon entitled NSC 68, gave President Truman the best analysis his administration could provide, one that drastically conflicted with policies he had previously established and that he had continued after the Soviet detonation.[76]

NSC 68 first considered Soviet intentions and the United States capabilities available to meet military challenges. The study did not break with assumptions and objectives outlined in NSC 14, but asserted more forcefully that "The Soviet Union is animated by a new fanatic faith, antithetical to our own, and seeks to impose its absolute authority over the rest of the world." Therefore, "to that end, Soviet efforts are now directed toward the domination of the Eurasian land mass."[77] The American military, continued the report, must first serve the national purpose by deterring attack upon the United States. Logically, the nation's forces must prepare for a variety of possible challenges. On this point, the planners expressed grave concern over United States insufficiency in conventional weapons; and, after introducing the subject of this deficiency early in its examination, the committee focused on it throughout the report.

The ad hoc committee now proceeded with a more detailed analysis of the situation in Western Europe. The JCS believed, continued the report, that the USSR retained the capability to overrun Western Europe and could drive toward the Near and Middle East oil fields or move into the Far East. Moreover, the Soviets could bombard the British Isles and their military installations by air and sea. The United States could rebuild the conventional forces of Western Europe to withstand such an attack, but little would emerge from current programs until 1952; and, without additional assistance, European governments would not achieve real defense capability before 1960. In any case, to deter war in Europe, the ad hoc committee considered it absolutely necessary to rearm the North Atlantic Treaty nations with conventional forces, as distance and national policy prohibited the Americans from building and maintaining an adequate force of their own on the European continent. Until that rearmament could be accomplished, the United States would lack the means of deterring limited conflict in the area it viewed as most important to its own interests, Western Europe.[78]

The committee also believed the United States atomic deterrent to be threatened. Intelligence reports recently estimated the USSR had between ten and twenty atomic bombs; but by mid-1954, the Russians would have 200. The Soviets maintained between 300 and 450 TU-4 aircraft, capable of delivering these weapons to North America.[79] Assuming a 50 percent success rate for attacking bombers, 100 well-placed atomic bombs in the United States could do devastating damage to American industrial and warmaking capability. Moreover, if the Soviets developed thermonuclear weapons first, the United States deterrence capability would further diminish. By breaking the atomic monopoly, the Soviets had comparatively weakened United States strength.

Ironically, this change placed new emphasis upon conventional military forces and higher defense spending. The ad hoc planners still considered containment a proper United States objective. But they questioned whether the nation had a commensurate military force, as conventional strength had also declined relative to the growing Soviet force. Without capability, the report warned, American policy would be "no more than a policy of bluff"—or, as Secretary Symington had just stated before Congress, a set of risks. Unless corrective steps followed, more weight would fall on the bluff. With a superior economic production base, "on the order of four to one," the United States certainly had great military possibilities; but the nation had realized little of that potential. Aided by their own specialists, the committee concluded that the United States could expand its military strength and that of its allies without endangering the economy or lowering the real standard of living. The USSR, in contrast, devoted nearly 14 percent of its GNP to military expenditures, twice the allocation ratio of the

United States. America had insufficient strength to deter war in Europe by conventional means, and existing programs would not meet our future requirements. There existed, warned the committee, "a sharp disparity between our actual military strength and our commitments."[80]

Committee planners stressed the shortcomings of current deterrence policy. If the Soviets applied pressure to any given area, the only strong United States reaction would lie in a willingness to initiate atomic conflict. But many possible situations would not warrant such an extreme response. Moreover, the United States needed allies, and the strengthening of Allied capabilities required sacrifices. "No people in history," noted the report, "have preserved their freedom who thought that by not being strong enough to protect themselves they might prove inoffensive to their enemies." The committee concluded the United States could presently deliver a serious atomic blow to the USSR, and in four years' time the Soviets would be able to launch a similar attack. Meanwhile, the nation needed to increase its number of atomic weapons and improve conventional capability in order to avoid excessive reliance on atomic bombs. The committee reconsidered the possibility of internationally controlled nuclear weapons and negotiations with the Soviets, but quickly discounted any hope for both. The report took the position that successful negotiations could come only from a strong military position.[81]

As planners examined existing objectives and capabilities, their discussion left little doubt about the proper corrective action: military expansion. The ad hoc committee concluded its study, however, by reviewing four possible alternatives left to the United States. It systematically rejected the first three. Two courses would bring about United States isolation, a deterioration of the world order, and finally, world conflict. First, the United States could maintain present levels of foreign assistance and military preparedness. In time, relative strength would decline, forcing the United States to retreat diplomatically and physically from Europe and limiting American influence to the Western Hemisphere. The second option, of initiating an isolation policy, offered some economic attraction but would present identical results. War would follow in both instances, the committee asserted, with fighting conducted at a grave disadvantage. The third alternative, briefly noted, concerned the possibility of attacking the USSR before the Soviets could develop a capability comparable to the United States. Americans, of course, would not accept this approach, nor would it prevent the Soviets from dominating most or all of Eurasia; therefore the planners quickly dismissed the idea of preventive war. The only remaining course lay in a rapid increase in atomic and conventional forces to cover the range of challenges the United States might encounter.[82]

The principal problem of implementing the recommendations of NSC 68 was their cost. The ad hoc committee deliberately avoided mentioning specific programs and attending costs and considered only the matter of requirements. Its members acknowledged that military expansion would require higher taxes, but they believed the nation could devote far more resources to defense without a decrease in its real standard of living. The United States held superior capability; but, without immediate expansion, that advantage would fade. In their view, "A cold war is a real war" and demanded resources and efforts as would any armed conflict.[83]

President Truman received the committee's report on 7 April 1950, and five days later sent the paper back to the NSC and the Bureau of the Budget, requesting information on specific programs and cost estimates. Aiming for a flash figure by 1 July 1950, government and military officials struggled with programming the recommendations. Soon a cost figure ranging between $35 billion and $50 billion appeared—a sum representing nearly three times Truman's current military budget.[84]

The president faced a dilemma. During these very weeks, preliminary work on the 1952 budget had begun, and Truman had hoped for yet another reduction, perhaps down to $12 billion.[85] Now his chief military, Defense Department, and State Department officials suddenly recommended a program far exceeding any cost he was prepared to assume. Yet the programs of containment, economic recovery, and military assistance he had initiated and urged for Western Europe demanded an increased outlay in order to continue.

Between 12 April and 26 June, Truman withheld comment on the report, while officials continued to program NSC 68. The document contained strong language and extensive support; the arguments no doubt made a deep impression upon the president. Yet he did not direct his budget planners to embrace any increased ceilings at this early point. Twice, in May, Truman held out for a reduced or stable budget for 1952.[86] But, whatever his feelings, he found himself left with little choice after 26 June, when North Korea shocked the Western world by invading South Korea and Truman decided containment had to extend to East Asia. Within months, the AF ballooned to more than 100 groups, while the military expenditures the president had so long opposed quickly followed.

By late 1949, Strategic Air Command had developed an atomic deterrent capability; and, with the signing of the North Atlantic Treaty, the United States had indicated willingness to use its military might to defend Western Europe. But in the eighteen months preceding their invasion, North Korean leaders found encouragement in United States actions. Although the Soviet achievement in atomic technology added a new element to the cold war, President Truman left his military force essentially unchanged, electing instead to develop thermonuclear weapons and to place more importance on atomic deterrence. Low defense budgets, increased attention to Western Europe, and diminished interest in South Korea and the Far East suggested the United States would not intervene in the Korean conflict. Truman's advisers warned the president that United States objectives had grown incompatible with the means available to support them, and a decision to bring the two into line was required soon. Before the president could make that decision, the Korean War erupted. The image and intent projected by United States actions in 1949 and 1950, rather than the extent of the nation's real or potential capability, had failed to discourage or deter the North Koreans from invading.

NOTES

1. For an analysis of causes leading to the Korean War and various historical interpretations, see Alexander L. George and Richard Smoke, *Deterrence in American Foreign Policy: Theory and Practice* (New York: Columbia University Press, 1974), pp. 140-80.

2. George F. Lemmer, "The Air Force and the Concept of Deterrence, 1945-1950," typescript, unpublished history by the USAF Historical Division Liaison Office, Washington, D.C., 1963, p. 51, Albert F. Simpson Historical Research Center, Maxwell Air Force Base, Alabama (hereafter cited as AFSHRC).

3. Record Group 218, "Records of the United States Joint Chiefs of Staff," CCS 381 7-5-49, Sec. 2. JCS 2032/4, Appendix "B," revised 23 August 1949, p. 56, National Archives, Washington, D.C.

4. Vannevar Bush, *Modern Arms and Free Men* (New York: Simon and Schuster, 1949), pp. 93-94.

5. Lemmer, pp. 49-50.

6. Lewis L. Strauss, *Men and Decisions* (Garden City, N.Y.: Doubleday and Company, Inc., 1962), pp. 201-4.

7. Strauss, pp. 204-5. See also Lemmer, p. 50.

8. Richard G. Hewlett and Francis Duncan, *A History of the United States Atomic Energy Commission*, vol. 2: *Atomic Shield, 1947-1952* (University Park: Pennsylvania State University Press, 1969), pp. 363-66.

9. David Lilienthal, *The Journals of David E. Lilienthal*, vol. 2: *The Atomic Energy Years, 1945-1950* (New York: Harper & Row, 1964), pp. 571-73.

10. Harry S. Truman, *Memoirs*, vol. 2: *Years of Trial and Hope* (Garden City, N.Y.: Doubleday and Company, Inc., 1956), p. 307.

11. Memorandum for Record, General Fairchild, 30 September 1949, Fairchild Collection, Library of Congress, Washington, D.C.

12. Then-secret testimony of General Vandenberg before the House Armed Services Committee, 14 January 1948, Vandenberg Collection, Library of Congress, Washington, D.C.

13. Memorandum, C/S USAF to JCS, subj: Air Defense of the United States, 16 November 1949, Fairchild Collection, Library of Congress, Washington, D.C.

14. Ibid.

15. Authorization came on 9 December 1949.

16. Record Group 341, Records of Headquarters United States Air Force. AF O.P.D./A/AE 391 (atomic warfare), National Archives, Washington, D.C. Memorandum for Maj. Gen. Schlatter, subj: Air Force Capability for Atomic Warfare, January 1950.

17. Record Group 341, Records of Headquarters United States Air Force, National Archives, Washington, D.C. Memorandum for Mr. Symington from S. E. Anderson, 11 April 1950.

18. Record Group 341, Records of Headquarters United States Air Force. O.P.D. 391 (12 October 49), Sec. 2, National Archives, Washington, D.C. Memorandum for Assistant for Programing et al, subj: JSPC 947/D, from Maj. Gen. Joseph Smith, 23 January 1950. The short-range emergency war plans fell under the 1844 series.

19. Strauss, pp. 216-17. See also David Alan Rosenberg's "American Atomic Strategy and the Hydrogen Bomb Decision," *The Journal of American History* 66 (1979): 78-87.

20. Lemmer, pp. 53-54. Admiral Souers, President Truman's military adviser doubted that even the president knew of the possibility of a thermonuclear weapon. See Hewlett, p. 374.

21. For a full and excellent treatment of the GAC deliberations, see Hewlett, pp. 373-88.

22. Lemmer, pp. 53-54. Secretary Acheson believed the Pentagon was pushing a crash program. See Dean Acheson, *Present at the Creation* (New York: W. W. Norton and Company, 1969), p. 346. See also Lilienthal, pp. 583, 590.

23. Lemmer, pp. 54-55. Also Hewlett, p. 400.

24. Lilienthal, pp. 587-90.

25. Acheson, p. 349. See also Lilienthal, pp. 632-33.

26. "History of Strategic Air Command January-June 1950." Typescript history prepared by Headquarters Strategic Air Command, Omaha, Nebr., October 1950, pp. 107, AFSHRC (hereafter cited as "SAC-50"). See also ltr., C/G SAC to C/S USAF, subj: Reorganization of Strategic Air Command, 15 February 1950, 416.01-50, AFSHRC.

27. "SAC-50," pp. 75-76, 92-94.

28. "SAC-50," p. 82.

29. "SAC-50," Operational Data, p. 6. SAC was able to maintain its manpower at between 57,000 and 59,000 men until the Korean War. All other commands, meanwhile, suffered personnel reductions.

30. Oral History Interview with Lt. Gen. C. S. Irvine by Robert Kipp, March AFB, Calif., 17 December 1970, Interview no. 734, AFSHRC.

31. "SAC-50," pp. 46-47.

32. General Orval Cook, director, Procurement and Industrial Planning, to CG/SAC, subj: Operational Suitability Test for the Flying Boom Refueling System, 5 May 1950, 416.01-50, AFSHRC. See also "SAC-50," pp. 67-69.

33. Record Group 218, "Records of the United States Joint Chiefs of Staff," CCS 092 8-22-46, Sec. 3. JCS 1769, 1 May 1947, pp. 115-19, National Archives, Washington, D.C. The State Department also judged Korea "not of decisive strategic importance to us." Department of State, PPS/13, "Resumé of World Situation" for Secretary of State from George Kennan, November 6, 1947, National Archives, Washington, D.C.

34. Record Group 218, "Records of the United States Joint Chiefs of Staff," CCS 092 8-22-46, Sec. 24. JCS 1925/1, 2 September 1948, p. 20-22, National Archives, Washington, D.C.

35. Record Group 218, "Records of the United States Joint Chiefs of Staff," CCS 092 8-22-46, Sec. 20 JCS 1868/62, 7 March 1949, p. 432, National Archives, Washington, D.C.

36. Ibid., pp. 444, 448.

37. Record Group 218, "Records of the United States Joint Chiefs of Staff," CCS 092 8-22-46, Sec. 23, National Archives, Washington, D.C. Ltr., President Truman to the Secretary of Defense, 13 April 1949. JCS 1868/72, 25 April 1949.

38. Ibid., Secretary of Defense to President Truman, 16 April 1949.

39. Record Group 218, "Records of the United States Joint Chiefs of Staff," CCS 092 8-22-46, Sec. 23. Press release (circa April 1949), National Archives, Washington, D.C.

40. Ibid. Memorandum, Secretary of Defense to General Lemnitzer, 19 April 1949.

41. Ibid., Part A. Revised statement of the Secretary of Defense before the Senate Foreign Relations Committee, 20 April 1949.

42. Secretary Johnson has usually been identified as Truman's strongest supporter on tight military spending, although his actions in mid-1949 conflict with this view. Only after Johnson became fully aware of Truman's future plans on defense spending did he fall in behind the president and, in fact, grow more conservative than Truman. Acheson believed Johnson's erratic change in attitude during this period could be attributed to mental illness. See Acheson, p. 374.

43. Record Group 218, "Records of the United States Joint Chiefs of Staff," CCS 370 8-19-45, Sec. 17, National Archives, Washington, D.C. Memorandum, Secretary of Defense to Secretary of the Navy, Air Force, and Acting Secretary of the Army, 25 May 1949.

44. Ibid. Memorandum, General Bradley for Generals Eisenhower and Vandenberg, and Admiral Denfeld, 25 May 1949.

45. Ibid., Sec. 18. Memorandum, General Eisenhower to the Secretary of Defense, 14 July 1949.

46. Ibid.

47. Ibid.

48. Ibid.

49. Ibid.

50. The Senate immediately rejected the president's proposal and attempted to force Truman into more specific and less costly programs. See Acheson, pp. 309-10.

51. Record Group 218, "Records of the United States Joint Chiefs of Staff," CCS 381 7-5-49, Sec. 2. JCS 2032/4, Appendix "B," revised 23 August 1949, p. 54, National Archives, Washington, D.C.

52. Record Group 218, "Records of the United States Joint Chiefs of Staff," CCS 370 8-9-45, Sec. 20, National Archives, Washington, D.C. Transcript, "Discussion Following Budget Presentation," 21 October 1949.

53. Robert F. Futrell, *Ideas, Concepts, Doctrine: A History of Basic*

Thinking in the United States Air Force 1907-1964 (Montgomery: Aerospace Studies Institute, 1971), pp. 261.

54. U.S. Congress, House, Committee on Appropriations, *Department of Defense Appropriations for 1951: Hearings before a subcommittee of the Committee on Appropriations*, 81st Cong., 2d sess., 1950, p. 43.

55. Ibid., p. 1220.

56. Ibid., p. 1215.

57. Memorandum, Secretary Symington to Secretary Johnson, n.d., Fairchild Collection, Library of Congress, Washington, D.C. Johnson and Truman added $500 million to the budget, and the House of Representatives added $85 million more before the bill went to the Senate. The Korean War, however, came before final consideration was made.

58. Record Group 218, "Records of the United States Joint Chiefs of Staff," CCS 452 11-11-48, Sec. 3, National Archives, Washington, D.C. Memorandum, Secretary Johnson to the Joint Chiefs of Staff, 5 April 1950, reproduced in JCS 1960/10.

59. Ibid. Memorandum, Joint Chiefs of Staff to Secretary Johnson, 13 April 1950, reproduced in JCS 1960/11.

60. George F. Kennan, *Memoirs 1925-1950* (Boston: Little, Brown & Company, 1967), p. 374.

61. Record Group 218, "Records of the United States Joint Chiefs of Staff," CCS 381 2-8-43, Sec. 12, National Archives, Washington, D.C. Message CX 65242 CINCFE (MacArthur) to Department of the Army, 9 November 1948.

62. Ibid.

63. Ibid.

64. Ibid., Sec. 15. JCS 2059, 31 August 1949.

65. Ibid., Sec. 19. JCS 521/39, 30 August 1949.

66. Ibid., Sec. 15. Message C 52346, CINCFE (MacArthur) to Department of Army, 6 September 1949.

67. Ibid.

68. Ibid., Sec. 15. JSPC 936/1 (circa September 1949).

69. Central Intelligence Agency, "Consequences of US Troop Withdrawal from Korea in Spring, 1949." ORE 3-49, 28 February 1949, p. 3. Annadel Wile, ed., *The Declassified Documents Quarterly Catalog*, vol. 4, no. 4, January-December 1978 (Washington, D.C.: Carrollton Press Inc., 1979), p. 16A.

70. Record Group 319, "Records of the Army Staff," G-3 091 Korea T.S. Sec. 1, case 18/2 (1949-50), National Archives, Washington, D.C. Ltr. to President Truman from President Syngman Rhee, August 20, 1949.

71. Acheson, p. 358. Acheson discounted charges that his speech a week earlier, defining United States defense lines in the Far East, had encouraged the North Koreans to attack. See pp. 355-57.

72. Record Group 218, "Records of the United States Joint Chiefs of Staff," CCS 381 2-8-43, Sec. 19. JCS 1906/16, 15 May 1950, National Archives, Washington, D.C.

73. See Paul Hammond's "NSC 68, Prologue to Rearmament," contained in Warner Schilling, Paul Hammond, and Glen Snyder, *Strategy, Politics, and Defense Budgets* (New York: Columbia University Press, 1962), pp. 293-94. Until the State Department declassified NSC 68 in April 1974, Hammond's description of the contents was one of the best. In writing his study, Hammond relied heavily upon personal interviews with many participants in the ad hoc committee and the executive branch. See also Samuel F. Wells, Jr., "Sounding the Tocsin: NSC 68 and the Soviet Threat," *International Securities* 4 (Fall 1979): 116-58.

74. Hammond, pp. 296-99.

75. Hammond, pp. 298-300.

76. In recent years, some scholars have focused on the "hawkish" nature of the document and have criticized its authors for failing to accurately assess the current situation. A review of JCS and NSC documents from 1945 to 1950, however, reveals a growing concern over perceived Soviet threats, heightened by the Berlin crisis, the Chinese revolution, and the Russian gains in atomic technology. NSC 68, although not supported by all officials, did not represent a radical departure from what most government leaders were thinking. Whatever its excesses or shortcomings, it must be remembered the authors did not have a solid intelligence base to rely upon. Quite simply, the report represented the best judgments of those trying to determine the Soviet threat to American interests and a proper United States response.

77. Record Group 341, "Records of Headquarters United States Air Force." National Security Council, "United States Objectives and Programs for National Security," 14 April 1950, pp. 4-6 (hereafter cited as NSC-68), National Archives, Washington, D.C.

78. NSC-68, pp. 17-21.

79. Record Group 218, "Records of the United States Joint Chiefs of Staff," CCS 381 2-18-46, Sec. 3. JCS 497/4, 7 May 1950, National Archives, Washington, D.C.

80. NSC-68, pp. 21-32.

81. NSC-68, pp. 36-40, 48.

82. NSC-68, pp. 48-56.

83. NSC-68, pp. 57-65.

84. Hammond, pp. 326, 331, 340-44.

85. Hammond, pp. 328, 331.

86. *Public Papers of the Presidents of the United States, Harry S. Truman, 1950* (Washington, D.C.: Government Printing Office, 1965), pp. 286, 440.

EPILOGUE

America's military tradition has never favored a large standing army or a powerful peacetime force. In the century following 1814, the United States faced no foreign threat and maintained a small army and navy. Nothing more was needed. Mobilization came during the Mexican and Civil Wars, but both were followed by massive demobilization when the fighting ended.

The United States entered World War I as an industrial power but militarily weak. Americans moved quickly to harness their potential for war; ultimately, the entry of the United States and its industrial resources into the conflict played a key role in Germany's decision to seek an armistice the next year. Disillusioned by the experiences and outcome of World War I, Americans returned to a small military force behind a foreign policy of isolation, but Hitler and Pearl Harbor brought America's industrial machine and population back to a wartime footing. Once again, Allied success during World War II stemmed largely from the ability of the United States to outproduce its enemies in war material and manpower. The same, of course, could be said of the Soviet Union in its Great Patriotic War. Victory in World War II, industrial might, and the atomic bomb gave Americans a sense of security after the war. The public accepted the idea that Americans could no longer avoid involvement in world affairs but still clung to the concept of maintaining a small peacetime force. Potential was considered preparedness.

While many Americans felt secure in this belief, others worried about Soviet potential. Because of its large population, dictatorial government, and geographic position, many defense leaders in 1947 came to believe that Russia could easily overrun Western Europe, the Middle East, or portions of East Asia. Though war damages sustained in World War II argued against this eventuality, the possibility underscored the thinking behind defense planning. To add to the dilemma, planners worked with poor intelligence and often resorted to worst-case analysis. They had to consider both the real as well as the potential capabilities of the United States and the Soviet Union and weigh the intent of the adversary, based on his actions and announced objectives. After some 175 years, Americans could no longer rest comfortably behind vast oceans or the conviction that their industrial and military potential alone could serve as an adequate defense.

The gap between potential and real capability during the early cold-war years raises many important and difficult questions. Although the American public knew little, if anything, about United States military deficiencies, how well did top governmental leaders understand American weaknesses? How did this knowledge, or its lack, affect their decision making? Did the military fully recognize its actual strength, both at the JCS and wing levels? How did our weakness influence military leadership? How well did Joseph Stalin's government evaluate American capability? Were the Soviets truly impressed with United States atomic monopoly, or did national pride cause them to downplay the atomic threat? Did Stalin's evaluation of American capability seriously affect his decisions? On the other hand, did Americans properly assess Soviet military potential to wage war after 1945 or were intelligence officials simply awed by numbers?

It may be possible that both powers overestimated one another's strength and perhaps these miscalculations prevented the eruption of a hot war. To answer these questions fully, future historians must first address the matter of capability and understand the marked gap that existed between real and potential strategic air power in the years of the United States atomic monopoly. Determining the exact impact of this hollow threat would add immeasurably to our understanding of the early cold war.

BIBLIOGRAPHY

PRIMARY SOURCES

Archival Material

Albert F. Simpson Historical Research Center, Maxwell Air Force Base, Alabama

Archival sources used from the Simpson Research Center are identified in the footnotes by title or index number. Note that the sources identified by the reference number 416.01 are compilations of original and reproduced primary documents used in writing annual Strategic Air Command histories. In addition, the Simpson Research Center maintains over eight hundred oral interviews with Air Force personnel and Defense Department officials. Most have been transcribed into manuscript form and are indexed by number, as some individuals have given several interviews. Those used in this study are therefore cited by name and index number.

Command and Service Histories (Typescripts)

Air Materiel Command. "Case History of Air-to-Air Refueling." Wright Patterson AFB, Ohio: AMC Historical Office, 1949.

Continental Air Forces. "Summary of CAF Activities." Bolling AFB, Md.: Hdg., Strategic Air Command, 1946.

Fifteenth Air Force. "History of the Fifteenth Air Force for 1947." Colorado Springs, Colo.: Hdq., Fifteenth Air Force, 1948.

——. "History of the Fifteenth Air Force for 1948." Colorado Springs, Colo.: Hdq., Fifteenth Air Force, 1949.

Lemmer, George F. "The Air Force and the Concept of Deterrence 1945-1950." Washington: USAF Historical Division Liaison Office, 1963.

Self, Mary. "History of the AMC Supply Support of the Strategic Air Command 1946-1952." Wright-Patterson AFB, Ohio: AMC Historical Division, 1954.

Strategic Air Command. "History of Strategic Air Command 1946." Offutt AFB, Nebr.: Hdq., Strategic Air Command, 1950.

——. "History of Strategic Air Command 1947." Offutt AFB, Nebr.: Hdq., Strategic Air Command, 1949.

——. "History of Strategic Air Command 1948." Offutt AFB, Nebr.: Hdq., Strategic Air Command, 1949.

——. "History of Strategic Air Command 1949." Offutt AFB, Nebr.: Hdq., Strategic Air Command, 1950.

——. "History of Strategic Air Command January-June 1950." Offutt AFB, Nebr.: Hdq., Strategic Air Command, 1950.

——. "Strategic Air Command Statistical Summary I, 1946." Andrews AFB, Md.: Hdq., Strategic Air Command, 1947.

——. "Strategic Air Command Statistical Summary September 1946." Andrews AFB, Md.: Hdq., Strategic Air Command, 1946.

——. "Strategic Air Command Statistical Summary 1947." Andrews AFB, Md.: Hdq., Strategic Air Command, 1948.

United States Air Forces in Europe. "A Five-Year Summary of USAFE History 1945-1950." Wiesbaden, Germany: Hdq., USAFE Historical Division, 1952.

Oral Histories

Finletter, Thomas K. Interviewed by Marvin Stanley, February 1967. Number 760.

Griswold, Lt. Gen. Francis. Interviewed by Robert Kipp, April 1970. Number 732.

Irvine, Lt. Gen. C. S. Interviewed by Robert Kipp, December 1970. Number 734.

Kingsbury, Maj. Gen. William C. Interviewed by Robert Kipp, December 1970. Number 733.

LeMay, Gen. Curtis E. Interviewed by John Bohn, March 1971. Number 736.

——. Unidentified interviewer, March 1965. Number 785.

Parrish, Brig. Noel F. Interviewed by James C. Hasdorff, June 1974. Number 744.

Power, Gen. Thomas S. Interviewed by Kenneth Leish, July 1960. Number 81.

Personal Files and Collections

LeMay, Gen. Curtis E. (168.64)
Whitehead, Lt. Gen. Ennis C. (168.6008-3)

Reports and Research Papers

AAF Scientific Advisory Group. *Toward New Horizons.* Washington, D.C.: Central Air Documents Office, 1945.
Headquarters Air University. "Report of Bombing Accuracy Conference, 1-2 November 1948." Maxwell AFB: 1948.
McCauley, Clarence. "Evaluation of Wing Organization." Air University, Maxwell AFB: 1949.
Martindale, Ward W. "An Analysis of the New Wing-Base Organization." Air University, Maxwell AFB: 1949.
Perry, William. "A Research Paper Submitted to the Faculty of the Air Command and Staff School of the Air University Regular Course Code Number 342." Air University, Maxwell AFB: 1949.
Smith, Maj. Gen. F. H. "History of B-36 Procurement." 1949.

Miscellaneous Files

AAF Letter 20-91. (168.116020-91).
AAF Letter 20-9. (415.01B).
Office of Public Relations, Hdq., AAF. (K141.2421).
Strategic Air Command. "Intelligence Briefs." (416.606).

The Library of Congress: Personal Collections and Papers

Fairchild, General Muir.
Quesada, Lt. Gen. Elwood.
Spaatz, General Carl.
Vandenberg, General Hoyt.

The National Archives

Record Group 218. Records of the United States Joint Chiefs of Staff.
Record Group 319. Records of the Army Staff.
Record Group 341. Records of Headquarters, United States Air Force.
Policy Planning Staff Papers. Diplomatic Branch.

Private Sources

Author's personal interviews. LeMay, General Curtis E., 1 October 1975. Montgomery, General J. B., 14 July 1975.
Fredette, Raymond. "Lindbergh Report." 14 September 1948. Personal copy.

Printed Sources

Government Documents

Hearings

U.S. Congress, House, Committee on Appropriations, *Military Establishment Appropriations Bill of 1947: Hearings before a subcommittee of the Committee on Appropriations*, 79th Cong., 2d sess., 1946.

——. *Military Establishment Appropriations Bill of 1948: Hearings before a subcommittee of the Committee on Appropriations*, 80th Cong., 1st sess., 1947.

——. *Department of Defense Appropriations for 1951: Hearings before a subcommittee of the Committee on Appropriations*, 81st Cong., 2d sess., 1950.

U.S. Congress, House, Committee on Armed Services, *Investigation of the B-36 Bomber Program: Hearings before the Committee on Armed Services*, 80th Cong., 1st sess., 1949, H. Rept. 234.

——. *Selective Service: Hearings before the Committee on Armed Services*, 80th Cong., 2d sess., 1948.

U.S. Congress, Senate, Committee on Military Affairs, *Department of Armed Forces Department of Military Security. Hearings before the Committee on Military Affairs*, 79th Cong., 1st sess., 1945, S. 84 and S. 1482.

Publications

Arnold, H. H. *Third Report of the Commanding General of the Army Air Forces to the Secretary of War.* Baltimore: Schneiderith & Sons, November 1945.

Bush, Vannevar. *Science, the Endless Frontier: Report to the President on a Program for Postwar Scientific Research.* Washington, D.C.: Government Printing Office, 1945.

Congressional Aviation Policy Board. *National Aviation Policy.* Washington, D.C.: Government Printing Office, 1948.

National Military Establishment. *First Report of the Secretary of Defense.* Washington, D.C.: Government Printing Office, 1948.

President's Air Policy Commission. *Survival in an Air Age.* Washington, D.C.: Government Printing Office, 1948.

Public Papers of the Presidents, Harry S. Truman, 1947. Washington, D.C.: Government Printing Office, 1963.

Public Papers of the Presidents, Harry S. Truman, 1950. Washington, D.C.: Government Printing Office, 1965.

Spaatz, Carl. *Report of the Chief of Staff United States Air Force to the*

Secretary of the Air Force. Washington, D.C.: Government Printing Office, 1948.
U.S. Advisory Commission on Service Pay. *Career Compensation for the Uniformed Forces.* Vol. 1. Washington, D.C.: Government Printing Office, 1948.
U.S., Department of Commerce, Bureau of the Census, *Statistical Abstract of the United States 1950.* Washington, D.C.: Government Printing Office, 1950.
The United States Strategic Bombing Survey Over-all Report, European War. Washington, D.C.: Government Printing Office, 1945.
The United States Strategic Bombing Survey Summary Report, Pacific War. Washington, D.C.: Government Printing Office, 1946.
Wile, Annadel, ed. *The Declassified Documents Quarterly Catalog,* vol. 3, no. 4, January-December 1977. Washington, D.C.: Carrollton Press Inc., 1978.
——. *The Declassified Documents Quarterly Catalog,* vol. 4, no. 4, January-December 1978. Washington, D.C.: Carrollton Press Inc., 1979.
——. *The Declassified Documents Retrospective Collection.* Washington, D.C.: Carrollton Press Inc., 1976.

Newspapers

New York Herald-Tribune. 27 March 1946.
New York Times. 13 October-30 December 1945, 7 April 1946, 26 April 1948.

SECONDARY SOURCES

Books

Acheson, Dean. *Present at the Creation.* New York: W. W. Norton and Company, 1969.
Arnold, H. H. *Global Mission.* New York: Harper and Brothers, 1949.
Baxter, James Phinney. *Scientists Against Time.* Boston: Little, Brown & Co., 1950.
Brodie, Bernard. *Strategy in the Missile Age.* Princeton: Princeton University Press, 1959.
——. *The Atomic Bomb and American Security.* New Haven: Yale Institute of International Studies, 1945.
Bush, Vannevar. *Modern Arms and Free Men.* New York: Simon and Schuster, 1949.
Chapman, John L. *Atlas: The Story of a Missile.* New York: Harper and Brothers, 1960.

Clay, Lucius D. *Decision in Germany*. Garden City, N.Y.: Doubleday and Company, Inc., 1950.

Congressional Quarterly Almanac, Vol. V, 1949. Washington, D.C.: Congressional Quarterly News Features, 1949.

Craven, Wesley, and Cate, James, eds. *The Army Air Forces in World War II*. Vol. 2: *Europe—Torch to Pointblank*. Chicago: University of Chicago Press, 1949.

——. *The Army Air Forces in World War II*. Vol. 5: *The Pacific: Matterhorn to Nagasaki*. Chicago: University of Chicago Press, 1953.

——. *The Army Air Forces in World War II*. Vol. 6: *Men and Planes*. Chicago: University of Chicago Press, 1955.

——. *The Army Air Forces in World War II*. Vol. 7: *Services Around the World*. Chicago: University of Chicago Press, 1958.

Davis, Vincent. *Postwar Defense Policy and the U.S. Navy, 1943-1946*. Chapel Hill: University of North Carolina Press, 1962.

Davison, W. Phillips. *The Berlin Blockade*. Princeton: Princeton University Press, 1958.

DuPre, Flint O. *U.S. Air Force Biographical Dictionary*. New York: Franklin Watts, Inc., 1965.

Freedman, Lawrence. *U.S. Intelligence and the Soviet Strategic Threat*. Boulder, Colo.: Westview Press, 1977.

Futrell, Robert F. *Ideas, Concepts, Doctrine: A History of Basic Thinking in the United States Air Force 1907-1964*. Montgomery: Aerospace Studies Institute, 1971.

Garthoff, Raymond L. *Soviet Strategy in the Nuclear Age*. New York: Frederick A. Praeger, 1958.

George, Alexander L., and Smoke, Richard. *Deterrence in American Foreign Policy: Theory and Practice*. New York: Columbia University Press, 1974.

Goldberg, Alfred, ed. *A History of the United States Air Force 1907-1957*. New York: D. Van Nostrand Inc., 1957.

Haynes, Richard R. *The Awesome Power*. Baton Rouge: Louisiana State University Press, 1973.

Herken, Gregg. *The Winning Weapon: The Atomic Bomb in the Cold War*. New York: Alfred A. Knopf, 1980.

Hewlett, Richard G., and Anderson, Oscar E., Jr. *A History of the United States Atomic Energy Commission*. Vol. 1: *The New World, 1939-1946*. University Park: Pennsylvania State University Press, 1962.

Hewlett, Richard R., and Duncan, Francis. *A History of the United States Atomic Energy Commission*. Vol. 2: *Atomic Shield, 1947-1952*. University Park: Pennsylvania State University Press, 1969.

Hurley, Alfred F., and Ehrhart, Robert C., eds. *Air Power and Warfare.* Washington, D.C.: Government Printing Office, 1979.

Kennan, George F. *Memoirs 1925-1950.* Boston: Little, Brown & Company, 1967.

Kenney, George C. *General Kenney Reports.* New York: Duell, Sloan and Pearce, 1949.

——. *The MacArthur I Know.* New York: Duell, Sloan and Pearce, 1951.

LeMay, Curtis E. *Mission with LeMay.* Garden City, N.Y.: Doubleday and Company, Inc., 1965.

Lilienthal, David E. *The Journals of David E. Lilienthal.* Vol. 2: *The Atomic Energy Years 1945-1950.* New York: Harper & Row, 1964.

MacArthur, Douglas. *Reminiscences.* New York: McGraw-Hill, 1964.

McClendon, R. Earl. *Unification of the Armed Forces.* Montgomery: Air University, 1952.

MacIsaac, David. *Strategic Bombing in World War Two.* New York: Garland Publishing, Inc., 1976.

——. *The United States Strategic Bombing Survey.* Vol. 1. New York: Garland Publishing, Inc., 1976.

Mackintosh, Malcolm. *Juggernaut.* New York: The Macmillan Company, 1967.

Mansfield, Harold. *Vision.* New York: Duell, Sloan and Pearce, 1956.

Millis, Walter, ed. *The Forrestal Diaries.* New York: Viking Press, 1951.

——. *Arms and Men.* New York: G. P. Putnam's Sons, 1956.

Mooney, Chase C., and Williamson, Edward C. *Organization of the Army Air Arm, 1935-1945*, USAF Historical Studies no. 10. Montgomery: Air University, 1956.

Nelson, Otto L. *National Security and the General Staff.* Washington, D.C.: Infantry Journal Press, 1946.

Quester, George H. *Nuclear Diplomacy.* New York: The Dunellen Company, Inc., 1970.

Rogow, Arnold A. *James Forrestal.* New York: The Macmillan Company, 1963.

——. *Victim of Duty.* London: Rupert Hart-Davis, 1966.

Schilling, Warner R.; Hammond, Paul Y.; and Snyder, Glen H. *Strategy, Politics, and Defense Budgets.* New York: Columbia University Press, 1962.

Sherry, Michael. *Preparing for the Next War: American Plans for Postwar Defense.* New Haven, Conn.: Yale University Press, 1977.

Smith, Jean Edward, ed. *The Papers of General Lucius Clay.* Vol. 2. Bloomington: Indiana University Press, 1974.

Smith, Perry McCoy. *The Air Force Plans for Peace 1943-1945.* Baltimore: Johns Hopkins University Press, 1970.

Sparrow, John C. *History of Personnel Demobilization in the United States Army.* Washington, D.C.: Office of the Chief of Military History, 1951.

Speer, Albert. *Inside the Third Reich.* New York: The Macmillan Company, 1970.

Stein, Herbert. *The Fiscal Revolution in America.* Chicago: University of Chicago Press, 1969.

Strategic Air Command. *The Development of Strategic Air Command 1946-1976.* Omaha: Headquarters Strategic Air Command, 1976.

Strauss, Lewis L. *Men and Decisions.* Garden City, N.Y.: Doubleday and Company, Inc., 1962.

Truman, Harry S. *Memoirs.* Vol. 2: *Years of Trial and Hope.* Garden City, N.Y.: Doubleday and Company, Inc., 1956.

Vandenberg, Arthur H., Jr., ed. *The Private Papers of Senator Vandenberg.* Boston: Houghton-Mifflin Company, 1952.

Von Karman, Theodore. *The Wind and Beyond.* Boston: Little, Brown & Co., 1967.

Webster, Charles, and Franklin, Noble. *The Strategic Air Offensive Against Germany 1939-1945.* Vol. 2: *Endeavor.* London: Her Majesty's Stationery Office, 1961.

Williams, William Appleman. *The Tragedy of American Diplomacy.* Cleveland: World Publishing Company, 1959. 2d ed., New York: Dell Publishing Company, Inc., 1962.

Wolfe, Thomas W. *Soviet Power and Europe 1945-1970.* Baltimore: Johns Hopkins University Press, 1970.

Wright, Gordon. *The Ordeal of Total War.* New York: Harper & Row, 1968.

Wright, Monte. *Most Probable Position.* Lawrence: University Press of Kansas, 1972.

Yergin, Daniel. *Shattered Peace: The Origins of the Cold War and the National Security State.* Boston: Houghton Mifflin Company, 1977.

Dissertations and Theses

Green, Murray. "Stuart Symington and the B-36." Ph.D. Diss., American University, 1960.

Johnson, Elliott. "The B-36 Controversy: A History of the Air Force-Navy Rivalry Over Strategic Bombardment." Master's Thesis, University of Wisconsin, 1961.

Parrish, Noel. "Behind the Sheltering Bomb: Military Indecision from Alamogordo to Korea." Ph.D. Diss., Rice University, 1968.

Shiner, John F. "The Air Arm in Transition: General Benjamin D. Foulois and the Air Corps, 1931-1935." Ph.D. Diss., Ohio State University, 1975.

Journal and Magazine Articles

Arnold, H. H. "Science and Air Power." *Air Affairs* 1 (1946): 184-95.

"The Balance of Power." *The Atlantic Monthly*, June 1951, pp. 21-27.

Eastman, James N. "Flight of the Lucky Lady II." *Aerospace Historian*, Winter 1969, p. 9.

Futrell, Robert F. "Preplanning the USAF." *Air University Review* 21 (1971): 63-68.

Greenwood, John T. "The Emergence of the Postwar Strategic Air Force, 1945-1953." *Air Power and Warfare*. Washington, D.C.: Government Printing Office, 1979, pp. 215-44.

Kennan, George F. "The Sources of Soviet Conduct." *Foreign Affairs* 25 (1947): 566-82.

Kenney, George C. "Strategic Air Command." *Military Review*, August 1947, pp. 3-7.

McFarland, Keith D. "The 1949 Revolt of the Admirals." *Parameters* 11 (1981): 53-63.

MacIsaac, David. "What the Bombing Survey Really Says." *Air Force Magazine*, June 1973, pp. 60-63.

Rosenberg, David Alan. "American Atomic Strategy and the Hydrogen Bomb Decision." *The Journal of American History* 66 (1979): 62-87.

Schlesinger, Arthur M., Jr. "Origins of the Cold War." *Foreign Affairs* 46 (1967): 22-52.

Smith, Gaddis. "Visions and Revisions of the Cold War." *New York Times*, Section 6, 29 April 1973, p. 13.

Spaatz, Carl. "Strategic Air Power." *Foreign Affairs* 24 (1946): 385-96.

"The Battlefields of Peace." *Time*, 8 March 1948, p. 26.

Wells, Samuel F., Jr. "Sounding the Tocsin: NSC 68 and the Soviet Threat." *International Security* 4 (1979): 116-58.

Wolk, Herman S. "Roots of Deterrence." *Aerospace Historian*, September 1972, pp. 137-44.

——. "The Defense Unification Battle, 1947-50: The Air Force." *Prologue*, Spring 1975, pp. 18-26.

INDEX

About the Author

HARRY R. BOROWSKI is Associate Professor of History at the United States Air Force Academy in Colorado Springs, Colorado. His articles have appeared in *Military Affairs, Air University Review,* and will be included in Greenwood's forthcoming *Dictionary of American Military Leaders.*